Managing IT Outsourcing

Outsourcing is a major international phenomenon in business today. IT represents a particular case for outsourcing both in benefits and in terms of potential inter-organizational problems. *Managing IT Outsourcing* combines theory, research and practice to explore how IT outsourcing partnerships can be managed successfully.

This ground-breaking book is supplemented with case studies drawn from a global network of companies involved in outsourcing, giving this book a firm grounding in real-world industrial experience. These partnerships include a range of industrial sectors such as manufacturing, telecoms, automotive and utilities. Unusually for books published on this topic, equal weight is given to both sides of the relationship, and the authors provide a unique governance model for outsourcing partnerships, exploring the risks and responsibilities involved for both partners.

Accessible and cutting-edge, this book provides an in-depth yet practical perspective on an important and far-reaching challenge in IT management, ideal for students, academics and practitioners alike.

Erik Beulen is a senior manager with Accenture and is associated with Tilburg University, the Netherlands.

Pieter Ribbers is Professor of Information Management at Tilburg University, the Netherlands.

Jan Roos is Emeritus Professor of Information Systems at Tilburg University, the Netherlands.

Managing IT Outsourcing

Governance in global partnerships

Erik Beulen,
Pieter Ribbers and
Jan Roos

Routledge
Taylor & Francis Group

LONDON AND NEW YORK

First published 2006
by Routledge
2 Park Square, Milton Park, Abingdon, Oxon OX14 4RN

Simultaneously published in the USA and Canada
by Routledge
270 Madison Ave, New York, NY 10016

Routledge is an imprint of the Taylor & Francis Group, an informa business

© 2006 Erik Beulen, Pieter Ribbers and Jan Roos

Typeset in Perpetua and Bell Gothic by
Book Now Ltd
Printed and bound in Great Britain by
MPG Books Ltd, Bodmin

British Library Cataloguing in Publication Data
A catalogue record for this book is available from the British Library

Library of Congress Cataloging in Publication Data
Beulen, Erik.
    Managing it outsourcing/Erik Beulen, Pieter Ribbers, and Jan Roos.
        p. cm.
    Includes bibliographical references and index.
    1. Information technology–Management. 2. Contracting out. 3. Electronic
    data processing departments–Contracting out. I. Ribbers, Pieter.
    II. Roos, Jan. III. Title.
HD30.2.B475 2006
004.068′7–dc22   2005031236

ISBN10: 0–415–36598–8 (hbk)
ISBN10: 0–415–36599–6 (pbk)
ISBN10: 0–203–01846–X (ebk)

ISBN13: 978–0–415–36598–7 (hbk)
ISBN13: 978–0–415–36599–4 (pbk)
ISBN13: 978–0–203–01846–0 (ebk)

Contents

Illustrations

FIGURES

TABLES

Preface

The business landscape is changing. Outsourcing plays an important role in this. At present, theories on how to manage inter-organizational relationships are developing. In this book we combine expertise in both practice and theory in information systems management. As a result, this work contains a blend of theory and practical insights in managing outsourcing relationships. Practical insight in this field is particularly important because of the newness of the phenomenon. The combination of theoretical development in management and economic disciplines with the emerging practice of how to manage inter-organizational relationships has resulted in guidance on managing outsourcing relationships.

This book contains a large number of (anonymous) case studies (see the Appendix). We would like to thank all the interviewees for sharing their insights with us. We would also like to thank Accenture and Atos Origin for providing the opportunity to write this book.

Erik Beulen
Pieter Ribbers
Jan Roos
September 2005

Chapter 1

Changing business models

- Strategic sourcing concentrates on long-term motives, such as making one's organization more agile or gaining access to important resources that are better supplied by external parties than developed internally.
- Competition puts pressure on efficiency, delivery times and product customization. Therefore suppliers must work together more closely: network organizations.

1.1 INTRODUCTION

Concentrating on core business has become the trend in many industries. This means that those activities that are not core to the business are outsourced to specialized suppliers. For companies doing this, decisions on how to acquire the basic products and services required to meet their customers' needs have come to be of strategic importance. They define the company's position in its competitive environment. The long-term relationships with suppliers that are the result of such sourcing practices are therefore included in the company's strategic planning processes.

Traditional sourcing was a matter of make-or-buy decisions, typically based on cost analysis and focused on limited numbers of specific goods and services, delivered for a limited number of times or over a limited period (rarely more than a year). Companies engaging in such transactions experienced little interdependence and their main motive was cost efficiency. Many such sourcing decisions are still taken, of course, on a day-to-day basis and all over the world. Strategic sourcing, however, is completely different. The dependence between the participants, their motives, the contract periods and many other characteristics are unlike those of traditional sourcing (Hvolby *et al.* 2000). Strategic sourcing concentrates on long-term motives such as making one's organization more agile or gaining access to important resources that are better supplied by external parties than developed internally. It therefore focuses on long-term relationships: the participants collaboratively plan their moves in what thus becomes a common competitive environment. They are therefore much more dependent on one another. And since the contract periods involved are consequently much longer, the decisions to be made concern the company's strategic planning horizons. Strategic sourcing, then, may be defined as the way in which organizations obtain products and services in exchange for returns while considering the long-term impact on the context, intensity and scope of their internal and external relationships (van der Zee and van Wijngaarden 1999).

In this chapter we will discuss strategic sourcing in the context of the changes in business models that may be observed throughout the world. To this end we first take a look at the competitive changes that force companies to rethink the way they do business (Section 1.2). Then, in Section 1.3, we focus on business models as a concept, and the importance of explicitly considering one's inter-company relationships. The evolution of such relationships from purely operational to strategic matters is described in Section 1.4.

1.2 THE CHANGING COMPETITIVE AGENDA

Up until recently, most companies usually decided for themselves which changes to make and when. If they decided to expand their market, they made small, carefully planned changes to their organization and strategy. If they wanted to modify their organization, they carefully considered the consequences for their customers and employees, trying to keep their company balanced. Today, they cannot afford such luxury. Companies constantly face unexpected developments that have a serious impact on their competitive environment and that occur with a startling and increasing frequency (Reijniers 2004). It is no longer the companies themselves but their environment that dictates most of the changes to be made, even internally (Parker 1999).

This transformation is driven by both business factors and technological developments. The primary business factors are the shift in power balance from supply to demand and the significantly fiercer competition that many companies experience in their industries, which D'Aveni (1994) described as hypercompetition. Business planning no longer begins with what one can deliver, but with what the customer wants – high-quality, customized goods and services. Demand-oriented markets set performance standards, and suppliers will either meet them or perish. Many authors have reported on the changes to business management that this transformation has caused (Parker 1996). In the early 1990s a *Harvard Business Review* editorial observed that modern business involved thinking like a customer, not a producer (Kanter 1992). Hence the concepts of mass customization and one-on-one marketing (Pine 1993; Peppers and Rogers 1993, 1997). Mass customization refers to the delivery of products and services meeting the specific needs of individual customers in mass markets. The idea is to compose one's products and services of standardized modules and to also modularize the assembly and distribution segments of one's supply chain, thus enabling the company to tailor its products and services to the needs of the individual. In one-on-one marketing the collective marketing activities of a company are targeted on individual customers who will thus receive individualized product offerings.

Technological developments — especially the application of information technology or IT — are as much a cause as an effect of the transformation to new ways of doing business. The convergence of IT and telecommunication, plus the increasing availability of bandwidth, has generated a highly competitive market environment and made new organizational designs possible. The Internet makes markets more transparent and helps customers locate the suppliers best suited to meet their expectations. It effectively cancels the former lack of information symmetry. IT also reduces many transaction and coordination costs, enabling companies to restructure their value chains and focus on their core competences. On the other hand, the global nature of the Internet also makes competition much fiercer, as one's competitors cross their former geographical boundaries.

When we look at the impact of IT on the business domain we may observe that initially its role in business organizations was reactive. Computer applications supported the existing managerial and operational processes, and IT investments were considered replacement investments which enabled efficiency improvements by replacing manual information-processing activities. From the mid-1980s, however, it became clear that IT could have a fundamental effect on the way the company's business was conducted. This was called the strategic impact of IT. On the basis of several hundreds of case studies four types of 'strategic systems' were identified (Ward and Peppard 2002):

- systems linking the company with customers and suppliers, thus changing the nature of these relationships;
- systems allowing a more effective integration of the organization's internal processes;
- systems enabling the organization to market new or improved information-based products and services;
- systems providing executives with high-quality information to support strategy development and implementation.

It is the last two strategic systems in particular that contribute to the innovations in the ways companies collaborate.

1.3 NEW BUSINESS MODELS

Increased competition forces companies fundamentally to rethink their position in their markets. Traditionally, they carried out all necessary activities for the

3

production and delivery of their products and services themselves, unless some were procured from external suppliers for specific reasons. But companies think differently nowadays. They feel there is no reason to do something themselves unless they really are uniquely good at it. And they therefore ask themselves which of their competences are unique and of core importance, which of their resources and functional capabilities really add value – and consequently, which might more efficiently be procured externally. Because of this change in their point of view, outsourcing and insourcing movements are expected to cause fundamental changes in the way companies are configured. Uniqueness and value-adding competences are the business drivers of the future (Gibson 1997).

In order to understand how companies develop their competitive positions we may profitably use the concept of the value chain (Porter and Millar 1985). It describes the series of activities connecting a company's supply side to its demand side, that is, its raw materials, inbound logistics and production processes to its outbound logistics, marketing and sales. This concept divides a company's activities into the technologically and economically distinct activities it performs to do business. We call these 'value activities' (Porter and Millar 1985: 150). Value chains generally are used to describe major lines of business and then show which activities are of primary importance and which have a supporting role. Primary activities are those that have a direct relationship – potential or actual – with the organization's customers. They contribute directly to its delivery of goods and services. Examples of such activities are inbound logistics, procurement, manufacturing, marketing and delivery. Support activities provide the necessary inputs and infrastructure to allow the company to perform those primary activities. This model is a tool to analyse and, if necessary, redesign the internal and external processes of companies in order to improve their efficiency and effectiveness.

As a result of the developments discussed in Section 1.2 traditional value chains are becoming unbundled. On the one hand, many support activities and some primary activities (logistics, operations) are being outsourced – even some parts of the company's infrastructure (accounting, financial services and human resources). In companies made up of many business units, shared service centres for specific activities such as human resources or IT are often set up as a first step towards out-sourcing. On the other hand, the outsourced activities have to be procured from one or more external suppliers, a process that rebundles them in another way. Clearly, this process causes the relationships between businesses to become increasingly complex.

The popular term used in business literature for these new ways of doing business is the 'business model'. Business models may be defined as descriptive representations of an enterprise's planned activities (also called business processes). They encompass three integral areas of attention, specifying (Papazoglou and Ribbers 2005):

1   the internal aspects of the business venture: what it does and how, and how it intends to make money from it;

2 the external aspects of the enterprise: its relationships with its business environment, including its effective knowledge of these relationships;

3 the way in which the company uses its information assets (such as information systems and effective business processes, typically grouped in the domains of customer relations management, supply chain management and core business operations) to do so.

These three components will now be discussed in further detail.

1.3.1 The internal aspects of a business venture

The first major area to which a business plan pays attention is the company's internal aspects. Specifying the internal matters of a business venture means defining, among other aspects, the following elements:

- The products and services the company delivers to its customers. These customers may be consumers or businesses that use these products and services as a part of their activities.
- The sources of revenue that indicate how and to what extent a business venture is viable economically.
- The activities the company performs to deliver its products and services and to realize its strategic objectives. These encompass both primary and support activities and concern physical activities like manufacturing as well as service activities like coordinating other parties' activities.
- The organization the company has established to realize its objectives: company structure (task allocation, for example) and its processes (the combinations of tasks leading to a specific outcome, like order acquisition). This part of the analysis must include the processes that cross the company's boundaries, such as collaborative actions with external business partners for product development, for instance.

Since the shift in managerial focus from vertical, functional activities to the final customer during the 1990s, interest in business processes and their management has grown (Davenport 1993). Business processes in this sense are taken to consist of one or more related activities that together constitute the response to a business requirement for action. Or, to put it another way, they are sets of interdependent activities designed and structured to produce a specific output for a customer or a market. A business process view therefore implies a horizontal look at the business organization. The role played by IT may differ widely, between insurance companies and health care organizations for example, but the process view applies to both. IT developments specifically oriented towards such a process view include workflow systems, workflow management systems and enterprise resource planning (ERP) systems.

5

1.3.2 The external aspects of the enterprise

As with internal aspects, the company's external relationships also must be defined. These involve several kinds of external actors, who are all in some way involved in the venture: customers, suppliers, shareholders, etc. Like the internal focus, this external focus includes structure and processes, since these are needed to maintain external relationships as well. The external aspects discussed must also include the potential benefits for those actors, indicating under which conditions the company may expect to enjoy their support.

Another kind of aspect to be included in this category is that of the new collaboration patterns enabling trading partners to respond to market demands successfully. Traditional arrangements such as buying and selling, subcontracting and joint product design still apply, but outsourcing and specialization are becoming increasingly important. Companies in the technology businesses, who work with very short product cycles, are taking the lead here. For instance, it has been reported that 70 per cent of electronics manufacturers are involved in contract manufacturing (Philips 2002).

Adopting an outsourcing model means developing a strategic vision of one's role and position in the value chain. Companies must ask themselves how they will add value for their customers and for those providing the inputs (Ward and Peppard 2002). They must also analyse their own and their partners' willingness to engage in long-term collaboration, as well as the strength of their collaborative links. Some external companies may want to be able to leave the partnership easily, in order to find new partners. Others are perhaps more willing to invest in close business relationships, integrating their business processes with those of their partners across their company boundaries. No company can afford to engage in outsourcing before it has analysed these aspects.

1.3.3 The use of information assets

Finally, the way in which the venture's information assets are to be used also must be included in the business model. Information technology is becoming an integral part of all business processes and organizational designs; it simply cannot be ignored on this level. An example may help to clarify this point: it makes a great deal of difference whether one sells books in a shop or through a website, and such differences must therefore be defined in one's business model. IT and the way it is used influences the company's internal processes as well as its external relationships, for even operational buying and selling activities may be pursued through e-markets.

The extent to which IT is interwoven with the company's business processes also affects its outsourcing decisions. Not only is significantly interwoven IT more important than IT only in a supportive role, but the role of its IT supplier increases if the company's IT is more highly integrated with its business. Thus, this aspect influences one's make-or-buy decisions, even though a greater degree of integration does not necessarily lead to a 'make' decision – after all, external parties may in fact be better able to guarantee services delivery than internal IT departments. In a similar way, the degree of integration affects the way in which outsourcing relationships are managed once they have been set up. Highly interwoven IT services will cause business managers to keep a close eye on their delivery. Such a situation therefore requires more IT knowledge on the part of the company's business managers and more business knowledge on the part of the supplier's IT professionals.

1.4 NEW FORMS OF INTER-COMPANY RELATIONSHIPS

A successful response to the new market situation described above demands not only new business models but also new trading patterns. The sell-and-buy relationships of old still exist, of course, but increasingly companies engage in all kinds of collaborative efforts, from joint product design to planning their market strategies together. Over the past 20 years or so, inter-company relationships have moved from the operational to the tactical level, and on to the strategic (Figure 1.1).

Originally, companies all operated independently from one another. They bought products, components, piece parts and services on the basis of their current needs, expecting there would be suppliers able to deliver, from which they would simply select the one with the lowest prices. Likewise, product and service offerings were based on forecasts derived from the current demand. Such business patterns may be characterized as operational-level relationships. Buyers and sellers exchanged no information beyond that directly concerning the orders placed.

Independence has its advantages, such as flexibility and the possibility to change suppliers quickly if the current one does not perform satisfactorily. However, it has also its price. It brings much uncertainty, which makes it impossible to plan far ahead. Hence the long delivery times, high inventories and low utilization levels per production unit (that is, production capacity standing idle). Hence also the

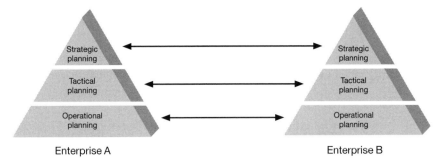

Figure 1.1 *Levels of inter-business relationships (Papazoglou and Ribbers 2005)*

dominance of standardized products: customer-specific components can only be offered after the customer order has been received.

When competition puts pressure on efficiency, delivery times and product customization, suppliers must work together more closely. Their relationships then move to the tactical level. They include longer-term agreements on the product types and quantities to be bought or sold, on the manufacturing of series and on production capacity, delivery moments, inventories and the like. As a result both organizations benefit from a more stable supplier–buyer relationship. Reduced uncertainty leads to reduced inventory levels[1] and improved delivery times. Tactical inter-company relationships induce the participants to plan collaboratively.

The final step in this development is towards strategic-level relationships. The partners involved then decide to act collaboratively for a long period, and strategic planning becomes a combined activity. In such relationships suppliers – on the basis of their specific expertise and skills – develop, design and produce specific components and services for their customers. These collaborative relationships are also called value-added partnerships (Johnston and Lawrence 1988). The stability they offer is even higher than on the tactical level. Collaboration is built around competence complementarities, and the partners share much information.

It is important to realize that companies engaging in higher-level collaboration still collaborate on the lower levels too. Operational-level and tactical-level relationships are always embedded in strategic-level collaboration. The result is that all three types of relationship can be found concurrently in almost every industry. In fact, almost every individual company nowadays engages in operational, tactical and strategic collaboration simultaneously.

- Companies buy and sell many goods and services on 'spot markets'. Here, relationships last only as long as the transaction and, although both parties are generally well informed about one another, they exchange little information. Spot market transactions are typically found in markets for basic raw materials and agricultural products.
- A regular need for specific products or services will usually be captured in a contract, specifying delivery conditions and volumes, and setting repeat provisions. Such longer-term relationships require the exchange of information for planning purposes.
- Finally, some relationships evolve into partnerships, in which the participants collaborate for a long period and even pursue a joint competitive strategy in their industry. Partnerships require an extensive exchange of information.

In this context of evolving business models, unbundling value chains and increasing collaboration, the concept of network organizations emerged. The term 'network' is generally used to describe a structure of ties among actors in a social system – actors being roles, individuals, organizations, industries or even nation states

(Nohria and Eccles 1992) – and these ties can be both intra-organizational and inter-organizational. In this book we are, of course, particularly interested in inter-organizational business networks.

The literature on network organizations provides a variety of definitions. For the purposes of this book we may define networked organizations as virtual partnerships formed by separate companies in order to enable them to operate as integral elements of a greater organization while retaining their own authority in major budgeting and pricing matters. The term 'network organization' is then roughly synonymous with such designations as modular organization, virtual corporation, organic network, value-adding partnership and inter-organizational configuration. Corporate networks are long-term arrangements among distinct but related profit-oriented organizations. Finally, inter-company networks may be defined as the relationships between a defined set of distinct organizations (the network structure) and their interactions (the network process) (Klein 1996). The inter-company networks in which we are primarily interested exhibit the following characteristics:

- the links between the network's participants are based on various types of exchange (of economic goods, money, information, knowledge, etc.);
- networks have a distinct boundary with their environments;
- network participants pursue a common goal;
- all network participants nevertheless also have their own diverse, specific goals;
- networks consist of relationships characterized by mutual investments or interdependences (that is, not just simple transactional links).

The potential variety of structures that may constitute network organizations is very large. Consequently, it is difficult to establish a single definition. Some authors even deny that inter-company networks represent a distinct way of organizing transactions at all; they believe they are simply another way to organize markets by new coordination mechanisms if their price mechanisms fail (Douma and Schreuder 1998).

NOTE

1 In order to form a buffer against uncertainty in supply and demand of goods and services, companies tend to keep safety stocks, thus avoiding stock-outs.

REFERENCES

D'Aveni, R. (1994) *Hyper-competition: Managing the Dynamics of Strategic Manoeuvring*, New York: The Free Press.

Davenport, T. (1993) *Process Innovation – Reengineering Work through Information Technology*, Boston, MA: Harvard Business School Press.

Douma, S. and Schreuder, H. (1998) *Economic Approaches to Organizations*, 2nd edn, London: Prentice Hall.

Gibson, R. (1997) *Rethinking the Future*, London: Nicholas Brealey Publishing.

Hvolby, H., Momme, J. and Trienekens, J. (2000) 'Planning and control in industrial networks – an outsourcing perspective', in *Proceedings of the 3rd Conference on Stimulating Manufacturing Excellence in SMEs*, April, Coventry, UK.

Johnston, R. and Lawrence, P. (1988) 'Beyond vertical integration – the rise of the value-adding partnership', *Harvard Business Review*, 66 (4): 94–101.

Kanter, R. (1992) 'Think like the customer: the new global business logic', *Harvard Business Review*, 70 (4): 9–10.

Klein, S. (1996) 'The configuration of inter-organizational relationships', *European Journal of Information Systems*, 5 (2): 75–84.

Nohria, N. and Eccles, R. (1992) *Networks and Organizations*, Boston, MA: Harvard Business School Press.

Papazoglou, M. and Ribbers, P. (2005) *E-Business: Organizational and Technical Foundations*, Chichester: John Wiley & Sons.

Parker, M. (1996) *Strategic Transformation and Information Technology: Performing while Transforming*, Upper Saddle River, NJ: Prentice Hall.

Parker, M. (1999) 'Theory and practice of business/IT organizational interdependencies', PhD thesis, Tilburg University.

Peppers, D. and Rogers, M. (1993) *The One to One Future*, New York: Currency Doubleday.

Peppers, D. and Rogers, M. (1997) *Enterprise One to One: Tools for Competing in the Interactive Age*, New York: Currency Doubleday.

Philips (2002) *Royal Philips Electronics NV Annual Report 2002*.

Pine, B. (1993) *Mass Customization: The New Frontiers in Business Competition*, Boston, MA: Harvard Business School Press.

Porter, M. and Millar, V. (1985) 'How information gives you competitive advantage', *Harvard Business Review*, 63 (4): 149–160.

Reijniers, J. (2004) 'Competent veranderen – operationele resultaten in een kortere tijd', PhD thesis, Tilburg University (in Dutch).

van der Zee, H. and van Wijngaarden, P. (1999) *Strategic Sourcing and Partnerships: Challenging Scenarios for IT Alliances in the Network Era*, Amsterdam: Addison Wesley Longman.

Ward, J. and Peppard, J. (2002) *Strategic Planning for Information Systems*, 3rd edn, Chichester: John Wiley & Sons.

Chapter 2

The IT outsourcing phenomenon

- This chapter opens with a typology of IT outsourcing.
- Next several important issues relevant to outsourcing decision-making are discussed. The first of these are reducing total cost of ownership and minimizing risks, the key considerations in the decision-making process.
- Business process outsourcing is the next important subject: what implications does it have for partnership governance?
- Then we take a look at offshore outsourcing. It supports total cost of ownership reduction, but in developed countries it has a social impact that must be addressed.
- Finally, shared service centres are discussed as a feasible option for in-sourcing.

2.1 INTRODUCTION

The first topic of this chapter is the typology of outsourcing solutions: the kinds of outsourcing relationships that are possible. The nature of the relationships involved and the services delivered are discussed. We then take a look at the aspects service recipients must consider when taking outsourcing decisions – the arguments for and against. In the last sections of this chapter three recent developments will be discussed: business process outsourcing, offshore outsourcing and shared service centres.

2.2 OUTSOURCING TYPOLOGY

A typology of outsourcing solutions may be introduced by looking at the nature of the relationships involved and the services to be delivered. The nature of the relationships involved depends on which IT services are outsourced and to how many providers. Distinctions may then be made between selective and total outsourcing and between single and multiple outsourcing. Likewise, depending on the services needed, companies may decide for information systems outsourcing or business process outsourcing.

2.2.1 The nature of outsourcing relationships

Currie and Willcocks (1998) distinguish between single outsourcing, in which the recipient hires one service provider to supply it with the information services needed, and multiple outsourcing, in which a number of providers are involved. We may refine this distinction by subdividing single outsourcing into multiple integrated IT outsourcing partnerships and joint IT outsourcing partnerships. If one of the client's suppliers serves as systems integrator too, and the other service providers subcontract to it rather than contracting directly to the client, the arrangement is called a multiple integrated IT outsourcing partnership. Akzo Nobel, Shell and DSM are examples of companies that have set up such partnerships. In joint IT outsourcing partnerships the recipient and its principal contractor set up a joint venture which provides the systems integration that the recipient needs but also offers its services to other clients as well. Examples of such relationships are those between General Motors and EDS and between Philips and Atos Origin.

Another distinction made by Currie and Willcocks is that between companies outsourcing all information services and those who outsource only a selection. The practice of total outsourcing is much criticized in business literature (Lacity and Hirschheim 1995; Willcocks *et al.* 1995; Cullen and Willcocks 2003) because it renders the client dependent on his service provider. This difficulty may be removed, at least partially, by outsourcing to several providers and managing their services as a portfolio (Peppard 2003).

2.2.2 The nature of outsourcing services

Outsourcing may be restricted to the company's information systems or it may encompass entire business processes (International Data Corporation 1997). In the first case the recipient sets targets for the performance of the information services only; it will itself remain responsible for the business processes in which these services are used. Business process outsourcing has a wider scope: now targets are set for entire business processes, of which the information systems are only a part. The service provider's responsibility is then much greater.

Companies outsourcing their information systems set up long-term contracts, transferring responsibility or partial responsibility for delivering the necessary information services to their provider. This provider may also take over some or all of the IT department's property and staff. Examples of such relationships are data centre outsourcing, network operations outsourcing, desktop outsourcing, applications outsourcing services, helpdesk outsourcing and disaster recovery.

Business process outsourcing means that the activities and knowledge needed to perform a department's tasks, processes or functions are all provided by an external service provider. Thus, the service provider also has responsibility for non-IT-related activities. These tasks, processes and functions may be administrative (billing, shareholder services and pension plans) or involve customer care (customer services and call centres), finance (cash management, receivables management and accounting), human resources (regulation compliance, benefits administration, workers' compensations and expatriate administration), logistics, manufacturing, marketing and sales. Section 2.5 deals with this kind of outsourcing in more detail.

2.3 ARGUMENTS IN FAVOUR OF IT OUTSOURCING

Many companies consider outsourcing their information services. There are many arguments to do so, used in the internal discussions leading to the decision. For this chapter we have selected the ten most frequently used, which will be discussed in detail below; they are summed up in Table 2.1. Remarkably, these arguments have changed relatively little with time. Another important remark has to be made: the order of importance of the arguments in favour of IT outsourcing is different for service recipients. The business strategy and the IT strategy have an impact on the order of the arguments. Van der Zee and van Wijngaarden (1999) address decreasing the total cost of ownership of the IT services, increasing IT services flexibility and achieving IT services innovativity as the most important arguments. Lacity and Hirschheim (1993) emphasize realizing a strategic focus on central competences and decreasing the total cost of ownership of the IT services. Cadwell and Young (2003) from Gartner also report on solving the problem of not being able to recruit qualified IT staff. The arguments in favour of outsourcing are:

1 decreasing the total cost of ownership of the IT services;
2 shortening time-to-market for new IT services;
3 increasing flexibility of IT services;
4 achieving innovativity in IT services;
5 facilitating the IT consequences of mergers and disentanglements;
6 achieving a 'technology shift';
7 realizing a strategic focus on central competences;
8 rendering the IT services costs variable;
9 improving the company's financial ratios;
10 solving the problem of not being able to recruit qualified IT staff.

13

1 Decreasing the total cost of ownership of the IT services

Information services suppliers must provide the same services as the company's IT department, but against lower costs. They can do so because of economies of scale, both on the delivery side and by using their buying power to obtain better hardware and software prices (Buck-Lew 1992). The condition for them to be able to do so is that their clients allow them to standardize their information services, which they probably will as long as their information needs are fulfilled (Klepper 1995).

The IT department manager of the Dutch subsidiary of Case I (see Appendix, p. 268, for all Case details) explains:

> Our company, which is a subsidiary of a large internationally operating concern, produces colour photographic paper, colour negatives and offset plates. I am responsible for a staff of fifty who provide the IT services to a total of 1300 people working here. Cost reduction being a central issue with our company, I am also held accountable for what we charge our business units. Nevertheless, since these business units are free to choose between our services and external contracts, they don't always select my department. Especially in the field of systems development we frequently use the services of an external party with whom a first-supplier agreement has been arranged. We also outsource network management. These decisions are all made on the basis of cost–benefit analyses, which are the business units' responsibility.
>
> (Beulen *et al.* 1994: 25)

Total cost of ownership (TCO) has been an important consideration since the 1990s. But as a consequence of the developments which made IT an integral part of companies' business processes, the focus of total cost ownership thinking has shifted from information services to business processes (David *et al.* 2002). This means that account must also be taken of the cost components that arise as a consequence of outsourcing, such as those for managing the IT service suppliers. This aspect is discussed more fully in Section 2.4.

2 Shortening time-to-market for new IT services

Many companies operate in markets whose already considerable dynamics have been increased by the globalization process. IT departments must therefore be able to react quickly, which means having substantial resources available. This makes it difficult for them to be cost-efficient. External suppliers, who as a rule have many more clients, are in a better position to handle fluctuations cost-efficiently (Cross 1995; Lander *et al.* 2004). Also, development and implementation often leave internal IT departments little time and resources to document the changes properly, again making outsourcing attractive (Travis 2003).

Achieving a short time-to-market is of the essence, especially for software development and implementation. One way of doing so is setting up a portal to make available all information stored by the company. By outsourcing the implementation and management of such portals, the time-to-market may be further shortened (Eckerson *et al.* 2000). Another possibility is provided by enterprise resource planning (ERP) software and the like: using standard instead of customized software speeds up the process significantly (Goldsmith 1994; Lander *et al.* 2004).

3 Increasing flexibility of IT services

IT departments must be able to react to changes in the services requested, both with respect to the quantity of these services and their nature. On the basis of their IT strategies, companies may decide to change from one information services platform to another. Such flexibility is needed to maintain their competitive positions (Buck-Lew 1992). Nevertheless, attention must be paid to the IT department's staff: where will they go if the company changes platforms (Tayntor 2001)?

An example is provided by the IT manager of Case I:

> We supply our products to several Fuji companies. It is they who decide the specifications, and these differ widely. Supplying many different products requires flexibility on our part. To meet a changing demand we outsource parts of our processes, and we don't feel bad about it at all. It isn't just our IT services that are procured externally; distribution and other processes are involved too. Working with a large number of contractors keeps us flexible and enables us to meet our clients' demands.
>
> (Beulen *et al.* 1994: 68)

Nowadays, flexibility is needed to keep up with the market's dynamics. Organizations are on the move and many companies join networks (Kanter 1994). Mergers and acquisitions are the order of the day. And paradoxically, it is mergers and acquisitions that require a certain amount of standardization in order to achieve flexibility. This is explained by the fact that connecting and disengaging whole departments is only possible if they all use the same standards (Brown and Renwick 1996).

4 Achieving innovativity in IT services

Since information services technologies are increasingly rapidly developed, IT departments face a growing complexity, certainly in companies operating on international markets. Keeping their companies' business processes connected requires much of the IT function's attention and much innovativity (Cross 1995; Klepper 1995).

A commercial manager recognizes the struggle:

15

> As an IT services provider we notice how the current rapid technological developments are a motive to consider outsourcing. I see many companies who can no longer justify making IT investments – it all changes so fast. Then they come to talk with us.
>
> (Beulen *et al.* 1994: 73)

One example of the innovations facing companies is the rise of the Internet and e-commerce. To keep up with these developments and to profit from them, outsourcing one's information services may be of use (Kraemer and Dedrick 2002).

5 Facilitating the IT consequences of mergers and disentanglements

Survival often requires selling parts of companies, which means that the IT functions of the separate parts must be disentangled. Such changes require much of the IT departments' attention. Likewise, integrating the IT functions of merging or acquired companies must be done very carefully to ensure good collaboration (Brown and Renwick 1996).

The IT manager of the technical department of an international airline (Case II) has experience with such changes:

> Our users' information needs constantly change. Information is important in our business, since it may offer strategic advantages over our competitors. So the company's objectives and the information needs following from them determine the objectives of my department. KLM used to have a central computing centre that supplied all the information needed, but things move so much faster now. Our environment is open and very dynamic; we have relations with many customers and suppliers and are constantly involved in merger and collaboration negotiations. We are always changing. Therefore, information must be available to the decision-makers much more quickly than before. This requires its processing at a lower level in the organization.
>
> (Beulen *et al.* 1994: 19)

6 Achieving a 'technology shift'

For years, IT departments have adapted their companies' information platforms – a sensible thing to do at first, but not always cost-effective in the long run. 'Legacy' problems are often the consequence. When it finally comes to transforming such platforms, this involves drastic operations, requiring substantial effort. Change is made even more difficult by the fact that during the transition two separate platforms must be kept working. Consequently, the risks to the continuity of the information services delivery are significant (Lacity and Hirschheim 1995; Cullen and Willcocks 2003).

Case II's IT manager states:

Being a large, internationally operating airline, we are well aware of the need to be flexible, to be able to react quickly to changes. I am constantly trying to achieve that flexibility in my department. Often our capacity is the bottleneck. Usually we are capable of doing the job but we simply haven't enough people available. A hardware platform change is an operation for which I could use double the staff I have now: one team to run the existing platform and one to set up the new one. Obviously, that is impossible. Outsourcing is then the solution. An external provider keeps the old platform in the air and makes sure our users get the information they need. Meanwhile my people and I develop the new platform. Once that's ready, the old platform is decommissioned and the new platform becomes operational. If all goes well, our users don't even notice what's going on, and I'll have managed to introduce a new platform without hiring extra staff.

(Beulen *et al.* 1994: 71)

A good example of a technology shift is the rise of m-commerce, which requires new development platforms and connections with the company's communication infrastructure, including GPRS standards. These connections must be capable of handling large amounts of data. The demands on the organizational architecture, in their turn, are very large as well (Frolick and Chen 2004).

7 Realizing a strategic focus on central competences

Delivering information services is a support activity that contributes to the recipient's primary business processes. IT's added value is limited, and the competitive advantage to be achieved with it is limited too (Buck-Lew 1992; Lacity and Hirschheim 1993).

The procurement manager of a chemical firm (Case III) remarks:

Since we are a large multinational in coatings, fibres, chemicals and pharmaceuticals, we consider IT a facilitator, not our real business. This applies especially to the operational aspects of information provisioning, for which we have set up a subsidiary called Information Services. It is still uncertain whether we will extend our IT outsourcing policy; but the fact that IT is no more than a facilitator will be an important argument in the discussion about it.

(Beulen *et al.* 1994: 73)

The trend to focus on central competences has passed the point where the question was whether information services should be considered core competences or not. Instead companies ask how collaboration may be achieved. Increasingly, global and partner-based alliances are established, evolving from the client-centred view of outsourcing (Lee *et al.* 2003).

8 Rendering the IT services costs variable

If a company's IT department is made responsible for information services delivery, the company will have to invest in information technology. But since the IT department has only that one company as its client, there is no way in which it can spread the investment costs over several clients when the information services demand fluctuates (Lacity and Hirschheim 1993). As a result, the IT costs are mostly fixed costs.

For one of the business managers of a truck manufacturer (Case IV), flexibility is all about volume:

> We are an almost single-product company. Since we produce capital goods, we are influenced directly by the economy's cycles. We must be very flexible in the volume we produce, since these cycles may cause our turnover to double in as little as five years.
>
> (Beulen 2000a: 227)

A good example of making costs variable is provided by application service providers (ASPs). These offer multiple users access to centrally managed applications, which their clients can use via the Internet and on the basis of subscriptions (Kern *et al.* 2002). However, the ASP concept is not very successful yet (Currie *et al.* 2004). Utility-based computing is another example: in this concept hardware providers make the hardware capacity investments needed, and their clients pay on the basis of their actual use. At the time of writing, utility-based computing is still mostly considered a marketing concept, used by companies such as IBM, Hewlett-Packard and Sun.

9 Improving the company's financial ratios

Many – especially listed – companies are assessed by investors and analysts on the basis of their financial ratios, such as turnover, profit per employee and market to book value. Outsourcing IT services may improve these ratios (since the service recipient reduces their book value, and then has fewer staff, for example) without influencing the company's primary processes (Loh and Venkatraman 1992). Improving financial ratios is an important motive for offshore outsourcing as well. This will be further discussed in Section 2.6 (Carmel and Agarwal 2002).

Table 2.1 *Arguments in favour of IT outsourcing*

Arguments	Rationale
1. Decreasing the total cost of ownership (TCO) of the IT services	• The IT department regularly overspends. • IT projects regularly overspend. • The IT services are insufficiently standardized. • The IT service levels are insufficiently standardized.
2. Shortening time-to-market for new IT services	• The IT department is unable to deliver, on time, the IT services the business units need. • The maintenance of the current information systems takes up too much of the budget. • Most of the IT department's staff are occupied keeping the current information systems working. • The IT department is too slow in realizing the connections between new information systems and their environment, which causes delays.
3. Increasing flexibility of IT services	• The IT department is unable to improve the level of their services temporarily (for example, by keeping the helpdesk open longer when new applications are introduced). • The IT department is unable to increase the volume of their services temporarily (when a new ERP system is introduced, for instance). • The IT department is unable to maintain the many different technologies used by all departments. • The IT department is unable to deliver IT services cost-effectively in new company locations.
4. Achieving innovativity in IT services	• The number of the IT department's staff is too small to assess the applicability of new technological developments. • The IT department's staff are insufficiently qualified to assess the applicability of new technological developments. • The IT department's objectives focus on operational excellence. • The IT department's budget does not include innovation.
5. Facilitating the IT consequences of mergers and disentanglements	• The IT services are insufficiently standardized. • There are no scenarios for disentangling the information systems when parts of the company are sold. • Consolidating information involves the use of a great number of interfaces, many of which are hand-operated. • Much of the information stored by the organization is redundant.
6. Achieving a 'technology shift'	• The IT department lacks sufficient knowledge to implement new technologies. • The IT department lacks the capacity to implement new technologies while keeping current systems working. • The IT department cannot implement new technologies within the time limits set by the company's business needs.

Continued

▓ *Table 2.1* *Continued*

Arguments	*Rationale*
	• The architecture of the current information systems hinders the implementation of new technologies.
7. Realizing a strategic focus on central competences	• The company's strategy includes focusing on central competences. • IT services are not part of the company's central competences. • The company collaborates with other enterprises in many fields already – in alliances, joint ventures and partnerships. • The company's business units all have their own profit and loss responsibility.
8. Rendering the IT services costs variable	• There are insufficient funds to invest in information technology. • The IT investments to be made are out of proportion to their use and utility. • The need for IT services will increase but is still limited. • The need for IT services is great but will soon diminish.
9. Improving the company's financial ratios	• The number of staff in relation to the company's turnover is high in comparison with that of other companies. • The costs of the IT services in relation to the company's turnover are high in comparison with those of other companies. • The investments in hardware and buildings needed for the IT department have a serious impact on the company's balance sheet. • The company's cash position must be improved.
10. Solving the problem of not being able to recruit qualified IT staff	• Local collective labour agreements offer little scope for incentive schemes with which to attract scarce IT specialists. • The company's salary structure offers little scope for incentive schemes (such as lease cars, bonuses) with which to attract scarce IT specialists. • The company's image is not attractive to IT specialists. • IT experts find insufficient development and education facilities within the company's IT department.

The IT manager of Case V, a manufacturer of copiers, computers and accessories, has experience with such decisions:

We have limited investment potential available for IT, and every penny invested must be put to maximum use. To get around this restriction, we often opt for outsourcing. It doesn't really matter financially: instead of investments you make other costs. But by evading the investment restriction we can get the IT we need without overstepping our investment limits.

(Beulen *et al.* 1994: 78)

10 Solving the problem of not being able to recruit qualified IT staff

IT experts are now less hard to find than a few years ago. Nevertheless, as the economy is slowly improving, the labour market is becoming tighter again (Beulen and Ribbers 2002). Recruiting qualified IT staff is therefore becoming more difficult, a trend that is reinforced by the rise of offshore outsourcing (Section 2.6). In order to be attractive for potential staff, much attention must be paid to education (Schambach and Blanton 2000).

According to an information services manager:

Many of our clients are unable to recruit full-time IT specialists. They are often too small for the considerable expenses of hiring specialists. Since we work for many clients, we enjoy advantages of scale and can afford to do so. This enables us to offer good IT services at reasonable prices.

(Beulen *et al.* 1994: 71)

Another aspect to be considered is staff turnover, which presents a considerable risk to service delivery continuity. Employees who leave take their knowledge and know-how with them. This is a serious problem in rapidly changing organizations (Longenecker and Scazzero 2003).

2.4 ARGUMENTS AGAINST IT OUTSOURCING

Companies who consider outsourcing must realize that there are also negative consequences. And like the arguments in favour of outsourcing, they have changed little with time. The five most important arguments are discussed below. Like those in favour of IT outsourcing, there is also no particular order in the arguments against outsourcing. Lacity and Hirschheim (1993) report mainly on increased dependence on suppliers and a loss of knowledge and know-how. In addition Cadwell and Young (2003) from Gartner address the confidentiality risk.

The arguments against IT outsourcing are:

1 increased dependence on suppliers;
2 a loss of knowledge and know-how;
3 higher costs;
4 confidentiality risks;
5 difficulty in selecting the right service provider.

These arguments are also listed in Table 2.2.

1 Increased dependence on suppliers

When information services are contracted out, the responsibility for their delivery is transferred to the service provider. This is a big step for many companies, since it renders them dependent on their service provider. Instead of managing an internal IT department, the company will now have to discuss its needs with outsiders. And the fulfilment of these needs is based on a contract, which narrows the recipient's elbowroom (Lacity and Hirschheim 1993; Feeny 1997).

The IT manager of Case VI reports:

> We have our reservations about outsourcing. Strategically important processes will never be outsourced – we cannot risk losing control over them since we don't want to lose our position as market leader. And the same goes for activities close to our primary business processes. A transfer to suppliers involves taking risks we'd rather avoid.
>
> (Beulen *et al.* 1994: 80)

2 A loss of knowledge and know-how

Outsourcing processes may transfer IT department staff to the company providing the services. Their knowledge and know-how then also leave the service recipient, and it will take much effort to acquire them again. This may well be an argument to keep one's information services in one's own hands (Grover and Teng 1993; Lacity and Hirschheim 1995; Cullen and Willcocks 2003).

The manager of Case VII's internal accounting department states:

> Recently, my department was involved in auditing the transfer of the responsibility for IT services delivery. For years, the company had been doing business with a supplier, but it was now switching to another. My people have identified the major risks. Our report led to serious discussions with our intended new supplier, whose transition plan we thought was in certain respects incomplete and insufficient ... The transfer of knowledge, processes and procedures was insufficiently addressed in the transition plan. ... As a result, the transition plan was improved. And so the continuation of the IT service delivery was guaranteed.
>
> (Beulen 2003: 154)

3 Higher costs

Many IT departments work with neutral budgets. Services providers, like all companies, want to make money. This means that outsourcing one's information services may mean increasing costs (Ketler and Walstrom 1993). Outsourcing also requires contract management, a task that is not only new to many companies but also costs money to perform. Generally, these costs are estimated at 3–8 per cent of the costs of information services performance (David *et al.* 2002).

The manager of the Dutch automobile leasing company (Case VIII) has seen his company decide against outsourcing:

> When our board of directors considered outsourcing the IT department of eight FTEs, two potential suppliers were invited for a tender. Both looked into the situation and drew the conclusion that outsourcing was well possible. Meanwhile, these investigations caused much emotion among the department's staff, who had for years worked hard and contributed loyally to their company.

In order to prevent his department's takeover, its manager then wrote a report explaining that the cost savings proposed by the external suppliers could only be realized if the entire department were transferred to the future supplier's computing centre. This, he argued, was inappropriate to the automobile leasing industry. He also showed that his customers, the company's business units, were very satisfied – especially with his staff's knowledge of the business units' environment, needs and processes. After careful consideration, the board of directors agreed with their information manager that their IT department had proved able to outbid external competition with respect to the cost effectiveness of IT service delivery (Beulen 2000b: 26).

With respect to outsourcing costs, governments and financial institutions have an extra problem. Their services usually are not subject to turnover taxes, which they therefore do not collect for transfer to the government. This means they cannot deduct the turnover taxes they pay to external suppliers, who have no such exemption. Consequently, outsourcing implies rising costs (Altinkemer *et al.* 1994).

4 Confidentiality risks

Much essential company information, including strategic plans, is stored in computers. Under no circumstances should such information fall into the hands of competitors. The security risks involved in outsourcing are therefore frequently cited as a reason for not contracting out one's information services delivery; these companies prefer to keep their internal IT departments (Willcocks and Fitzgerald 1994; Klepper and Jones 1998).

The IT procurement manager of Case III explains:

> Our primary processes of producing coatings, fibres, chemicals and pharmaceuticals are supported by IT, which consequently has very much added value. Contracting out activities so close to our primary processes is not desirable. The risk of production secrets falling into the hands of our competitors by way of external suppliers is far too great.

(Beulen *et al.* 1994: 80)

Table 2.2 *Arguments against IT outsourcing*

Arguments	Rationale
1. Increased dependence on suppliers	• Managing the IT service delivery of service providers on the basis of contracts is more difficult and less flexible than managing an IT department by internal agreements. • Price changes during a contract period may significantly affect the recipient's total cost of ownership. • Companies performing their own information services delivery can independently decide to invest in technological innovations specific to their industry or situation; if IT services are delivered by service providers, these will have to be convinced of the need to make the investments.
2. A loss of knowledge and know-how	• By transferring IT experts to the service provider, knowledge of the business is lost as well as technical IT expertise. • Experts working for internal IT departments usually are all-round technicians with much knowledge of the business. • Staff sent by service providers usually have a narrower technical expertise and much less knowledge of the business; they are also generally quickly rotated between clients. • For a service recipient it is difficult, costly and time-consuming to acquire IT knowledge and know-how after the expiration of an outsourcing contract.
3. Higher costs	• Unlike internal IT departments, external service providers do have profit objectives. • Turnover taxes increase the costs of outsourcing for governments and financial institutions. • Managing service providers is more expensive than managing an internal IT department.
4. Confidentiality risks	• IT departments work for their own company only. Service providers may also work for the company's direct competitors, which causes serious security risks. • IT service delivery may be too directly connected to the company's primary processes. • Outsourcing, while it improves the service provider's competitive position, may decrease the service recipient's competitive power.
5. Difficulty in selecting the right service provider	• Future information needs are unforeseeable for service recipient. • Future mergers and acquisitions in the IT outsourcing service provider market are unforeseeable for service recipient. • Future changes in the service provider strategy are unforeseeable for service recipients.

5 *Difficulty in selecting the right service provider*

Based on today's information needs, a service recipient is able to select the right service provider. This requires a thorough selection procedure including pre-defined objectives of the outsourcing and requirements (Lacity and Hirschheim 1993; Cullen and Willcocks 2003). For service recipients it is very difficult to predict future information needs; future information needs might impact today's outcome of the selection procedure. Also future mergers and acquisitions in the IT outsourcing service provider market might impact today's outcome of the selection procedure. Also changes in the service provider strategy might have an impact.

2.5 BUSINESS PROCESS OUTSOURCING[1]

Growing business maturity has conveyed many companies from information systems outsourcing to the next phase: business process outsourcing (BPO) (Dain *et al.* 2004). This involves not only delivering information services, but taking responsibility for the execution of the service recipient's business processes as well. Generally, the business processes concerned are so-called IT-centred services, which are heavily based on information services. In order to provide such services effectively, service providers must have in-depth knowledge of the specific business processes involved. Business process outsourcing therefore requires more investment by the service provider and more business knowledge than does information systems outsourcing. It entails shifting the focus to the functionality required, and using specific applications in order to deliver it. Therefore, application maintenance capabilities are of crucial importance to BPO service providers.

Two types of business process outsourcing may be identified: supportive BPO, which is rather loosely linked to the recipient's business, and core BPO, which involves activities much closer to the recipient's primary processes. The differences between the two are outlined in Table 2.3. Supportive business process outsourcing started slowly in the 1980s and matured in the 1990s. Its beginnings, with payroll services, show that the difference between supportive BPO and outsourcing specific services is not always very clear. Supportive business process outsourcing is there-fore sometimes simply called process outsourcing (International Data Corporation 1997). It is provided on a one-on-one basis and therefore highly customized. An excellent example is provided by UK Network Rail, which entails the processing of more than 315 million ticket transactions per year. Other examples are provided by the British Department of Health, Work and Pensions, which has outsourced the processing of medical services delivered to more than 850,000 cases per year; and Hydro One, which has contracted out its billing process involving 1.2 million customers.

Core BPO is only recently starting to be adopted. By contrast with supportive business process outsourcing, in these relationships processes are provided to

Table 2.3 *Characteristics of supportive and core business process outsourcing, from the service recipient's point of view*

Supportive BPO	Core BPO
Exclusive, one-on-one partnerships on the basis of contracts	Non-exclusive partnerships on the basis of contracts
The outsourced processes are loosely linked to the primary processes of the service recipient	The outsourced processes are much closer to the primary processes of the service recipient
A high degree of customization	A limited degree of customization
Greater effectiveness by managing an automated customized environment	Cost efficiency (as a result of economies of scale) and innovation (by implementing the shared services centre concept)

multiple services recipients on a therefore less customized basis. The most important difference with supportive BPO, however, is that core business process outsourcing is much more closely interwoven with the primary processes of the service recipient. Take, for instance, the mortgage processes of DBV Verzekeringen, an insurance company of the Credit Suisse Group, active in the Netherlands. They have outsourced the processing of 400,000 mortgages. Likewise, British Petrol has outsourced the processing of over 15,000 invoices per month.

Bert Halm, vice-president of RCC (a Dutch information services provider that is now a subsidiary of PinkRoccade), explained in 1994:

> Facilities management and service management come in many shapes and sizes. Sometimes even data management is outsourced. My company recently began processing the staff and salary administration for our national museums, part of the culture department of the Dutch ministry of public transport.
>
> (Beulen *et al.* 1994: 34)

The current focus in the BPO world is on back-office processes such as human resources administration and payment services. Customer care, supply chain management, billing, and finance and accounting are growing in importance too – in fact, the whole financial sector is emerging strongly. By outsourcing some business processes, companies are able to deal simultaneously with business issues, such as global competition and privatization, and IT issues, such as maintaining legacy systems.

Market analysts consider business process outsourcing an emerging market: the Compounded Annual Growth Rate over the 2002–08 period was 18 per cent (Metcalfe 2004). To take advantage of this potential growth area, traditional IT out-sourcing suppliers are joining forces with business partners, consulting companies and process specialists, positioning themselves to market BPO. The original strength

Table 2.4 *The advantages and disadvantages of BPO compared with IT outsourcing, from the service recipient's point of view*

Advantages of BPO	Disadvantages of BPO
BPO costs are more directly related to the profits, through business-related accounting mechanisms	There is a greater interdependence with the recipient's primary processes, increasing the recipient's dependence on his provider
IT investments needed because of legacy problems are made by the service provider	Apart from IT knowledge and know-how, business competence also gradually slips away to the provider

of traditional information services outsourcing suppliers was their capability to execute; now they also have substantial business knowledge, as a result of their taking over IT staff from service recipients. This enables them to offer BPO successfully. And their experience with contract work makes for a smooth implementation of business process outsourcing contracts.

Essentially, information systems outsourcing and business process outsourcing share the same advantages and disadvantages. In Table 2.4 the differences – which are in accent only – are listed as the pros and cons of BPO with respect to IT outsourcing, as seen from the recipient's point of view.

2.6 OFFSHORE OUTSOURCING

Offshore outsourcing is a special kind of outsourcing, in which the services to be delivered (hardware and software availability, in particular) are performed from another geographical location to where they are used (Carmel 1999). Generally, service performance is located in developing countries. This means offshore outsourcing governance must always include a local customer interface near the recipient's location, in order for the service provider to be able to react adequately and in a timely fashion to changing demand and to reduce the risks presented by culture clashes, time-zone differences and language barriers (Marriot 2004). Offshore service providers also need extra capacity and must put in extra coordination effort to manage their relationships with their clients, since these are located far away (Lacity and Hirschheim 1993; Klepper 1995; Beulen *et al.* 2005). Additional coordination is required.

In regular offshore outsourcing, service providers and recipients belong to different companies and have customer–supplier relationships; if the provider is part of the same legal entity as the recipient, this is called captive offshore outsourcing (Carmel and Agarwal 2002). Another distinction may be made between so-called native service providers, who are based in developed countries and have subsidiaries in developing countries for the actual delivery of the services, and

Table 2.5 *The advantages and disadvantages of offshore outsourcing compared with IT outsourcing, from the service recipient's point of view*

Advantages of offshore outsourcing	Disadvantages of offshore outsourcing
Greater cost advantages caused by geographical differences in prices and salaries	Higher coordination costs due to geographical distance
Access to large pools of IT experts	Geopolitical risks
Certified processes (especially in the field of application development; for example, CMM level 5)	Communication (language and culture) barriers, which impede quality, costs and speed

foreign service providers, who have their headquarters in developing countries and subsidiaries in developed countries functioning mainly as sales offices. Well-known native service providers are companies such as Accenture, Atos Origin (in France), CSC, EDS and IBM (all in the United States), and Logica CMG (in Britain). Most foreign service providers are based in India (Cognizant, Satyam, Tata Consultancy Services and Xansa), which shows the subcontinent's dominance in the offshore outsourcing market (Carmel and Beulen 2005).

As with business process outsourcing, the pros and cons of offshore outsourcing are not essentially different from those of IT outsourcing. There are differences in accent, though, and these are listed in Table 2.5 as the advantages and disadvantages of offshore outsourcing for the recipient.

2.7 SHARED SERVICE CENTRES

Shared service centres (SSCs) are organizational units that centrally execute services shared by the recipient's divisions and business units. The services delivered are generally standard, process-driven, transactional activities (Goold *et al.* 2001), which support the company's primary processes (Cullen and Willcocks 2003) and usually involve much information technology. Accounting services and e-procurement exchanges are examples of such services.

The difference with outsourcing is that shared service centres remain part of the recipient's organization; they are the result of delivery concentration. This means that only large companies can have them. It also implies that their governance involves not only contractual agreements but hierarchical connections between them and the company's divisions and business units as well. Yet setting up a shared service centre can be a first step towards independence and thus possibly to outsourcing.

Elizabeth Arden International, a skin care, cosmetics and perfume company that is currently part of Unilever, was one of the first companies to set up a shared service centre in the mid-1990s in Geneva. From here, customer services as well as marketing, order processing, finance, treasury, supply chain and information services were provided for all 12 national divisions (Krempel 1999). Another example is Dupont's Global Business Services, set up in 1999. It offers accounting and legal services, people processes and sourcing and value chain processes and employs a staff of 6,000, which is more than 6 per cent of the company's total workforce (Goold *et al.* 2001).

2.7.1 The advantages and disadvantages of shared service centres

The most important advantages of shared service centres are cost savings and quality improvement. Both are the result of concentration, in the case of cost savings because concentration causes economies of scale (Krempel 1999). Companies who decide to locate their shared service centres in developing countries can increase their cost savings still further, as rates and salaries are lower there (Carmel and Agarwal 2002). This has now become a trend (Metcalfe 2004), as evidenced by companies such as Ford, which transferred its European accounting services to Chennai in India (500 employees) (Rickel 2004), and the World Bank, which transferred its entire back office to India (Choudhury 2004).

Another advantage is the possibility of head count reduction, which improves a company's financial ratios (Section 2.3) (Loh and Venkatraman 1992). When shared service centres are set up, staff reductions of more than 40 per cent are not unusual (Goold *et al.* 2001). Concentration also helps reduce the profusion of different systems that the many divisions and business units of large concerns would otherwise use. Thus, many costly and risky interface issues are eliminated (Krempel 2000), like having to adapt all interfaces when one IT system is changed somewhere. Ford has realized substantial cost savings by integrating its IT systems (Rickel 2004) and at the World Bank these savings have been in excess of 35 per cent (Choudhury 2004).

Of course, shared service centres have their disadvantages too. The recipient's business processes must conform to the standards developed by the service centre. This lowers the business units' flexibility, which is a problem especially in large conglomerates operating many different processes (Krempel 1999). Then there are the communication problems introduced by having a service centre far away from the business; these difficulties are similar to those encountered in offshore outsourcing.

Finally, while reducing the company's head count may be good for its financial ratios, it does of course present a personnel problem. Many employees will not be willing to move to another country simply because their activities move there. And it does not always make economic sense to move them either: generally, only those staff whose skills are not available at the new centre's location should move, which usually means less than 5 per cent of the employees, mostly subject experts and

29

managers, but rarely operational staff. Consequently, the question arises of where most of the current staff should go. Often it is difficult to find new positions for them in the recipient's organization and therefore they will have to be laid off. But this is costly too, and in economically difficult times may damage the company's image and cause negative publicity.

NOTE

1 This section is based on a White Paper on outsourcing published by Atos Origin (Beulen *et al.* 2004), which is also available on the Internet. A short version of the White Paper was published in Dain *et al.* (2004).

REFERENCES

Altinkemer, K., Chaturvedi, A. and Gulati, R. (1994) 'Information systems outsourcing: issues and evidence', *International Journal of Information Management*, 4 (4): 252–268.

Beulen, E. (2000a) 'Beheersing van IT-outsourcingsrelaties: een beheersingsmodel voor uitbestedende bedrijven en IT-leveranciers', PhD thesis, Tilburg University (in Dutch).

Beulen, E. (2000b) *Kostenbeheersing*, Den Haag: Ten Hagen en Stam (in Dutch).

Beulen, E. (2002) *Uitbesteding van IT-dienstverlening*, Den Haag: Ten Hagen en Stam (in Dutch).

Beulen, E. (2003) 'Lessons learned voor de beëindiging van uitbestedingscontracten', in J. van Bon (ed.) *IT-beheer Jaarboek 2003*, Den Haag: Ten Hagen en Stam.

Beulen, E. and Ribbers P. (2002) 'Managing complex IT outsourcing – partnerships', paper presented at HICSS 2002 conference, Hawaii, 0–7695–1435–9/02, January 2002.

Beulen, E., Ribbers, P. and Roos, J. (1994) *Outsourcing van de IT-dienstverlening: een make or buy beslissing*, Deventer: Kluwer Bedrijfswetenschappen (in Dutch).

Beulen, E., Baas, R., Dain, J., Hudson, J., Reitsma, E., Symonds, M. and van der Zee, H. (2004) 'Outsourcing: the Atos Origin outsourcing lifecycle – building successful outsourcing relationships', White Paper, Atos Origin (www.atosorigin.com/corporate/viewpoint/vp_270104.htm) Accessed 29 August 2004.

Beulen, E., van Fenema, P. and Currie, W. (2005) 'From application outsourcing to infrastructure management: extending the offshore outsourcing service portfolio', *European Management Journal*, 23 (2): 133–144.

Brown, C. and Renwick, J. (1996) 'Alignment of the IS organization: the special case of corporate acquisitions', *The Database for Advances in Information Systems*, 27 (September): 25–33.

Buck-Lew, M. (1992) 'To outsource or not?', *International Journal of Information Management*, 12: 3–20.

Cadwell, B. and Young, A. (2003) 'Cost, caution and consolidation unsettle the outsourcing market, market trends', research report, Gartner.

Carmel, E. (1999) *Global Software Teams, Collaboration Across Borders and Time Zones*, Englewood Cliffs, NJ: Prentice Hall.

Carmel, E. and Agarwal, R. (2002) 'The maturation of offshore sourcing of Information Technology work', *Management Information Systems Quarterly Executive*, 1 (2): 65–76.

Carmel, E. and Beulen, E. (2005) 'Managing offshore transition', in E. Carmel and P. Tjia (eds) *Offshore Outsourcing of Information Technology Work*, Cambridge: Cambridge University Press.

Choudhury, F. (2004) 'Migrating the back office offshore – a World Bank perspective', proceedings of 'Successful Business Process Outsourcing Strategies' conference, European Networking Group, Amsterdam, 25 and 26 February 2004.

Cross, J. (1995) 'IT-outsourcing: British Petroleum's competitive approach', *Harvard Business Review*, 73 (3): 94–104.

Cullen, S. and Willcocks, L. (2003) *Intelligent IT Outsourcing: eight building blocks to success*, Oxford: Butterworth-Heinemann.

Currie, W. and Willcocks, L. (1998) 'Analysing four types of IT-outsourcing decisions in the context of scale, client/server, interdependency and risk migration', *Information Systems Journal*, 8 (2): 119–143.

Currie, W., Desai, B. and Khan, N. (2004) 'Customer evaluation of application services provisioning in five vertical sectors', *Journal of Information Technology*, 19 (1): 39–58.

Dain, J., Beulen, E., Baas, R., Hudson, J., Symonds, M. and van der Zee, H. (2004) 'Building successful outsourcing relationships', Achieving Competitive Advantage Collaborative Partnerships, Middlesex: CxO Research Ltd (www.cxoeurope.com/documents.asp?d_ID = 27) Accessed 29 August 2005.

David, J., Schuff, D. and Louis, R. (2002) 'Managing your IT total cost of ownership', *Communications of the Association for Computing Machinery*, 45 (1): 101–106.

Eckerson, W., Hayward, G., Palmer, N. and Simpson, T. (2000) 'Outsourcing speeds portal development, saves resources', *I/S Analyzer*, 39 (8): 1–16.

Feeny, D. (1997) 'The five-year learning of ten IT directors', in L. Willcocks, D. Feeny and G. Islei (eds) *Managing IT as a Strategic Resource*, London: McGraw Hill.

Frolick, M. and Chen, L. (2004) 'Assessing M-commerce opportunities', *Information Systems Management*, 21 (2): 53–61.

Goldsmith, R. (1994) 'Confidently outsourcing software development', *Journal of Systems Management*, 45 (4): 12–17.

Goold, M., Pettifer, D. and Young, D. (2001) 'Re-design the corporate center', *European Management Journal*, 19 (1): 83–91.

Grover, V. and Teng, J. (1993) 'The decision to outsource information systems functions', *Journal of Systems Management*, 44 (11): 34–38.

International Data Corporation (1997) 'European consulting and management services: riding the wave: an analysis of outsourcing market leaders in Western Europe', research report, International Data Corporation.

Kanter, R. (1994) 'Collaborative advantage: the art of alliances', *Harvard Business Review*, 73 (July/August): 96–108.

Kern, T., Kreijger, J. and Willcocks, L. (2002) 'Exploring ASP as sourcing strategy: theoretical perspectives, propositions for practice', *Journal of Strategic Information Systems*, 11 (2): 153–177.

Ketler, K. and Walstrom, J. (1993) 'The outsourcing decision', *International Journal of Information Management*, 13 (6): 449–459.

Klepper, R. (1995) 'The management of partnering development in I/S outsourcing', *Journal of Technology*, 10 (4): 249–258.

31

Klepper, R. and Jones, W. (1998) *Outsourcing Information Technology Systems and Services*, New York: Prentice Hall.

Kraemer, K. and Dedrick, J. (2002) 'Strategic use of the Internet and e-commerce: Cisco Systems', *Journal of Strategic Information Systems*, 11 (1): 5–29.

Krempel, M. (1999) 'The pan-European company – restructuring for a new Europe', *European Business Journal*, 11 (3): 11–27.

Krempel, M. (2000) 'Restructuring for a new Europe', *Strategic Direction*, May: 13–15.

Lacity, M. and Hirschheim, R. (1993) *Information Systems Outsourcing*, Chichester: Wiley.

Lacity, M. and Hirschheim, R. (1995) *Beyond the Information Systems Outsourcing Bandwagon*, Chichester: Wiley.

Lander, M., Purvis, R., McCray, G. and Leigh, W. (2004) 'Trust-building mechanisms utilized in outsourced IS development projects: a case study', *Information & Management*, 41 (4): 509–528.

Lee, J.-N., Huynh, M.Q., Kwok, R.C.-W. and Pi, S.-M. (2003) 'IT outsourcing evolution: past, present, and future', *Communications of the Association for Computing Machinery*, 46 (5): 84–89.

Loh, L. and Venkatraman, N. (1992) 'Stockmarket reaction to information technology outsourcing: an event study', working paper no. 3499–92BPS, Massachusetts Institute of Technology.

Longenecker, C. and Scazzero, J. (2003) 'The turnover and retention of IT managers in rapidly changing organizations', *Information Systems Management*, 20 (1): 58–63.

Marriot, I. (2004) 'Offshore Sourcing: a framework for success', presentation at Outsourcing and IT Services Summit 2004, Gartner, Royal Lancaster Hotel, London, 26–27 April.

Metcalfe, D. (2004) 'The future viability of business process outsourcing', Proceedings of 'Successful Business Process Outsourcing Strategies' conference, European Networking Group, Amsterdam, 25 and 26 February 2004.

Peppard, J. (2003) 'Managing IT as a portfolio of services', *European Management Journal*, 21 (4): 467–483.

Rickel, J. (2004) 'Successful business process outsourcing strategies', Proceedings of 'Successful Business Process Outsourcing Strategies' conference, European Networking Group, Amsterdam, 25 and 26 February 2004.

Schambach, T. and Blanton, J. (2000) 'The professional development challenge for IT professionals', *Communications of the Association for Computing Machinery*, 45 (4): 83–87.

Tayntor, C. (2001) 'A practical guide to staff augmentation and outsourcing', *Information Systems Management*, 18 (1): 84–91.

Travis, L. (2003) 'To reduce partner management burden', research note Outsource EDI INT AS2, 25 July.

van der Zee, H. and van Wijngaarden, P. (1999) *Strategic Sourcing and Partnerships: Challenging Scenarios for IT Alliances in the Network Era*, Amsterdam: Addison Wesley.

Willcocks, L. and Fitzgerald, G. (1994) *A Business Guide to Outsourcing IT*, London: Business Intelligence.

Willcocks, L., Fitzgerald, G. and Feeny, D. (1995) 'Outsourcing IT: the strategic implications', *Long Range Planning*, 28 (5): 59–70.

Chapter 3

Structuring responsibilities

- This chapter opens with a discussion on IS/IT planning.
- Next it presents an overview of IT services responsibilities, activities and roles, which are found on all organizational levels – strategic, tactical and operational.
- Attention is also paid to the implications outsourcing has for implementing service delivery processes, and to the governance of relationships with IT service providers.
- The chapter ends with a discussion of the responsibilities that may be outsourced profitably to service providers.

3.1 INTRODUCTION

First we must take stock of the responsibilities related to IT services, and assign them to the respective organizational levels of strategy, tactics and operations. This is the subject of Sections 3.2 and 3.3. Next we will discuss whether strategic decisions should be made on a central level or should be decentralized. For this purpose, in Section 3.4 a distinction is made between information systems (IS) and information technology (IT), the strategies for each requiring their own considerations. Then, in Section 3.5, we link IT responsibilities with activities and roles, on each of the organizational levels mentioned above. And finally, in Section 3.6, we will discuss which responsibilities may be outsourced and which would be best kept by service recipients.

3.2 RESPONSIBILITIES FOR IS/IT PLANNING

In every organization the responsibilities to be held, the activities to be carried out and the roles to be played are allocated to specific people. This allocation is based on common organizational principles of division of labour, which aim at balancing the benefits and costs of specialization and coordination. In this way functional areas have emerged like Marketing, Production and Human Resources. This holds not only for business issues, but also for information systems and information technology. Assuring that the appropriate information and information systems are available to the organization is the responsibility of the Information Systems or IS function (Feeney and Willcocks 1997). The service delivery responsibility is with the internal IT department or, in the case of outsourcing, with the service provider. This requires alignment with the company's business functions as well as with its IT services suppliers.

Management of any business function, and of the business itself, can be described by the classical management cycle, which encompasses strategy and planning, organizing and leading, execution of plans and monitoring. Although these terms have been known for decades in the management and organization literature, the definition of responsibilities and tasks in the IT domain is still confusing and not crystallized (Earl 1989; Galliers and Leidner 2003).

With regard to the management of information and information resources, a distinction is made between demand and supply, and so between demand management and supply management (Ward and Peppard 2002). Demand management is business oriented and is about specifying the organizational needs for information, and consequently for information systems. Demand management is typically a business responsibility. Supply management has a technology focus and is about managing the information resources – people, assets and processes – in such a way that demand for information exerted by the organization is met effectively in a cost-efficient way. Being an integral business responsibility, demand typically is not a candidate for outsourcing. As supply is about installing and managing the technology in order to deliver the needed information, which often will be an activity quite different from the (core) business of the company requiring different knowledge bases and skills, it may be a typical candidate for outsourcing. Philips, an international manufacturer, decided in the late 1980s to structure demand and supply management. In the 1990s, Philips outsourced first the application part of the internal IT department and at a later stage their infrastructure management. The initial structuring and the phased approach enabled the implementation of an adequate demand management (Beulen et al. 1994).

Related to the distinction above is the difference between information systems (IS) and information technology (IT), and with that between IS strategy and IT strategy (Earl 1987; Ward and Peppard 2002). The UK Academy of Information Systems[1] defines IS as 'the means by which people and organizations, utilizing technology, gather, process, store, use and disseminate information'. IT is then taken to refer especially to the technology involved, including software, hardware and networks. IT facilitates the processing, storing and delivery of information. In Europe the term ICT (Information Communication Technology) was often used instead of IT. Communication was originally held to be a separate discipline; in this book we will conform to international standards and use IT.

How does this relate to strategy? There are many definitions of strategy. We define strategy as a set of decisions that drives future plans and principal policies and defines the range of the business (Andrews 1980; Smits *et al.* 1997). In general the concept of strategy refers to corporate strategy, which is the strategy that drives the corporation or enterprise as a whole. Business units within larger corporations have business strategies related to their specific product-market environment (Porter 1987). From corporate or business strategies are derived the notion of functional strategies such as marketing strategy, manufacturing strategy, personnel strategy. As suggested above, with regard to the information systems function a distinction is made between the IS strategy and IT strategy. IS strategy may be defined as the plan an organization uses in providing IS (Pearlson 2001). It specifies investments in the application portfolio (e.g. strategic applications, necessary applications, business critical systems, infrastructure, etc.), the benefits expected from them and the necessary changes to deliver the benefits (Ward and Peppard 2003). The IS strategy focuses on IS demand management. IT strategy specifies how the required application portfolio will be supported by technology. It encompasses choices with regard to hardware, software, databases, networks and related standards and defines the services to be delivered, like computer operations, data management, software development, maintenance and user support. As such, it focuses on IT supply.

Both IS and IT strategy relate to formal applications and technology. Some stress the necessity to consider the need for information separately from the need for the applications and technology that deliver it (Smits *et al.* 1997). From this perspective Information Strategy may include implicit or explicit visions, goals, guidelines and plans as part of the supply and demand of formal information in an organization. These are sanctioned by management and intended to support the objectives of the organization in the long run. In addition these allow adjustment to the environment (Smits *et al.* 1997; Galliers and Leidner 2003).

In fact an Information Strategy is demand oriented and would precede an IS and IT strategy. Contrary to the other definitions, this definition does not focus attention on applications and technology, but on information required to enable the implementation of the business strategy, and which would provide managers with information that would enable the questioning of assumptions on which strategy and plans are based. This implies external information from the business and technological environment and internal feedback information on the effect of strategies and plans once implemented (Galliers and Leidner 2003).

Of interest are the linkages between the functional strategies and the business strategies, particularly the linkage between the information strategy and the business strategy in an organization (Parker *et al.* 1989). This linkage may be visualized by the strategic alignment model proposed by Henderson and Venkatraman (1993) (based on Parker *et al.* 1989), covering the linkages between four domains in an organization:

1 the business strategy domain;
2 the business process domain;
3 the IT strategy domain;
4 the IT processes domain.

The term IT governance has arisen in recent literature (Weill and Ross 2004), which in general refers to the way responsibilities related to information provisioning are allocated in the organization. IT governance may be defined as 'specifying the decision rights and accountability framework to encourage desirable behaviour in the use of IT' (Weill and Ross 2004: 2). IT governance addresses three fundamental questions:

1 What decisions must be made to ensure effective management and use of IT?
2 Who should make these decisions?
3 How will these decisions be made and monitored?

3.3 THREE PLANNING LEVELS FOR IS/IT

The management of any business activity can be described on the basis of Anthony's traditional planning and control framework (Anthony 1965; Wiseman 1988). This framework discerns three levels of management decisions:

1 Strategic level: strategic decisions typically relate to the (long-term) objectives of the organization, changes in those objectives, resources needed to attain those objectives, and policies that are to govern the acquisition, use and disposition of those resources.
2 Tactical or management level: this level concerns the management activity through which managers assure that the planned resources are obtained and used to accomplish the stated objectives in an effective and efficient way.
3 Operational level: operational level activities are about assuring that specific tasks are carried out according to plan.

Along a variety of dimensions, these planning levels form a hierarchy, with the strategic level at the top and the operational level at the bottom (Wiseman 1988). The longer the effect of a plan, the more difficult to reverse and the more strategic it is. The higher the hierarchical level that takes the decision, the more strategic it is. The more judgement is needed and the higher the importance of a decision, the more strategic it is. However, in practical situations distinctions are not always that clear. Decisions that seem strategic to one person may appear tactical to another, which suggests that the distinction is much more relative than absolute (Ackoff 1970).

1 Strategic-level responsibilities

Obviously, information systems strategy and information technology strategy belong on a strategic organizational level. IS strategies are derived from the company's overall business strategy, and the two must be aligned with one another (Henderson and Venkatraman 1993; Brown and Magill 1994; Luftman 2000). This is all the more essential because the importance of IS and IT is steadily increasing, and strategic decisions about them in return influence the company's business strategy. Therefore, two-way strategic alignment is required (Rockart *et al.* 1996).

On the basis of the IS strategy, an IT strategy is then set up. This includes a sourcing strategy, which defines which IT services will be delivered by the company's internal information technology department and which will be outsourced to external service providers (Quinn and Hilmer 1994). For those services that are outsourced, a choice must be made between contracting a single provider or several (Currie and Willcocks 1998).

The IT strategy also includes choices about the architecture needed, which involves the layout of applications and infrastructure – aspects that both require attention and that also influence each other (Aerts *et al.* 2004). This architectural element is also derived from the IS strategy (Sankar *et al.* 1993; Duncan 1995), and it includes choices for development platforms, operating systems, databases and middleware solutions as well as for hardware suppliers (Luftman 2000; Applegate *et al.* 2003).

2 Tactical-level responsibilities

Planning the quantity and type of IT services to be delivered during the upcoming planning period and assuring the proper utilization of these services (e.g. through training) is a matter for tactical organization levels (Morton 1991). The way in which IT services are managed is derived from the IS and IT strategies (Feeny and Willcocks 1998). Whether some or all delivery has been outsourced is less relevant at this level, since agreements with internal departments and external suppliers must both always be laid down in contracts (Kraljic 1983; Heckmann 1999). In the case of outsourcing, the need for watertight contracts is of course greater, since there is no hierarchic relationship but only a contractual one between the parties (Lacity and Hirschheim 1993). Nevertheless, in practice it is often impossible to foresee every eventuality and make arrangements ahead of time.

3 Operational-level responsibilities

Finally, the responsibility for the actual delivery and proper use of IT services is an operational matter (Earl 1987). Contractual obligations entered into on the tactical level point the way here. Nevertheless, the dynamics of such obligations have always been a source of trouble (Dickson *et al.* 1984; Niederman *et al.* 1991) and still are (Cullen and Willcocks 2003). And the situation continues to grow even more complex, with the ever-increasing number of companies involved in mergers and acquisitions (Brown and Renwick 1996) and the rise of technological developments. These technological developments, such as enterprise resource planning (ERP) systems in the 1990s, e-business around 1995 and recently m-business,[2] introduce new possibilities in the field of IT services that must somehow be made to fit into the contractual framework agreed upon. This is called 'technology push'. To be able to handle such changes, it is important that the processes involved are treated seriously (Luftman 2000). Change processes such as that of the IT Infrastructure Library (ITIL) can be of help here. They anchor the implementation of the changes in the plans made (Johnson and Andrew 1994).

3.4 STRATEGY CENTRALIZATION AND DECENTRALIZATION

Strategic decisions may be taken in a centralized or a decentralized manner. Since both information systems and information technology strategies involve strategic decision-making, the question of centralization or decentralization must be answered for both (Earl 1987). A centralized IS strategy means that decisions about the architecture needed for the business are taken on a corporate level, for the whole company. The specifics of individual business processes are of little influence then, as are both internal and external IT providers. Instead, there is a goal of enterprise-wide commonality, both for applications and business processes. For a decentralized IS strategy architecture decisions are taken separately for each part of the company, which means that the input of the business processes and of internal or external IT suppliers is needed.

Likewise, a centralized IT strategy means making technology choices for the entire company at once, on the basis of the structure derived from the IS strategy. Internal IT departments and external providers are managed in a centralized manner, as are choices for one provider or another. For a decentralized IT strategy, technology choices are made for each of the company's parts separately, on the basis of their individual information needs. IT department and provider governance is then decentralized and so are supplier choices.

Centralization and decentralization both have advantages and disadvantages. These will now be discussed. This discussion culminates in the proposal of a grid, which is the result of combining the centralization questions for IS and IT.

3.4.1 Centralizing or decentralizing the IS strategy

There are companies for which information systems strategy centralization is the only choice. Sometimes a company's divisions are simply too small to have IS strategies of their own. They lack the scale to acquire the knowledge and know-how needed. Then the company's central head office must take all the decisions required.

For larger companies, IS strategy centralization offers the advantage of 'internal co-alignment' (Luftman 2000), which means that all parts of the company work from the same basic principles. Internal co-alignment has the advantage of making internal information exchange easier. Companies whose activities encompass large segments of the value chain will find this especially important: data from one of the value chain's elements is then easily transferred to the next, which results in efficient and effective internal information processing and provision.

Naturally, such standardization also makes advantages of scale possible in the field of IT services. If the company's divisions have less choice in their procurement of IT technology, cost advantages may be achieved. Furthermore, companies involved in frequent mergers and acquisitions will paradoxically find it easier to disentangle divisions if their IT processes are standardized. They will also have less trouble integrating new divisions if there are clear corporate IS standards (Brown and Renwick 1996).

The CIO of a global agricultural supplier (Case IX; see Appendix, p. 268, for all Case details) gives an example:

> We sell products based on potato, wheat, tapioca and waxy maize starches. Our plants and sales offices are located all over the world. Nevertheless, our IT requirements are limited in terms of scope, such as the number of servers and desktops, and in terms of the need for technology innovation. Our processes are, after all, fairly straightforward. The IT knowledge of many of our local plants and sales offices is therefore limited. So we set the IS strategy at our international head office.

Flexibility is a prime argument in favour of decentralizing IS strategy. This holds especially for companies that consist of widely different components. In decentralized environments, however, it is very important to prevent legacy problems (Applegate *et al.* 2003). If the infrastructure and the applications are not managed as a portfolio, there will not be enough flexibility in the long term to provide all business processes with the information they need (Ward and Peppard 2002).

The CIO of a global process industry company (Case III) explains:

> I'm responsible for the implementation of the IS strategy within my company. I limit myself to setting architecture guidelines. Since the company consists of

three divisions with totally different information needs, setting too many central standards is no use. And besides, since the divisions have their own profit and loss responsibility, they also have the power to take many such decisions for themselves.

3.4.2 Centralizing or decentralizing the IT strategy

Centralizing the company's IT strategy enables it to achieve advantages of scale in IT services. The resources available – IT professionals, hardware and software – are all scarce and much may be saved on costs if they are deployed to optimum effect. Another advantage of centralization is the improved ease of internal data exchange that results from everyone using the same technology, provided that everyone uses the same data-definitions (which is a matter of IS strategy). And in the IT strategy field, too, there is an advantage to centralization and the consequent standardization if the company is involved in frequent mergers and acquisitions – although the advantage is admittedly somewhat less important than for IS strategy (Brown and Renwick 1996). Centralization enables the integration and disentanglement of parts of the company: interface issues can be addressed more effectively.

Decentralization, on the other hand, allows a better match with the demands of the users in all parts of the company (George and King 1991). As in the area of IS strategy, flexibility is a serious argument in favour of IT strategy decentralization. It is an especially strong argument for companies whose divisions exchange much information with external parties: flexibility with respect to their interfaces with other organizations enables them to process and provide information efficiently and effectively.

In the days of mainframe computing, centralization was usually the only possibility. The investments and costs were simply too high to allow decentralization. But the rise of personal computers made decentralization possible, at least for service recipients (Buchanan and Linowes 1980). And in practice many companies have indeed chosen to decentralize, with the result that many hardware platforms, development platforms and applications are part of the company's IT services. Lacking a powerful IS strategy, some companies have come to the point where even their IT strategy is decentralized.

The CIO of a global consumer package goods company (Case X) tells us about his dilemma:

As a member of the company's corporate organization I have only limited say over our many national operating companies. They have profit and loss responsibility and can organize their business processes as they see best, including information technology. All I can do is try to get the operating companies to pool their resources, and see if a business case can be made for organizing some IT services together. That is no easy task, certainly not when legacy systems are involved, but in some cases it is worthwhile. For instance: I am now working with one of our suppliers to establish a business case to introduce SAP, a pre-eminent example of a change that must be supported from the centre.

The centralization versus decentralization choice is not only important for companies with internal IT departments. If one's IT services are outsourced, there still is the choice of outsourcing to one or to several providers. On the one hand, there is the possibility that autonomous business units approach different service providers for the same type of service. This is a situation we would label as decentralization. The advantage of this approach is the reduced dependency on one supplier, however at the cost of a loss of buying power. On the other hand there is the possibility of approaching multiple service providers for different services, which is utilizing the specific competencies of specialized suppliers.

Atos Origin's service delivery manager for one of their major clients (Case XI) explains:

My customer, who is active in the telecommunication industry, chose to spread the responsibilities of their IT services. We do helpdesk, desktop and LAN services as well as Unix systems and technical application management for supply chain applications. Other tasks are left to some of our competitors. This portfolio approach may cost my client money because he cannot profit from advantages of scale, but the ongoing competition between his providers does get him a good price-quality ratio. One important aspect here is that the total contract value exceeds 20 million euros; perhaps such an approach would not work for smaller contracts.

3.4.3 The IS and IT strategy centralization–decentralization grid

We may now set up an IS and IT strategy centralization–decentralization grid (see Table 3.1), combining these approaches with the respective IS and IT strategy levels. Only in the case of a centralized approach are both IS and IT strategy managed in a centralized manner; and only in the case of a decentralized approach are both treated in a decentralized manner.

A centralized technology approach is a kind of bottom-up approach. The company's component parts have only limited freedom in making information technology investments as most are done on a corporate level, even though there are no central IS guidelines to that effect. The benefits of such a set-up are that advantages of scale may be achieved and a certain degree of standardization is reached. The centralized architecture approach, on the other hand, does include clear IS guidelines. Within these guidelines, however, every division can make the IT investments it considers necessary, which guarantees a certain degree of flexibility.

Table 3.1 *The IS and IT strategy centralization–decentralization grid*

		Information technology strategy	
		Centralized	Decentralized
Information systems strategy	Centralized	Centralized approach	Centralized architecture approach
	Decentralized	Centralized technology approach	Decentralized approach

This grid is meant to help service recipients in positioning their IS and IT strategies and in determining the future organizational structure of their company. It does this by facilitating the company's internal discussions.

3.5 IS/IT PLANNING RESPONSIBILITIES, ACTIVITIES AND ROLES

With regard to the effective exploitation of IT in the business, three key areas of management responsibility can be distinguished (Feeny and Willcocks 1997). First, the appropriate alignment of IT and business requires the development of a vision of how IT should support the business, and also of how IT may enable new innovative strategies and organizational designs. These two effects have been labelled alignment and impact, respectively (Parker 1987). The second area of responsibility concerns the design of the appropriate IT architecture, the choices of the technical platform on the basis of which IT services will be delivered. These choices, though technical in nature, are closely related to current and future business models. Networked business models and blurring organizational boundaries pose new challenges for choices regarding the right IT architectures and how to cope with new needs for inter-operability and integration. Finally, there is the challenge of delivery of low-cost and high-quality IS services. The functioning of modern businesses is increasingly dependent on the availability of high-quality IS services. Choosing the right supplier, either internal or external, is a key decision.

These responsibilities can be separated into activities and roles, which in turn can be assigned to each of the organizational levels – strategic, tactical and operational (see Table 3.2). Such an analysis is the subject of this section, and is based on the work of Feeny and Willcocks (1997) and our experience with large outsourcing deals. The results are presented in Table 3.3, p. 55. The analysis must begin with the definition of the roles to be played, that is, people's functions with respect to information technology. At the service recipient's side (also called the IS function) there are six roles: those of business manager; chief information officer (CIO); information manager (IM); service delivery supervisor; purchaser; and business analyst.

Table 3.2 *Overview of roles and responsibilities in outsourcing relationships*

Role		Description
Service recipient (IS function)	Business manager	Business managers carry final responsibility for the execution of business processes.
	Chief information officer (CIO)	CIOs carry final responsibility for the IT services and for the development and implementation of their company's IS and IT strategies.
	Information manager (IM)	IMs are responsible for the IT services and the implementation of their company's IS and IT strategies. They serve as contact persons for the company's divisions who must define their information needs. In large companies there may be several IMs, each with responsibility for part of the company. IMs report to the CIO.
	Service delivery supervisor	Service delivery supervisors manage external IT providers and, if applicable, the internal IT department. They report to their IM.
	Purchaser	Purchasers support their IM and the service provider's contract manager in selecting and managing external IT providers and, if applicable, managing the internal IT department. They represent both the IS function's interests and those of the company's divisions. They do not report to any official within the IS function.
	Business analyst	Business analysts implement the IS and IT strategies. They serve as contact persons for the company's divisions who must define their information needs. In large companies there are several business analysts, each with responsibility for part of the company. They report to their respective IMs.
Service provider	IT director	IT directors carry final responsibility for the delivery of IT services as well as for the continuity of service delivery by external and, if applicable, internal IT providers. They are the IS function's strategic-level contact persons. If the IT services are outsourced, this role is played by the supplier's general manager.
	Account manager	Account managers maintain relationships with the IS function (and the managers of the recipient company's divisions). Their contacts partly focus on widening the scope and increasing the scale of their contracts. They are held accountable for the scale of the services

Continued

Table 3.2 *Continued*

Role	Description
	delivered and for customer satisfaction. Account managers serve as tactical-level contact persons for the IS function; together with the contract managers they are the provider's front office.
Contract manager	Contract managers are responsible for delivering the IT services contracted and for reporting and invoicing. For these aspects contract managers serve as contact persons for the IS function; together with the account managers they are the provider's front office.
Service delivery manager (SDM)	Service delivery managers manage the IT professionals who deliver the IT services. They report to the contract managers.
Process manager	Process managers set up and maintain the processes and certification of the IT services delivered. This responsibility does not pertain to any specific contract but to the IT services delivered for all the supplier's contracts. Process managers report to their IT director.
Competence manager	Competence managers investigate the potential of new technologies. This responsibility does not pertain to any specific contract but to the IT services delivered for all the supplier's contracts. The intention is to ascertain delivery continuity. Competence managers report to their IT director.
IT professional	IT professionals deliver the IT services and investigate the potential of new technologies. They report to either the service delivery manager or to the competence manager.

At the service supplier's side seven roles may be distinguished, those of IT director; account manager; contract manager; service delivery manager (SDM); process manager; competence manager; and IT professional. The content of these roles is described in Table 3.2. Naturally, while there is always only one CIO and usually only one IT director, there may be several business analysts, account managers, etc. And the provider may be an internal IT department, an external partner, or both.

We can now move on to the activities that must be carried out, and assign them to the three organizational levels and to the functional roles just defined. This is the subject of the following three sub-sections. For the purpose of this analysis, four levels of responsibility for the activities will be used. Final responsibility means that the company's general manager will hold the person involved directly accountable for the accomplishment of the tasks. This highest level of responsibility is called A, from approves or accepts. Next is the level called responsible (R), which entails carrying out the activity and involves being held accountable by the person in the A role. Sometimes A and R are combined (A/R), in which case the incumbent is again held directly accountable by the company's general manager. The letter S signifies delivering support to the persons in the R role. Finally, C stands for people who must be consulted by the persons in the R role before the activity is carried out, because their expertise is needed to decide how it must be done.

3.5.1 Strategic-level activities and roles

On a strategic level, five activities may be distinguished:

1   business systems thinking;
2   IS/IT leadership;
3   relationship building;
4   architecture planning;
5   making technology work.

(Feeny and Willcocks 1998)

These will now be discussed and assigned to the roles just described. Activities on a strategic level are mostly the responsibility of the service recipient's managers.

1 Business systems thinking

Business systems thinking is about envisioning how modern business management can be supported and how business processes may be reshaped exploiting the functionality of modern IT.

The CIO's most important task is making sure the company's business information requirements are met. They must therefore deploy information technology so that it makes a maximum contribution to business management. This means CIOs must know the developments in the field of information technology as well as in their company's markets, and consequently they must also maintain good relations with the company's business manager. These tasks are carried out on the basis of perceptions laid down in the company's IS and IT strategies.

The importance of having well-aligned business processes has become increasingly clear. And since many business processes require much information, CIOs must also contribute to their alignment. Virgin Mobile UK's chief information officer position, for instance, has evolved into that of a business improvement director. Says the current incumbent, Jon Kandiah (Case XII): 'The question I keep asking myself is: How can the value of the business be increased by changing the operations?'

It follows that CIOs must remain at their post for relatively long periods to be able to carry out these tasks well. Estimates of the time needed to make a significant contribution differ from 36 to 60 months (Cullen and Willcocks 2003). Unfortunately, CIOs often resign after much shorter periods – their job title is sometimes jokingly explained as 'career is over'. Another difficulty is that it is quite hard to find the right people for this position. Listen to an expert's observations:

> Three months ago I was doing a presentation at a conference where resourcing the information management office was one of the major discussion subjects. Many vendors were present, as well as major user companies. These latter kept saying it was very hard to find people with experience or expertise in the field of supplier management, in particular people who would be able to manage multiple providers.
>
> (Beulen 2000: 197)

Nevertheless, because of the importance of business systems thinking, it is the company's CIO who is ultimately accountable (A) for business systems thinking. Their information managers, next in line, carry out this activity (R), supported (S) by the company's business manager. Business analysts play a consulting (C) role.

2 IS/IT leadership

IS/IT leadership is needed to integrate IS/IT with the business and its activities. Leadership sets out the vision and the direction in which to go. IS/IT leadership bridges the gap between the business domain and IT domain, through the creation of shared understanding and a shared vision. The first person in the organization to address this capability is the CIO. He holds both final and executive responsibility (A/R). He is supported (S) by the company's information managers. Together they develop and implement the company's IS and IT strategies (Klepper 1995). They also serve as ambassadors who must alert their business manager to the potential of IT services. The question, therefore, is which position CIOs should have in their companies' organizations. Up until the year 2000, there was a tendency to promote CIOs to board members, but considering the board's integral business responsibility it is now usually considered better policy to put CIOs in staff positions, which would allow them to fulfil their leadership tasks better. This is confirmed by an expert in the field, who uses a CIO asked to become a board member as an example:

> He told us, 'I'm not interested in a board position. The board doesn't take any useful decisions. Actually, I'm far better employed forming relations with the people who really do make the decisions in the business.' This CIO just wasn't

interested, and showed that much depends on the board's role. Is it a really powerful decision-making body? If it is, then it's always important to be there. If it's not, then go where the decisions really are made.

(Beulen 2000: 205)

3 Relationship building

IT groups and business functions are differentiated in terms of departmental structures and mindsets of employees (Lawrence and Lorsch 1973). Mental models differ between the 'techies' and the business people. Building collaborative relationships based on shared understanding of IT/business issues is a requisite for the effective development, deployment and utilization of IT systems. Chief information officers must, together with their information managers and the company's business manager, make sure people collaborate. Of course, the people involved must have good interpersonal skills in order for this to succeed, which means there is a need to 'develop effective relations with line management' (Rockart *et al.* 1996). There is a clear difference with the task of achieving alignment, but both are needed to attain good governance in IT outsourcing partnerships. It is important that all perceptions and points of view are talked through.

An account manager (Case XIII), who as external IT provider has experience with such relationships, explains:

> Our IT forum is a kind of awareness club bringing together several of our client's business functions, such as purchasing, sales and transport. During excursions and thematic discussions they are brought into contact with what goes on in IT. The result is that they ask how and where they can use these new developments, how they can make a match between them and their business processes and improve those processes using these developments. They learn not only to think from their business point of view but from an IT point of view as well. There is, therefore, a political aspect to such a forum. These forums are a smart idea introduced by our client's finance and IT departments, with the object of getting the organization's support for IT.

(Beulen 2000: 195)

As with leadership, the company's CIO combines final and executive responsibility (A/R) for relationship building. Both his information manager and the company's business manager support (S) him, as do the provider's IT director and account manager.

4 Architecture planning

Architecture planning refers to bringing about the technical platform that supports current and future business models. The close interplay of the development of

47

modern technologies and the demands posed by new business models require a close collaboration between IT groups and business management. Architecture planning is a technical activity that belongs to both the IS and IT strategies. It involves an analysis of the development of current into future business management practice in order to establish how the information architecture should be adapted to meet the demands expected. This includes both hardware and software (Keen 1991), and it means that trend analyses of technological developments must be made. Since the current architecture plays a role in this planning activity, service providers too must be included in these deliberations.

Aligning the interests of service recipients and service providers often is not easy (Khosrowpour 1995); on the contrary, it requires much effort. An expert states: 'Common issues like architecture must be discussed together; they cannot be left to a central staff. Therefore, company-wide steering groups are often involved which include division business managers and division IT portfolio managers' (Beulen 2000: 195). To keep this activity on track for the longer term, companies usually formulate policies. Individual projects and investment proposals can then be assessed on the basis of these policies (Earl 1987). These policies often become part of the company's IT strategy (McFarlan and Nolan 1995).

Here, again, the CIO carries final responsibility (A). Executive responsibility (R) rests with the information managers, who are supported (S) by the company's business analysts. The service provider's contract manager and service delivery manager play a consulting role (C).

5 Making technology work

This capability addresses how to pick up problems that arise with the technical platform quickly and how to serve business needs that cannot be addressed by the standard solution offered by the system. Making technology work, an activity Rockart *et al.* (1996) call 'building high performance', rather resembles architecture planning. Compared with the other strategic-level activities, however, it has many operational aspects. The information office, which consists of the CIO and the company's corporate information managers, must therefore be involved closely, certainly in the case of major projects and when short-term decisions must be taken (as is often the case).

Information technology knowledge is of essential importance for this task, as is the involvement of the company's service provider. Service providers must contribute knowledge and know-how concerning IT possibilities and risks, while the service recipient's information office makes sure its business information requirements are met. It also takes the decisions, on the basis of the information provided by its supplier. Thus, the information office has final responsibility.

This activity is complicated by the dynamics of the interaction between business requirements and technology developments. These two must remain well tuned, which requires constant effort. According to one expert in the field:

> We intend to move away somewhat from aligning business and IT because it sounds so static, and because it is quite possible to be aligned but still go wrong. It is more important to have a good 'conversation' between IT and business. In a dynamic conversation there is tension because the future is unsure and you don't know what you should do. But while this tension shows that the service recipient and his provider are not exactly aligned, being able to have an open and respectful conversation about future developments and needs is much more important than being in close agreement all the time.
>
> (Beulen 2000: 206)

Again, the CIO is ultimately responsible (A) for this activity, which is carried out under the executive responsibility (R) of the information managers. They in their turn are supported (S) by the company's business analysts. The contract manager, service delivery manager and competence manager contribute (C) to this activity.

3.5.2 Tactical-level activities and roles

The tactical organizational level involves another five activities:

1. formulating information needs (Beulen 2000);
2. informed buying;
3. contract facilitation;
4. contract monitoring;
5. vendor development.

(Feeny and Willcocks 1998)

These tasks are shared between the service recipient and his suppliers.

Typical activities on this level to be taken care of by the service provider are:

6. setting up, maintaining and certifying delivery processes;
7. investigating and developing the potential of new technologies.

The importance of these processes may even have a strategic dimension for the service provider. The execution of the service processes takes place on an operational level.

1 Formulating information needs

Feeny and Willcocks (1998) consider this activity a part of what they call 'informed buying'. But there is a big difference between knowing which IT *services* are available in the market and knowing which information *needs* the business units experience. The first of these presupposes a technical profile, the second business management insight (Beulen 2000), and the two are rarely found in a single person. Therefore, the task of formulating information needs, called 'the stewardship role' by Lowrey (1996), is mentioned separately here. To carry out this activity you need both technology experts and subject experts. They can contribute knowledge of their business and define their business management's information needs.

> What you really need is a subject expert – who understands how the department functions, what are its purpose and role, and how it fits within the rest of the business. For it is their thinking that needs changing, and you must get them to consider that issue.
>
> (Beulen 2000: 190)

Final accountability (A) for this activity resides with the company's information managers. It is carried out (R) by the service delivery supervisor, with the support (S) of the service recipient's purchaser and business analysts and the service provider's account manager. The service recipient's contract manager and competence manager play a consulting (C) role.

2 Informed buying

Purchasing IT services requires market knowledge and insight. The buyer must also maintain good relations with their IT suppliers, setting up transparent tendering procedures and open communications. An important aspect is the willingness to let one's provider have his share of the profits too. It is a myth that one should drive the hardest commercial bargain possible, assuming that the supplier will look after their own profit margin. On the contrary, relationships with one's providers are all-important (Cullen and Willcocks 2003: 10). Says one expert:

> If the outsourcing company is too successful in its negotiations with its suppliers, driving down the margin to the point where their suppliers make no money, this will in the end ruin their relations with them. A provider who is given no room to manoeuvre will have to charge you for every last little extra. Eventually, this breaks down what should be friendly relations – poverty kills relations. If, on the other hand, the outsourcing company demands lower costs while insisting that his provider make an adequate margin too, trust develops which is beneficial for both parties.
>
> (Beulen 2000: 231)

Informed buying is part of the information manager's final responsibility (A). It is carried out (R) by the service delivery supervisor, who is supported (S) by the purchaser and the service recipient's account manager.

3 Contract facilitation

The objective of contract facilitation is to warrant the success of existing contracts for IS/IT services. Sourcing relationships and contracts are becoming increasingly complex. Service agreements are not perfect, and neither are services suppliers nor the recipients. It is important that upcoming problems can be solved swiftly and fairly within the framework of agreements and relationships. To facilitate contacts both the service recipient and the service provider must make the effort to 'lubricate' their outsourcing relationship (Grönroos 2000). Personal trust is very important (Klepper 1995). An external IT provider's contract manager, whose client is a major energy producing company (Case XIII), explains:

> My client's IT manager must trust me personally for our relation to work. They must know that what I say is true. If that trust is absent you have a serious problem. And while it is relatively easy to correct one another on the operational level if something should go wrong, in the tactical and strategic domains this is very difficult, so trust is even more important there.
>
> (Beulen 2002: 215)

The service recipient's service delivery supervisor holds both final and executive responsibility (A/R) for contract facilitation. He is supported (S) by the purchaser. The service provider's contract manager and service delivery manager may be consulted (C).

4 Contract monitoring

Through contract monitoring the service recipient's current and future contractual position is protected. It involves keeping suppliers on track by gearing their performance to the existing contracts and developments in the service market. To monitor a contract well, good reporting is essential (Lacity and Hirschheim 1993; Klepper 1995). Regular reporting, usually monthly and on the basis of key performance indicators, is needed. To this end a balanced scorecard may be used to assess the service provider's performance (Lacity and Willcocks 2001). Nevertheless, if the service recipient and their provider trust one another, fewer checks are needed (Fukuyama 1995), both in IT projects (Sabherwal 1999) and in continuously delivered services (Grover et al. 1996). The service recipient's service delivery supervisor holds both final and executive responsibility (A/R) for contract monitoring. He is supported (S) by their purchaser and by the service provider's IT director and account manager.

51

5 Vendor development

It is important for the service recipient to exploit the potential added value of its current service suppliers. Selection of a supplier, arriving at a contract and the subsequent implementation require substantial efforts and costs. Changing from one supplier to another may require the same level of effort. As a result, it is in the recipient's interest to maximize the contribution to its business by its existing suppliers. This requires looking beyond existing delivery agreements at how the IS/IT service needs will evolve and how the suppliers might contribute to these. However, apart from the company's relationships with its current service providers, contacts with other suppliers must be maintained too. They may be able to supplement one's current IT services or make a proposition to improve them or their price. Also in the situation that existing suppliers cannot satisfy a company's need, a logical alternative may be to try to create a supplier that can. Service recipients would therefore do well to manage their IT services as portfolios. This makes it easier to transfer the responsibility for them to another supplier (Anderson and Stampe Christensen 2002).

This activity is carried out (R) by the information manager, under the final responsibility (A) of the company's CIO. The information manager is supported (S) by his business analysts. Of course, the service recipient's IT director and account manager also support (S) this activity.

6 Setting up, maintaining and certifying service delivery processes

To ensure service delivery continuity, attention must be paid to setting up, maintaining and certifying service delivery processes – quite apart from the tasks already assigned to contract and service delivery managers. This activity must be the responsibility of a staff member. And it is important that service provisioning is organized as a process (Beulen 2000). For certification, the infrastructure management guidelines of the International Organization for Standards (ISO) may be followed, or the application development guidelines of the Capability Maturity Model (CMM).[3] As one might expect, certification plays an important role in service-provider selection. 'Certification – ISO, CMM and BS7799, for example – is essential in outsourcing and offshore outsourcing relationships. Customers pre-select their potential suppliers on the basis of their being certified', remarks one expert (Beulen *et al.* 2004).

The service provider's process managers hold final and executive responsibility (A/R) for this activity. They are supported (S) by their IT professionals, and the service recipient's information and service delivery supervisors may be consulted (C).

7 Investigating and developing the potential of new technologies

This activity, also called 'reskilling the IT organization' (Rockart *et al.* 1996), is linked with the outsourcing company's IS and IT strategies. By assessing the potential of new technologies and sharing that knowledge with their clients, service providers may contribute to their clients' competitive positions. This process is called 'technology push'. To improve their own positions, service providers may also enter into partnerships. The account manager of an IT provider to an energy producer explains:

> If our IT suppliers enter into strategic alliances with parties who can deliver resources we absolutely lack, this may be very advantageous. Of course, then we're not talking about subcontracting but about real partnering, which means adding to one another's strengths and growing together.
>
> (Beulen 2000: 252)

Final and executive responsibility (A/R) for this activity rest with the service provider's competence manager. Their IT professionals and the service recipient's information managers, service delivery supervisors and business analysts support (S) them.

3.5.3 Operational-level activities and roles

Finally, on the operational level, there are three activities:

> 1 maintaining relationships with the tenderer;
> 2 creating a skills base;
> 3 managing IT professionals.
>
> (Rockart *et al.* 1996)

These activities are mostly the responsibility of the service provider.

1 Maintaining relationships with the tenderer

In order to maintain their relationships with their tenderer (important to ensure the proper delivery of the services contracted), service providers must set up an unambiguous contact interface (Cross 1995). This is usually a combination of the provider's account manager and their contract manager (Magee 1998). The importance of this activity is illustrated by the following anecdote:

> An outsourcing company was buying desktop hardware from a commodity supplier. By the time it arrived, however, they had moved on and were thinking

of using Lotus Notes for their business processes – an application that requires working methods very different from the way they used to do things, and that was supplied by a very innovative and collaborative service provider. But their hardware provider's account manager, used to working in a commodity environment, didn't understand what they were talking about, and was enormously difficult to persuade to cooperate. In the end, he had to be removed from his post before they (the outsourcing company) could get any sense out of their supplier again; while he was still there, he effectively blocked their communications.

(Beulen 2002: 240)

Maintaining relationships with one's tenderer is the ultimate responsibility (A) of the provider's IT director. It is carried out (R) by the recipient's account manager and the provider's contract manager. The contract manager supports (S) the account manager, as the service delivery manager sometimes does too. The service recipient's information manager and service delivery supervisor in turn support (S) all of them. Finally, the purchaser can play a consulting (C) role.

2 Creating a skills base

The supplier must have the right resources available to deliver the contracted services. Rockart *et al.* (1996) distinguish between application development and infrastructure management, which they call 'delivering and implementing new systems' and 'building and managing infrastructure', respectively. Most IT outsourcing contracts, however, do not distinguish between these two kinds of services. It is therefore important that the right people are available to deliver the services. But if staff are moved from one project to another regularly, discontinuities may be the result. 'Creating a skills base can be a headache. Sometimes the best people available have to be taken away from other projects, which disrupts business developments there', one expert remarked (Beulen 2000: 247).

Final responsibility (A) for this activity rests with the service provider's contract manager. Their service delivery manager is responsible (R) for carrying it out, while their IT professionals and the service recipient's service delivery supervisor support (S) it. The service recipient's purchaser may be consulted (C).

3 Managing IT professionals

Gottschalk (2004) assigns the task of managing professionals who deliver IT services to systems development managers, systems operation managers and helpdesk managers. An important aspect of this management task is ensuring sufficient career and development perspectives for the professionals involved. This may be done by offering training or by assigning new responsibilities, that is, by arranging for the possibility of in-depth specialization or of broadening horizons. From the

Table 3.3 Overview of responsibilities, activities and role in demand and supply management

Level	Responsibility	Activities	Demand management						Supply management						
			Business manager	CIO	IM	Service delivery supervisor	Purchaser	Business analyst	IT director	Account manager	Contract manager	Service delivery manager	Process manager	Competence manager	IT professional
Strategic	IS/IT strategy	Business systems thinking	S	A	R			C							
		Leadership		A/R	S										
		Relationship building	S	A/R	S				S	S					
		Architecture planning		A	R			S				C		C	
		Making technology work		A	R			S				C		C	S
Tactical	Managing IT services	Formulating information needs		A	A	R	S	S							
		Vendor development				A/R	S		S	S					
		Informed buying		A	A	R	S			S					
		Contract facilitation		A	A	R	S			S	C	C			
		Contract monitoring				A/R	S				S	S			
		Investigating the potential of new technologies			S			S							S
Operational	Delivering IT services	Maintaining relations with the tenderer			S	S	C	S	A	R	S	(S)			
		Delivering the contracted IT services				S	C		A	R	A	R			
		Creating a skills base									A	R		A/R	
		Setting up, maintaining and certifying IT delivery processes			C	C							A/R		S

Notes: A: approves; R: responsible; S: support; C: consulted.

service recipient's point of view, however, the result is an unpleasant increase in staff dynamics, as IT professionals are removed from one project and assigned to another. To maintain the knowledge base needed for a proper service delivery, the personnel situation preferably should be stable. This is especially important when the services delivered involve management tasks. The contract manager of an external IT provider to an energy producer (Case XIII) explains:

> In IT maintenance organizations, IT professionals must usually do their work for a longer period in order to acquire the experience they need. The processes involved are continuous processes, in which knowledge and especially experience are very important indeed. Many other IT services, on the other hand, involve rather more short-term delivery processes: you come, build something, and when it's finished you can leave.
>
> (Beulen 2000: 251)

Managing IT professionals is an activity for which the service provider's contract manager holds the final responsibility (A). The service delivery manager executes this activity (R).

3.6 THE FEASIBILITY OF OUTSOURCING

Outsourcing has different implications on each of the organizational levels discussed. Generally speaking, strategy cannot be outsourced, so neither can IS and IT strategy (Lacity and Hirschheim 1993; Feeny and Willcocks 1998). Outsourcing companies must maintain control over their IT services, and have clear guidelines for managing their IT providers. The minimum attention that outsourcing companies must spend on IT is called the 'residual in-house IS function' (Lacity *et al.* 1996). IT service delivery can, of course, be outsourced, since this involves rather more operational tasks.

3.6.1 Outsourcing strategy-level responsibilities

Despite the statement above, to the effect that strategy cannot be outsourced, some strategic aspects are in fact sometimes provided by service suppliers. An example given by an expert:

> In one project in which I was involved, the staff seconded by the service provider regarded it as their role to manage affairs in the interests of the outsourcing company. They *went native*, you might say. It was sometimes quite difficult to tell who was employed by whom. Outsourcing one's strategy processes is not, apparently, necessarily disastrous.
>
> (Beulen 2000: 193)

Manning the strategic level can be difficult (Cullen and Willcocks 2003). Service recipients sometimes resort to hiring external staff in order to fill vacant positions. These external staff must never be employed by the company's service provider, of course. Generally, they are independent freelancers who have previous experience with service demand or provisioning management in large companies. The costs of such external consultants, however, are substantial; and they usually do not have previous ties with the service recipient, which makes it difficult for them to assess its internal politics. Besides, by hiring external consultants, the service recipient still does not build knowledge or know-how with which to carry on after they leave. And yet there are situations in which there is no other way than hiring external consultants. Jon Kandiah, CIO with Virgin Mobile UK, explains: 'We started this company from scratch in 1999. There was no alternative to hiring temporary staff, including positions in the IS function' (Case XII).

Service recipients may also adopt a mix of their own staff and external consultants (Beulen 2000). They keep the responsibility for and control over strategy to themselves, but hire external staff to supply extra capacity when there are peaks in the tasks to be carried out. An example of such a mix is hiring extra capacity to write out or adapt the company's IS and IT strategies – a periodic activity involving the writing of a document in which the strategy is laid down. This may even be more cost-effective than using only internal staff. Likewise, external staff may be hired to supply specific expertise, which is then absorbed by the company's own employees.

3.6.2 Outsourcing tactical-level responsibilities

Service providers increasingly include tactical-level activities in their offerings. This enables them not only to increase their turnover but also to strengthen their grip on their clients – and then hopefully to generate their own turnover growth, as it were. For this reason, outsourcing tactical-level activities is not always a good idea (Lacity and Hirschheim 1993).

It can, however, be a good idea to hire external expertise for specific activities, such as the tendering process. Tendering is a project activity, which means that hiring external staff can be appropriate.[4] Besides, the purchasing department and the company's information managers often have too little time or even know-how to carry out a tendering process themselves. Nevertheless, it is important that the service recipient's own staff remain involved in the process. While external consultants may have a helpfully broader market perspective (Cullen and Willcocks 2003), they often lack the specific business knowledge of the service recipient's own staff, which is of particular importance if service delivery also has been outsourced.

And then there are situations in which hiring external consultants is actually to be preferred over using internal staff. This is especially so in the case of auditing and mediation – incidental activities for which the independence of the staff carrying them out is of crucial importance (Beulen 2000) (and that should never, of course, be carried out by the same people). An experienced employee of a consulting firm tells about his company's preference for mediation over audits:

> We don't do audits. We prefer to set up contacts between our clients and mediators. This is well appreciated by our clients, since it often takes only small interventions to achieve much better results than would have been possible had the problem been approached from an audit angle.
>
> (Beulen 2000: 211)

3.6.3 Outsourcing operational-level responsibilities

Provided that the strategic-level and tactical-level activities are carried out by the service recipient itself, operational activities are candidates to be outsourced to external service providers (Apte 1990; Lacity and Hirschheim 1993; Quinn and Hilmer 1994; Earl 1996). The former managing director of the Information Systems Center of the Dutch government stated:

> In 1990 the governmental data centre (Rijks Computercentrum) was privatised in the context of an overall cost cutting program of the Dutch government. The Dutch government was also focusing on their core competences. The governmental data centre transformed into PinkRoccade NV, currently noted on the Euronext stock exchange as GetronicsPinkRoccade.

Whether in a specific company situation these will be outsourced or not depends on a number of external and internal factors. Examples of these are the extent to which the activity belongs to the core of the organization, the business criticality of the applications involved and consequently in the case of outsourcing the dependence of the outside provider, the existing market for the services to be procured, the increase of transaction costs in the case of outsourcing, etc. Selecting external service providers is not easy. Their competences and prices must be taken into consideration as well as their flexibility and the extent of their knowledge of the service recipient's industry. A service provider must also have a company culture matching that of their client. This does not mean their company cultures must be the same – in fact, certainly when changes must be made it can be helpful if the service provider has an entirely different style. And finally, service provider and service recipient must be of a similar size (measured by turnover, for example) to prevent unwanted forms of dependence. If a service provider is much larger than its client, any problems arising on the recipient's side may not be given enough priority to reach an adequate solution. And if the service provider is much smaller than its client, it may not be able to deliver what is needed or to achieve advantages of scale.

When outsourcing operational activities, care must be taken with several of the new relation's aspects. For one, good contractual agreements are very important.

Preferably, these include output obligations. It is also important that the service provider submits regular reports on the services delivered, in a manner that is unambiguous and that matches the thought processes of the client (Cullen and Willcocks 2003).

> Usually, all-over outsourcing deals involve loads and loads of – technical – details, most of which are of very little relevance to the businessman even though their measurement is important to keep service delivery on track. Business managers only want to know what they need for their business. Perhaps a comparison of the results achieved with a simple scorecard containing the top seven most important items would be a good idea.
>
> (Beulen 2000: 225)

Finally, attention must also be paid to setting up a good interface between client and supplier. This becomes increasingly complex when more service providers are involved. It must always be absolutely clear who are the contact officials, on both the recipient's and the provider's side. These staff must have in-depth knowledge and know-how of the services involved.

NOTES

1 See www.ukais.org, 'definitions of information systems'.
2 Essentially, e-business using mobile telephones rather than personal computers.
3 CMM guidelines for outsourcing are being developed at present (www. itsqc.cs. cmu.edu).
4 Many companies are active in this field, such as TPI (www.tpi.net), Morgan Chambers (www.morgan-chambers.com), Gartner (www.gartner.com) and Quint Wellington Redwood (www.quintgroup.com).

REFERENCES

Ackoff, R. (1970) *A Concept of Corporate Planning*, New York: John Wiley & Sons.

Aerts, A., Goossenaerts, J., Hammer, D. and Wortmann, J. (2004) 'Architectures in context: on the evolution of business, application software, and ICT platform architectures', *Information & Management*, 41 (6): 781–794.

Anderson, T. and Stampe Christensen, M. (2002) 'Contract renewal under uncertainty', *Journal of Economic Dynamics & Control*, 26 (4): 637–652.

Andrews, K. (1980) *The Concept of Corporate Strategy*, Boston, MA: R.D. Irwin.

Anthony, R. (1965) *Planning and Control Systems: A Framework for Analysis*, Cambridge, MA: Harvard University Press.

Applegate, L., Austin, R. and McFarlan, F. (2003) *Corporate Information Strategy and Management: Text and Cases*, 6th edn, Boston, MA: McGraw-Hill/Irwin.

Apte, U. (1990) 'Global outsourcing of information systems and processing services', *The Information Society*, 7: 287–303.

Beulen, E. (2000) 'Beheersing van IT-outsourcingsrelaties: een beheersingsmodel voor uitbestedende bedrijven en IT-leveranciers', PhD thesis, Tilburg University (in Dutch).

Beulen, E. (2002) *Uitbesteding van IT-dienstverlening*, Den Haag: Ten Hagen en Stam (in Dutch).

Beulen, E., Ribbers, P. and Roos, J. (1994) *Outsourcing van de IT-dienstverlening: een make or buy beslissing*, Deventer: Kluwer Bedrijfswetenschappen (in Dutch).

Beulen, E., Baas, R., Dain, J., Hudson, J., Reitsma, E., Symonds, M. and van der Zee, H. (2004) 'Outsourcing: the Atos Origin outsourcing lifecycle – building successful outsourcing relationships', White Paper, Atos Origin (www.atosorigin.com/corporate/viewpoint/vp_270104.htm) Accessed 29 August 2004.

Brown, C. and Magill, S. (1994) 'Alignment of the IS functions with the enterprise: toward a model of antecedents', *Management Information Systems Quarterly*, 18 (4): 371–403.

Brown, C. and Renwick, J. (1996) 'Alignment of the IS organization: the special case of corporate acquisitions', *The Database for Advances in Information Systems*, 27 (4): 25–33.

Buchanan, J. and Linowes, R. (1980) 'Making distributed data processing work', *Harvard Business Review*, September/October.

Cross, J. (1995) 'IT-outsourcing: British Petroleum's competitive approach', *Harvard Business Review*, 73 (3): 94–104.

Cullen, S. and Willcocks, L. (2003) *Intelligent IT Outsourcing: Eight Building Blocks to Success*, Oxford: Butterworth-Heinemann.

Currie, W. and Willcocks, L. (1998) 'Analysing four types of IT-outsourcing decisions in the context of scale, client/server, interdependency and risk migration', *Information Systems Journal*, 8 (2): 119–143.

Dickson, G., Leitheiser, R. and Wetherbe, J. (1984) 'Key information systems issues for the 1980s', *Management Information Systems Quarterly*, 8 (3): 135–159.

Duncan, N. (1995) 'Capturing flexibility of information technology infrastructure: a study of resource characteristics and their measure', *Journal of Management Information Systems*, 12 (2): 37–57.

Earl, M. (1987) 'Information systems strategy formulation', in R. Boland and R. Hirschheim (eds) *Critical Issues in Information Systems Research*, New York: John Wiley & Sons.

Earl, M. (1989) *Management Strategies for Information Technology*, London: Prentice-Hall.

Earl, M. (1996) 'The risks of outsourcing IT', *Sloan Management Review*, 37 (3): 26–32.

Feeny, D. and Willcocks, L. (1997) 'The IT-function: changing capabilities and skills', in L. Willcocks, D. Feeny and G. Islei (eds) *Managing IT as a Strategic Resource*, London: McGraw-Hill.

Feeny, D. and Willcocks, L. (1998) 'Re-designing the IS function around core capabilities', *Long Range Planning*, 31 (3): 354–367.

Fukuyama, F. (1995) *Trust*, London: Hamish Hamilton.

Galliers, R. and Leidner, D. (2003) 'Introduction to Part One', in R. Galliers and D. Leidner (eds) *Strategic Information Management, Challenges and Strategies in Managing Information Systems*, Oxford: Butterworth-Heinemann.

George, J. and King, J. (1991) 'Examining the computing and centralization debate', *Communications of the Association for Computing Machinery*, 34 (7): 63–72.

Gottschalk, P. (2004) 'Managing IT functions', in W. van Grembergen (ed.) *Strategies for Information Technology Governance*, Hershey, PA: Idea Publishing.

Grönroos, C. (2000) *Service Management and Marketing. A Customer Relationship Management Approach*, New York: Wiley.

Grover, V., Cheon, M. and Teng, J. (1996) 'The effect of service quality and partnership on the outsourcing of information systems functions', *Journal of Management Information Systems*, 12 (4): 89–116.

Heckmann, R. (1999) 'Organizing and managing supplier relationships in information technology procurement', *Journal of Information Management*, 19: 141–155.

Henderson, J. and Venkatraman, N. (1993) 'Strategic alignment: leveraging information technology for transforming organisations', *IBM Systems Journal*, 32 (1): 4–16.

Johnson, B. and Andrew, M. (1994) *The Infrastructure Library: An Introduction*, London: HMSO.

Keen, P. (1991) *Shaping the Future: Business Design Through Information Technology*, Boston, MA: Harvard Business School Press.

Khosrowpour, M. (1995) *Managing Information Technology Investments with Outsourcing*, Harrisburg: Idea Group Publishing.

Klepper, R. (1995) 'The management of partnering development in I/S outsourcing', *Journal of Technology*, 10 (4): 249–258.

Kraljic, P. (1983) 'Purchasing must become supply management', *Harvard Business Review*, 61 (5): 109–117.

Lacity, M. and Hirschheim, R. (1993) *Information Systems Outsourcing*, Chichester: Wiley & Sons.

Lacity, M. and Willcocks, L. (2001) *Global Information Technology Outsourcing: In Search of Business Advantage*, New York: John Wiley & Sons.

Lacity, M., Willcocks, L. and Feeny, D. (1996) 'The value of selective outsourcing', *Sloan Management Review*, 37 (3): 13–25.

Lawrence, P. and Lorsch, J. (1973) *Organization and Environment, Managing Differentiation and Integration*, Homewood, IL: Irwin.

Lowrey, R. (1996) '"Owning" IT: the stewardship role', *Managing Information Technology (Nolan Norton Institute)*, 1: 5.

Luftman, J. (2000) 'Assessing IT-business alignment maturity', *Communication of the Association for Information Systems*, 4, article 14: 1–51.

McFarlan, F. and Nolan, R. (1995) 'How to manage an IT outsourcing alliance', *Sloan Management Review*, 36 (2): 9–23.

Magee, M. (1998) 'What does a relationship manager actually do?' Gartner research report.

Morton, S. (1991) *The Cooperation of the 1990s: Information Technology and Organizational Transformation*, New York: Oxford University Press.

Niederman, F., Brancheau, J.C. and Wetherbe, J.C. (1991) 'Information systems management issues for the 1990s', *MIS Quarterly*, 15 (4): 474–500.

Parker, D.B. (1987) 'Information crime and security', *Computer Fraud and Security Bulletin*, 9 (5): 1–5.

Parker, M., Trainor, H. and Benson, R. (1989) *Information Strategy and Economics*, New York: Prentice Hall.

Pearlson, K. (2001) *Managing and Using Information Systems: A Strategic Approach*, New York: John Wiley & Sons.

Porter, M. (1987) 'From competitive advantage to corporate strategy', *Harvard Business Review*, 65 (95): 43–59.

Quinn, J. and Hilmer, F. (1994) 'Strategic outsourcing', *Sloan Management Review*, 35 (4): 43–55.

Rockart, J., Earl, M. and Ross, J. (1996) 'Eight imperatives for the new IT organization', *Sloan Management Review*, 38 (1): 43–55.

Sabherwal, K. (1999) 'The role of trust in outsourced IS development projects', *Communications of the Association for Computing Machinery*, 42 (2): 80–86.

Sankar, C., Apte, U. and Palvia, P. (1993) 'Global information architectures: alternatives and tradeoffs', *International Journal of Information Management*, 13 (2): 84–93.

Smits, M., van der Poel, K. and Ribbers, P. (1997) 'Assessment of information strategies in insurance companies in the Netherlands', *The Journal of Strategic Information Systems*, 6: 129–149. Also in R. Galliers and D. Leidner (eds) *Strategic Information Management, Challenges and Strategies in Managing Information Systems*, Oxford: Butterworth-Heinemann.

Ward, J. and Peppard, J. (2002) *Strategic Planning for Information Systems*, 3rd edn, Chichester: John Wiley & Sons.

Weill, P. and Ross, J. (2004) *IT Governance: How Top Performers Manage IT Decision Rights for Superior Results*, Boston, MA: Harvard Business School Press.

Wiseman, C. (1988) *Strategic Information Systems*, Homewood, IL: Irwin.

Chapter 4

Partnership risk management

- This chapter discusses the ten most important partnership risks that must be managed in global IT outsourcing, and the circumstances under which they occur most often.
- As cost reduction is one of the key drivers for outsourcing, the risk of overspending requires extra attention – especially since it happens very easily, despite the cost-cutting objective.
- During the discussion it will become clear that both service recipient and service provider are responsible for managing these risks.

4.1 INTRODUCTION

Engaging in partnerships involves taking certain risks, and IT outsourcing is no exception. It is these risks and their management that we will discuss in this chapter. First, in Section 4.2, the subject of risk management is treated in a general way. We look into the processes and procedures that both service providers and service recipients must set up to keep the risks of IT outsourcing relationships under control. We will see that there is a difference between the risks involved in setting up such relationships and contracts, and the risks of managing these relationships. Since the focus in this book is on partnership management and not on their acquisition, we only briefly look at the first category of risks (Section 4.3). Then, in Section 4.4, partnership management risks will be studied more thoroughly. This entails a subdivision into ten kinds of risks, each of which will be discussed in some detail. Once we are aware of the risks involved, we can move on to Chapter 5 to study the governance of IT outsourcing relationships.

4.2 RISK MANAGEMENT

Outsourcing IT services causes organizational risks that service recipients must pay serious attention to. About a decade ago, very few companies had any experience with the contracting processes involved (Klepper 1995; McFarlan and Nolan 1995). But since then a lot has changed. Much experience has been gained outsourcing non-core processes such as catering, security, logistics, and treasury and archive services. This helps when IT services must be outsourced (Beulen 2000). In fact, many companies now have some experience with IT outsourcing itself, since they have contracted out their IT services before – sometimes even to several consecutive suppliers. Nevertheless, the contracting process is important and it still involves certain risks that must be addressed. These issues are discussed in Section 4.3.

Once an outsourcing relationship has been set up, however, it must be managed. And since the interrelation between business management and IT service provision has greatly increased (Henderson and Venkatraman 1993; Cullen and Willcocks 2003), IT service providers have acquired a direct influence on their clients' business management. The risks this entails must be managed.

Increasing IT systems integration and Internet communication have amplified the risk of service provision disruptions caused by information leaks and spreading viruses. After all, once IT systems are outsourced they are no longer only linked internally but to the provider's systems too. Then trust is essential but not sufficient. Service providers must set up processes and procedures such as ISO, ITIL and CMM[1] in order to minimize the risks (Sherwood 1997; Fenn et al. 2002). Service recipients would do well to set up agreements allowing them to audit or assess the services delivered, or to let them be audited and assessed. This will give them insight in the extent to which service provision continuity is guaranteed (Willcocks et al. 1995a).

Other important aspects are the capabilities and geographical coverage of the service provider. These may change during the contract period, so developments in the service provider's market must be watched closely. Concentration in that market, for instance, has serious consequences for competition and may lead to provision monopoly situations (Cullen and Willcocks 2003). Examples of such concentrations are the merger of Hewlett Packard and Compaq in 2001 and the take-over of PWC Consulting by IBM in 2002. Likewise, Atos Origin acquired SchlumbergerSema in 2004, after having earlier bought parts of KPMG Consulting UK and The Netherlands.

4.3 CONTRACTING RISKS

Contracting IT outsourcing relationships involves certain specific risks, which we will discuss here briefly. The most important risk, obviously, is that of selecting the wrong provider. It is essential that the service provider chosen is capable of delivering the services needed (Willcocks and Kern 1998). This means they must have the necessary knowledge and experience and must be able to deliver these when and where the service recipients needs them. It is also important that the service provider is of roughly the same size as the recipient. A provider that is much larger than his client may not give them sufficient priority if there are service provision disruptions or other problems. A small provider, on the other hand, may lack the size to realize advantages of scale for his client (Lacity and Hirschheim 1995) and may even become too dependent on the service recipient. Third, when outsourcing contracts are made, service levels and specifications must be defined clearly and unambiguously. If this is not done properly, the contract cannot be used to manage the outsourcing relationship, for which it should be an important instrument (Lacity and Hirschheim 1993).

An important element in the contracting process is the selection of the provider. The selection process must be transparent in order to encourage potential providers to make good offers (de Looff 1996). Potential providers who think that the current provider's contract is going to be renewed anyway will not take the trouble to do so: the costs of making an offer run to a substantial 1.5–3 per cent of the contract value, so being used as only a benchmark is not attractive. Even in Europe, where authorities must follow Union regulations with respect to tendering out processes that focus on transparency and objectivity,[2] current providers have an information advantage since they are responsible for the present state of affairs. Service recipients must therefore do everything in their power to provide potential suppliers with the information they need.

4.4 MANAGEMENT RISKS

Since this book concentrates on partnership management, we will now take a closer look into the risks involved in managing IT outsourcing relationships. After a contract has been agreed upon and signed, running the contract requires close attention. For the sake of clarity, the risks involved in having IT partners may be divided into ten categories. Essentially, these concern aspects of the IT outsourcing relationship that must be managed. They are summed up in Table 4.1 and then treated in detail in the following subsections.

4.4.1 Cost control

Many service recipients consider cost advantages an important argument to out-source IT services. And yet cost advantages are not always achieved (Lacity and Willcocks 2001). Therefore, it is important for service recipients that the way in which providers calculate their costs and invoice their work is specified clearly in the outsourcing contract. In other words: the contract must define which services are to be delivered at what prices. Since the IT services needed may change from time to time, this may be a complex matter. These dynamics and the consequent

Table 4.1 *Partnership management risk categories*

Risk category	Aspects requiring attention
Cost control	IT service delivery costs must be controlled.
Management control	The service recipient must clearly define the role of the service provider and manage the details and specifics of their service delivery.
Demand management	Service recipients need service delivery interfaces, both for their company's divisions and the provider.
Priority	The service provider must assign sufficient priority to the recipient's needs.
Confidentiality	No confidential information may be divulged to outsiders or unauthorized persons.
Information requirements definition	Service recipients must be able to define which IT services their providers must supply.
Business knowledge	Service providers must have sufficient knowledge of their clients' business to ensure continuity in the delivery of the services needed.
Business dynamics	Service providers and the contracts made with them must never hinder the recipient adapting the delivery requirements as a consequence of business management changes.
Innovation	Service providers must regularly introduce new technologies in order to make possible and stimulate the recipient's innovation processes.
Vendor lock-in	Service recipients must always be able to change providers, and must not become dependent on any one supplier.

cost control risks may be managed using a service portfolio, in which the recipient and the provider lay down which services may be required against what prices. Such a portfolio offers a framework for the outsourcing relationship, giving the service recipient a grip on the costs involved.

From a cost control perspective, it is also important that the rates remain in accordance with the market (Willcocks *et al.* 1995b), certainly in the case of long-term contracts. To ensure market conformity, the contract may include agreements on benchmarking. But benchmarking is expensive. It is therefore probably better to include agreements on price developments during the contract period: a yearly rate increase of *x* per cent due to efficiency and effectiveness measures, for example, or *y* per cent per annum inflation correction. Nevertheless, if either recipient or provider considers it necessary, it must be possible to benchmark the services delivered (Beulen 2000). In such cases, the benchmark has to be carried out by an independent third party. And the service provider should be included in the process:

It is essential for the IT supplier to be involved in the benchmarking process. . . . They may be able to provide additional information . . . and, even more important, are more likely to accept the conclusions of a benchmark analysis if they were involved. This makes any discussions on this subject far easier for the outsourcing organization.

(Beulen 2004: 327)

4.4.2 Management control

In order for an outsourcing partnership to work well, the service provider's role must be clear, allowing the recipient to manage the details and specifics of the services delivered. To achieve such management control over the partnership, recipients primarily use their IT and sourcing strategies as management instruments. The IT strategy, which is derived from the company's general business strategy and must be aligned with it (Henderson and Venkatraman 1993), sets out the major guidelines for the IT services required. These must be shared with the company's providers (Khosrowpour 1995) so as to achieve 'complementary or shared goals' (Lacity and Hirschheim 1995). The recipient's divisions must also be involved, for the company's IT strategy is not just a matter for its CIO: 'the whole organization must be aware of the objectives. This does not involve only the CIO, but corporate management too' (Beulen 2004: 320).

On the basis of the IT strategy a sourcing strategy is developed (Currie and Willcocks 1998), detailing which IT services may be outsourced and which must be taken care of by the recipient itself. This is called identifying core capabilities for insourcing (Lacity and Hirschheim 1993: 117). The idea used to be that strategically important services could never be outsourced safely. In practice, however, they are.

An example is provided by the IT manager of a major oil company (Case XIV; see Appendix, p. 268, for all Case details):

We produce, refine and sell oil and oil products. Having good information is very important for our decision processes, so we need good IT services. Some of these we deliver ourselves, some are provided by external suppliers. In the past there was always the question of whether a supplier could guarantee delivery, and it often kept services from being outsourced. Since we've begun to ask ourselves whether we are any better able to guarantee delivery, such 'soft' criteria are increasingly irrelevant. IT outsourcing decisions are now more and more taken on the basis of rational business arguments, although for a new process such as IT services delivery it takes a while to achieve the change. We now use the transaction cost approach. This was already used for other outsourcing decisions, and it fits our company's objective: maximizing profit in the long term.

(Beulen et al. 1994)

67

The outsourcing strategy involves some other matters as well. For one: how many service providers should be contracted? If the choice is made to work with many small providers, for instance, they will have difficulty achieving advantages of scale for their client. Also, this will require much experience and management attention from both the providers and the recipient. Another issue is whether providers should be allowed to subcontract some of the services. Since doing so involves risks, service recipients would do well to list the subcontractors they find acceptable. Says the account manager of a company working for a major electronics manufacturer (Case VII):

> In order to provide our services we use a limited number of subcontractors. Sometimes these are not on the list, but all are approved by the recipient prior to service provision. Nevertheless, my company always remains responsible for the provision of the services to our customer.
>
> (Beulen 2004: 326)

4.4.3 Demand management

As we have seen in Chapter 2, demand management is responsible for the formulation of the recipient's requirements with respect to IT services; supply management is then responsible for meeting that demand (Beulen *et al.* 1994). It must be understood that demand management is still needed when service recipients do not outsource their IT service delivery.

The costs of setting up and running demand management adequately are estimated at between 2 and 10 per cent of the total value of the services delivered (Aylott 2002; Cullen and Willcocks 2003), a substantial amount that service recipients must reckon with. And it is not easy to find the people who can carry it out. Listen to an expert's observations:

> I was doing a presentation on a conference where resourcing the information management office was one of the major discussions subjects. Many vendors were present, as well as major user companies. These latter kept saying it was very hard to find people with experience or expertise in the field of supplier management, in particular people who would be able to manage multiple providers.
>
> (Beulen 2004: 322)

If the recipient has to hire external expertise to carry out their demand management, the costs will increase sharply.

Nevertheless, the consequences of not carrying out adequate demand management are even less attractive. Service providers are then unable to deliver the services needed in a way that matches the recipient's needs. Information managers must therefore support their business managers on the basis of the company's strategic views on IT services. This means they must facilitate good relations between these business managers and their service provider. The better the dialogue, the better providers will be able to deliver the IT services requested.

4.4.4 Priority

We have already noted that it is important that the service recipient's needs are treated with sufficient priority by their provider. This is important during the selection process, of course, but a close watch must also be kept after a contract has been agreed upon. Contracts are not enough to ensure getting sufficient attention, and penalty clauses are only a partial solution. It is better to collaborate and achieve a balanced relationship. Then the provider will assign sufficient priority to their client and to finding solutions for delivery problems or differences of opinion. In order to do so, contact persons must be designated by both recipient and provider (Kern and Willcocks 2002), for all organizational levels involved. There should be a clear distinction between contract managers and service delivery managers, as is acknowledged by an account manager working for a major electronics manufacturer (Case VII):

> In our provider's organization, the delivery manager and the contract manager were one and the same person. This was wrong, because it entailed a conflict of interests. Contract managers should be able to hold delivery managers account-able and say, 'This is not what we agreed to do.' If one person plays both roles, this correction mechanism doesn't work and service delivery will become slack.
>
> (Beulen 2000: 242)

On the recipient's side, account management is important for maintaining service delivery quality (Goles 2003; Levina and Ross 2003).

Another important issue is staff changes. The frequency with which providers change the staff working for a client is an indication of how important that client is for them. If personnel are moved elsewhere, the other client is apparently more important. And changing staff obviously does not improve delivery continuity either (a matter that applies to service recipients as well). On the other hand, it is not realistic to expect that there will be no changes at all during the contract period. Generally speaking, key staff should remain in their posts for some 30 months at a time in order to guarantee continuity. This holds for relationship managers as well as IT professionals. And it is certainly important if these professionals are involved in maintenance work, which involves much tacit knowledge that is difficult and therefore expensive to transfer to other people. Service providers, then, should keep their staff in place for longer periods. In recognition of this fact, outsourcing contracts often stipulate the conditions for changing the professionals who execute the service delivery.

4.4.5 Confidentiality

No company can take the risk that its essential business information falls into the hands of outsiders or unauthorized persons. Therefore, confidentiality is of the greatest importance for outsourcing relationships. It must be addressed in contracts containing guarantees that ensure the security of the recipient's information (Burnett 1998). Even more important is the way in which confidentiality measures are actually carried out, the processes and procedures involved (Levina and Ross 2003). Infrastructure management services require ISO and BS7799 certification. Providers usually find it easier to certify processes than do internal IT departments, who often lack the size and experience. Remarks the CIO of a major beverages producer (Case X):

> Our ERP system is of critical importance to our business, and it contains confidential information. And yet we have chosen to outsource running the system. We trust our supplier and his processes and procedures. Only application support remains in our hands, since it is too close to our primary business processes. And besides, I don't see how a provider could easily improve performance there.
>
> (Beulen and Ribbers 2004: 294)

Application development also requires certification. A well-known standard in this field is the Capability Maturity Model (Paulk *et al.* 1993). A contract manager working for a major electronics manufacturer (Case VII) says:

> A portion of our software is developed in India, in a CMM Level 5 certified development process. This certification was the deciding factor for our client to select us as their supplier. But being certified has other advantages as well. Because of it our processes have been set up such that the quality of our services is high and that we are able to work efficiently.
>
> (Beulen 2004: 329)

Apart from certification, recipients may also ask their providers for Third Party Maintenance declarations. These provide extra security, since they are issued by independent institutions. If the data processing involved in the services to be delivered is not carried out in the same country where the recipient is established, differences in local laws and regulations may be of influence. This is especially important for service recipients in the European Union whose data are processed outside the Union ('offshore outsourcing'). Before outsourcing agreements are made, the limitations and conditions must be examined carefully.

4.4.6 Information requirements definition

We have seen that demand management is important in establishing which information needs must be serviced. In doing so, it is important not to lose sight of the original objectives of the outsourcing relationship (Lacity and Hirschheim 1993). These objectives may not be the same for everyone. End users may have entirely different needs from those of their company's managers. Users generally want specific IT services, while the standardization that is often the result of striving for lower costs (a common management objective) instead imposes limits. Standardization is a common result, too, when several geographically widespread locations are involved – a situation in which it is difficult to establish the organization's information needs. Says the CIO of a major beverages producer (Case X):

> To ensure that the information needs of all operating companies in many countries are met, we have made a corporate contract with our service provider. The contract is the framework of our outsourcing relation. All operating companies can now have their own separate contracts with this provider, and are billed separately. This allows them to define and obtain the information services they need.
>
> (Beulen and Ribbers 2004: 296)

It is important to check periodically whether the IT services contracted still meet the needs of the service recipient. Apart from demand management, representatives of the end users should be involved. Consultation meetings must therefore be held. Representatives of the service providers may also be invited to these meeting, since this will increase their commitment and make it easier for them to understand their client's needs.

4.4.7 Business knowledge

IT services are increasingly interwoven with the recipient's business, so business knowledge is an increasingly important aspect of outsourcing relationships. The recipient's demand managers must have business knowledge and the business managers must have IT knowledge. A business manager who works for an electronics manufacturer states: 'IT must be integrated in the business. The IT manager must never be the only one with IT knowledge' (Beulen *et al*. 1994: 184).

Service providers must also know their clients' business. Providers may group their IT professionals according to their technical expertise. Their contribution to business knowledge is minimal, but they can achieve maximum advantages of scale and thus costs savings. On the other hand, if they are grouped according to the industries they have worked in, this maximizes the business knowledge available in their outsourcing relationships. In practice, most providers opt for a hybrid method:

71

most business knowledge is contributed by senior IT professionals and especially consultants, while technical experts concentrate rather more on technology. Providers also tend to bundle their expertise internationally. Very senior experts are then flown in when their contribution is needed. This allows the expertise available to be used to maximum effect.

Of course, the service provider's account managers must also have business knowledge of their clients' industries (Beulen 2000; Goles 2003) since they are the interface between the provider and the recipient. They need business knowledge to build and maintain the outsourcing relationship.

4.4.8 Business dynamics

One of the difficulties of establishing an outsourcing relationship is that it is almost impossible to set up a contract that includes everything (Beulen and Ribbers 2003). Many things change during the contract period that are unforeseen, which is why both partners should 'embrace the dynamics of the relationship' (Lacity and Willcocks 2003: 123). Service recipients as well as service providers should have the 'willingness to cooperate on all organizational processes' (Barnard 1938). To this end, the concept of ex-post negotiations was introduced (Hart 1995; Segal 1999). It includes a procedure for reaching agreement about issues that are as yet unclear. It is also called the Liaison Model (Burnett 1998). Open communication and clear points of departure are obviously very important (Beulen and Ribbers 2003). Then these concepts enable one to establish what is reasonable for both parties involved when an unforeseen situation arises. Examples of unforeseen changes are technological developments and developments in the service recipient's industry or market. These changes may be so far-reaching that it is necessary to terminate the contract. This is exceptional, but even in such cases problems may be avoided if the original contract includes a 'termination for convenience clause'. Damages must then still be paid, of course. They generally include costs made by the provider that cannot now be recouped – hardware investments, for example – and profit losses incurred by the discontinuation of the contract. But these are often substantially lower than the costs of continuing a useless contract.

Service recipients with steep growth curves face serious business dynamics. 'The influence of the growing market for mobile telephones is very great', Virgin Mobile's technical services manager John Melton says.

Two years ago our growth was some 200 per cent per annum. This meant we could simply build capacity and then wait for demand to grow and use it. The worst that could happen was that the capacity would be available too soon. Now our yearly growth is around 25 per cent. Therefore, when IT investments are discussed, we will first examine if it can't be done with the capacity already available. Nevertheless, a 25 per cent growth is still enormous so our business' dynamics are too. Our IT department must keep up with it. These dynamics have made us decide to outsource part of our business processes.

4.4.9 Innovation

Innovation is the responsibility of both the service recipient and the service provider. Service recipients define the direction in which innovation is needed on the basis of their IT strategy. Their greatest difficulty is legacy systems, that is, current systems that represent major investments and that are closely integrated with their business processes. Such systems cannot be replaced overnight, even if something better becomes available.

In order to prevent making investments in systems that will soon be outdated, it is important that information managers are closely involved in the business and its changes. Then they can contribute by finding systems that will stay up-to-date and will even facilitate innovation. This is called 'making technology work' (Feeny and Willcocks 1998). Such involvement may go quite far. A business manager with chemicals company AkzoNobel tells us: 'We specifically involve our information managers in our product creation process. This helps us prevent IT from becoming a bottleneck when we are ready to introduce new products' (Beulen 2004: 321). This is not surprising, coming from a company with a very innovative profile. Other industries in which information managers are involved in product development processes at an early stage are those in which large quantities of data are processed, such as financial institutions. In such industries IT services are of major importance. Less innovative companies will be slower to involve their information managers in product development.

On the service provider's side, account managers and competence managers are responsible for the implementation of innovations in outsourcing relationships. Account managers try to get a feel for their clients' needs and thoughts. This means dealing with both demand managers and business managers. The latter's input is the more important with respect to innovation. 'I maintain intensive contacts with the managers of my client's competence centres', says the account manager of a provider working for a major electronics manufacturer (Case VII). 'I very much want to discuss the innovations developed there. However, it is the service delivery units that deliver the actual services when a contract is signed' (Beulen 2000: 329). Competence managers must investigate new technologies. Those that can be used are then added to the provider's service portfolio. The provider's service delivery managers can then pass them on to the recipients they do business with.

4.4.10 Vendor lock-in

Outsourcing relationships are usually entered into for the long term. Both recipients and providers should therefore practise restraint if there are differences of opinion.

As one expert put it: 'If there is a dispute, you don't go straight to court. You find some other way of settling the matter' (Beulen 2000: 230). Consultation is the best way to resolve any problems. If that does not work, arbitration by an independent third party may help.

Nevertheless, both parties know one thing for certain right from the start: one day their partnership will end. They should therefore always be prepared for this to happen (Bahli and Rivard 2003). Virgin Mobile UK, for example, outsourced its IT services three years ago and is now in the process of either renewing the contract or selecting a new provider. Their current provider's offer is not bad, but that of its competitor Atos Origin is better and radiates more confidence. And yet Virgin's CIO has his doubts. 'Do I really have the choice of partnering with a new provider? Can I convince my CEO that the risks of changing partners are containable?'

Developing contract management capability is something that requires further attention. For example, the delivery of IT services may profitably be managed as a portfolio: selective sourcing, as it is called (Lacity and Hirschheim 1995). The advantage of portfolio management is clear: it reduces the dependence of the recipient on the provider. It does, of course, make heavy demands on the recipient's contract management capacity, since they must manage multiple IT suppliers (Beulen 2000). So far, we have found only one instance of true portfolio IT management (Case XI). In that case, an external consulting bureau provides contract management support to the outsourcing organization (Beulen and Ribbers 2003). Portfolio management can be made easier by contracting out to a provider that already subcontracts to one's current supplier. Then there is the advantage of an existing communication format, and the current contract may serve as a basis for the new agreement. Such a solution, however, does not reduce the recipient's dependence on his provider as much as proper portfolio management would.

NOTES

1 These are further discussed in Chapter 7.
2 Among other things, no potential providers may be excluded from the tendering process.

REFERENCES

Aylott, B. (2002) 'Questions and answers', research report, Montgomery Research Europe, ISSN 1476–2064.

Bahli, B. and Rivard, S. (2003) 'The information technology outsourcing risk: a transaction cost and agency theory-based perspective', *Journal of Information Technology*, 18: 211–221.

Barnard, C. (1938) *The Functions of the Executive*, Cambridge, MA: Harvard University Press.

Beulen, E. (2000) 'Het beheersen van IT-outsourcingsrelaties: een beheersingsmodel voor uitbestedende bedrijven en IT-leveranciers', PhD thesis, Tilburg University (in Dutch).

Beulen, E. (2004) 'Governance in IT outsourcing partnerships', in W. van Grembergen (ed.) *Strategies for Information Technologies*, Hershey, PA: Idea Group Publishing.

Beulen, E. and Ribbers, P. (2003) 'IT outsourcing contacts: practical implications of the incomplete contract theory', paper presented at Hawaii International Conference on Systems Sciences, Hawaii, January 2003.

Beulen, E. and Ribbers, P. (2004) 'Value creation in application outsourcing relationships: an international case study on ERP outsourcing', in W. Curry (ed.) *Value Creation from e-Business Models*, Oxford: Elsevier Butterworth-Heinemann.

Beulen, E., Ribbers, P. and Roos, J. (1994) *Outsourcing van IT-dienstverlening, een 'make or buy' beslissing*, Deventer: Kluwer Bedrijfswetenschappen (in Dutch).

Burnett, R. (1998) *Outsourcing IT: The Legal Aspects*, Aldershot: Gower.

Cullen, S. and Willcocks, L. (2003) *Intelligent IT Outsourcing: Eight Building Blocks to Success*, Oxford: Butterworth-Heinemann.

Currie, W. and Willcocks, L. (1998) 'Analysing four types of IT-outsourcing decisions in the context of scale, client/server, interdependency and risk migration', *Information Systems Journal*, 8 (2): 119–143.

de Looff, L. (1996) *A Model for Information Systems Outsourcing Decision Making*, Harrisburg, PA: Idea Publishing.

Feeny, D. and Willcocks, L. (1998) 'Re-designing the IS function around core capabilities', *Long Range Planning*, 31 (3): 354–367.

Fenn, C., Shooter, R. and Allan, K. (2002) 'IT security outsourcing, how safe is your IT security?', *Computer Law & Security Report*, 18 (2): 109–111.

Goles, T. (2003) 'Vendor capabilities and outsourcing success', *Wirtschaftsinformatik*, 45 (2): 199–206.

Hart, O. (1995) *Contracts and Financial Structure*, Oxford: Oxford University Press.

Henderson, J. and Venkatraman, N. (1993) 'Strategic alignment: leveraging information technology for transforming organisations', *IBM Systems Journal*, 32 (1): 4–16.

Kern, T. and Willcocks, L. (2002) 'Exploring relationships in information technology outsourcing: the interaction approach', *European Journal of Information Systems*, 11: 3–19.

Khosrowpour, M. (1995) *Managing Information Technology Investments with Outsourcing*, Harrisburg, PA: Idea Group Publishing.

Klepper, R. (1995) 'The management of partnering development in I/S outsourcing', *Journal of Technology*, 10 (4): 249–258.

Lacity, M. and Hirschheim, R. (1993) *Information Systems Outsourcing*, Chichester: Wiley & Sons.

Lacity, M. and Hirschheim, R. (1995) *Beyond the Information Systems Outsourcing Bandwagon*, Chichester: Wiley & Sons.

Lacity, M. and Willcocks, L. (2001) *Global Information Technology Outsourcing: In Search of Business Advantage*, Chichester: John Wiley & Sons.

Lacity, M. and Willcocks, L. (2003) 'IT sourcing reflections: lessons for customers and suppliers', *Wirtschaftinformatik*, 45 (2): 115–125.

Levina, N. and Ross, J. (2003) 'From the vendor's perspective: exploring the value proposition in information technology outsourcing', *Management Information Systems Quarterly*, 27 (3): 331–364.

75

McFarlan, F. and Nolan, R. (1995) 'How to manage an IT outsourcing alliance', *Sloan Management Review*, 36 (2): 9–23.

Paulk, M., Curtis, B., Averill, E. *et al.* (1993) 'Capability Maturity Model, version 1.1', *IEEE Software*, 10 (4): 18–27.

Segal, I. (1999) 'Complexity and renegotiation: a foundation for incomplete contracts', *Review of Economic Studies*, 66 (1): 57–82.

Sherwood, J. (1997) 'Managing security for outsourcing contracts', *Computer & Security*, 16: 603–609.

Willcocks, L. and Kern, T. (1998) 'IT outsourcing as strategic partnering: the case of the UK Inland Revenue', *European Journal of Information Systems*, 7: 29–45.

Willcocks, L., Fitzgerald, G. and Feeny, D. (1995a) 'Outsourcing IT: the strategic implications', *Long Range Planning*, 28 (5): 59–70.

Willcocks, L., Lacity, M. and Fitzgerald, G. (1995b) 'Information technology outsourcing in Europe and the USA: assessment issues', *International Journal of Information Management*, 15 (5): 333–351.

Chapter 5

Governance of IT outsourcing

- Because of the increasingly dominant influence of IT services, the importance of IT governance is also growing.
- IT governance frameworks such as COBIT, ISO17799, ITIL/BS15000 and CMMi provide support for service providers setting up IT governance structures.
- The steadily increasing number of laws and regulations influence not only corporate governance but also IT governance.
- In order to structure governance of IT sourcing relationships, we present a descriptive framework that has three dimensions: that of the service recipient, that of the service provider, and that of their relationship as a whole.
- In each of these dimensions we distinguish four governance factors.

5.1 INTRODUCTION

Corporate governance has been an important subject of discussion and research for decades. Recently, the interest in IT governance, which may be considered a special kind of corporate governance, is also growing. The relationship between the two will be discussed in Section 5.2. IT governance is the implementation of governance for IT by the service recipient and will be defined in Section 5.3. Service providers and service recipients are obviously both responsible for ensuring good IT governance; nevertheless, it is the recipient who retains final responsibility. Several frameworks, developed especially for the purpose of IT governance, will be discussed in Section 5.4: COBIT, ISO17799, ITIL/BS15000 and CMMi. Such frameworks help recipients and providers set up their IT governance structure. Section 5.5 presents an overview of the steadily growing number of laws and regulations concerning IT governance. Section 5.6 contains a conceptual framework to structure governance of IT outsourcing relationships. Especially in global sourcing relationships, culture is an important factor that affects governance. Theoretical foundations are presented in Section 5.7. Finally, in Section 5.8, we present a case study on IT outsourcing governance in a multicultural setting.

5.2 CORPORATE GOVERNANCE VS IT GOVERNANCE

Corporate governance may be defined as the organizational expression of the company's business objectives, a structure that therefore includes the means of attaining those objectives as well as guidelines for performance monitoring. Good corporate governance provides incentives for the company's board and managers to pursue objectives that are in its own and its stakeholders' interests. It therefore also facilitates effective monitoring, thus encouraging companies to use their resources more efficiently (OECD 2004). An important goal of corporate governance is to prevent conflicts of interest between the company's employees (including its managers) and its stockholders (Berle and Means 1932; Fama and Jensen 1983). It is, therefore, a subject that remains important (Shleifer and Vishny 1997; Gugler *et al.* 2004).

To set up a properly functioning corporate governance structure, the integrated enterprise risk management (ERM) framework, developed by the Committee of Sponsoring Organizations of the Treadway Commission (COSO),[1] may be used. This framework describes the essential concepts, principles and components of enterprise risk management and it applies to all organizations, regardless of size. In a world of heightened concern and with many people focusing on risk management, the framework provides boards of directors as well as managers with a clear roadmap for identifying risks, avoiding pitfalls and seizing opportunities to grow stakeholder value. To this end, the framework consists of a process that is implemented by the organization's board of directors, managers and other personnel, and that is applied in strategy setting for the whole of the enterprise. It is designed to enable the organization's staff to identify potential events that may affect the organization, to manage the risks involved such that they remain within the limits of its risk appetite, and to provide reasonable assurance regarding the achievement of the organization's objectives (see www.coso.org).

IT governance may be considered a special kind of corporate governance. Its importance increases because IT services are becoming more dominant and because IT services and business management are increasingly integrated. In order to set up a good IT governance structure, it must be well anchored in the organization's corporate governance set-up. According to the strategic alignment model (Henderson and Venkatraman 1993), this connection should be achieved on the strategic organizational level.

The question of how large organizations manage the complexity from global business operations and IT infrastructures remains one of the most pressing issues facing management (Brown and Magill 1994; Sambamurthy and Zmud 1999; Doh

2005; King 2005). Traditionally, research on IT governance has focused on the design of decision-making structures for the control of IT (Brown and Magill 1994; Sambamurthy and Zmud 1999). Most of this literature about how to organize IT focused on choices between centralization, decentralization and federal models. These studies indicate that a federal IT governance structure, i.e. a hybrid design of centralized infrastructure control and decentralized application control, is the dominant model in many contemporary enterprises. However, in current hyper-competitive environments and with the emergence of new electronic network organizations (El Sawy *et al*. 1999), the classical hierarchical design of IT governance becomes obsolete and inadequate to deal with the information processing and coordination demands posed (Galbraith 1993; Galbraith and Cohen 1998; Sambamurthy and Zmud 1999). So later the focus shifted to coordination, by introducing the issues of relational architectures and integration architectures as building blocks for the Organizing Logic for IT activities (Brown and Magill 1994; Sambamurthy and Zmud 1999). The governance problem is pertinent when IT and its department form a legal part of the (business) organization, and it is even more complex when IT is largely outsourced to one or more service providers. The latest development in IT governance is the recognition of the importance of accountability (Weill and Ross 2004). Financial scandals have caused authorities to issue stricter laws and regulations. A well-known example of the latter is the Sarbenes Oxley Act (USA, 2002). Other countries have adopted similar regulations and laws; an overview will be presented in Section 5.5.

Governance of IT outsourcing relationships has to result in realizing the mutually set goals of the relationship. This situation differs from insourcing and as a result is more complex, as there is no common hierarchy (the companies are legally and economically independent of each other) and their respective goals may not be aligned. An example of the latter is the cost-saving goal of the service recipient vs the return-on-investment goal of the services provider. IT outsourcing partnerships involve an allocation of responsibilities to either the service provider or the service recipient. This split of course also influences IT governance, even though this always remains the recipient's responsibility. Service recipients should ensure that their outsourcing contracts contribute to the realization of their IT governance objectives. In fact, you might say that meeting the recipient's IT governance objectives is just one more of the requirements that service providers must meet and that service recipients must therefore monitor. This monitoring is the task of the recipient's information management. Naturally, if the recipient's IT services are insourced rather than outsourced, this responsibility remains; but in such circumstances it concerns the recipient's internal IT department rather than an external provider.

Because of the link between corporate and IT governance, service recipients outsourcing their IT services to partners must give their providers insight into their corporate governance structure. Doing so requires trust. In reality, not many companies like sharing such information with outsiders, so the increasingly strong link between corporate and IT governance effectively renders IT outsourcing partnerships less attractive. At the very least IT governance requires the partners to set up extra organizational structures and processes, in order to realize a good alignment between the business and IT. These will be further discussed in Chapters 6–9.

5.3 IT GOVERNANCE DEFINITIONS

Many definitions of IT governance have been presented (see Table 5.1). As the demands made on service recipients changed, so did these definitions. The most important of them will be briefly discussed here. At first only the locus of IT decision-making in the organization was included (Brown and Magill 1994). Then decision-making processes were added (Luftman 1996; Sambamurthy and Zmud

Table 5.1 Definitions of IT governance

Researchers	IT governance definition
Brown and Magill (1994)	IT governance describes the locus of responsibility for IT functions.
Luftman (1996)	IT governance is the degree to which the authority for making IT decisions is defined and shared among management, and the processes managers in both IT and business organizations apply in setting IT priorities and the allocation of IT resources.
Sambamurthy and Zmud (1999)	IT governance refers to the patterns of authority for key IT activities.
Van Grembergen (2002)	IT governance is the organizational capacity by the board, executive management and IT management to control the formulation and implementation of IT strategy and in this way ensure the fusion of business and IT.
Weill and Vitale (2002)	IT governance describes a firm's overall process for sharing decision rights about IT and monitoring the performance of IT investments.
Schwarz and Hirschheim (2003)	IT governance consists of IT-related structures or architectures (and associated authority patterns), implemented to successfully accomplish (IT-imperative) activities in response to an enterprise's environment and strategic imperatives.
IT Governance Institute (2004)	IT governance is the responsibility of the board of directors and executive management. It is an integral part of enterprise governance and consists of the leadership and organizational structures and processes that ensure that the organization's IT sustains and extends the organization's strategies and objectives.
Weill and Ross (2004)	IT governance is specifying the decision rights and accountability framework to encourage desirable behaviour in using IT.

1999): which IT decisions should the recipient's IT and business managers take, and which priorities should they define? The next addition was that the return on their IT investments should be monitored (Weill and Vitale 2002). And it was then stressed that companies should ensure the organizational capacity to formulate and implement an IT strategy, in order to align IT and business (van Grembergen 2002).

Meanwhile, two interesting observations were made. The first is that the set-up of a company's IT governance structure depends to a large degree on its environment, which means that there is no one way of doing it right. A more dynamic environment requires a more flexible IT governance structure, for example. The second observation concerns the importance of the perceptions that the IT organization and the rest of the company have of one another (Schwarz and Hirschheim 2003). These perceptions play a serious role in the realization of a good governance structure. Communication is, therefore, an important success factor – but not necessarily something at which IT professionals excel. And so it is all the more important to achieve a good alignment between business and IT.

Finally, the importance of accountability was recognized (Weill and Ross 2004). In this area, laws and regulations clearly influence the way in which IT governance is implemented.

5.4 IT GOVERNANCE FRAMEWORKS

In IT governance structures several mechanisms may be distinguished: decision-making structures, alignment processes and communication approaches (Weill and Ross 2004). In outsourcing situations communication is of prime importance. After all, external providers are involved who, because of their greater distance to the recipient's business management, are always behind with respect to the information they need to do their job well. Only good communication can provide them with this information.

Another suggestion made is that IT governance requires the constant attention of the recipient's management. They should know when to redesign the IT governance structure and how to assign ownership and accountability. This feedback loop is also mentioned in the 'platform logic model' of Schwarz and Hirschheim (2003). On the basis of a metric, the capabilities included and the architecture decisions made must constantly be adapted.

To set up an IT governance structure, several frameworks are available: COBIT, ISO17799, ITIL/BS15000 and CMMi. These will now be discussed more fully.

5.4.1 COBIT

COBIT, or 'control objectives for information and related technology', is an IT control framework first issued in 1996 by ISACA.[2] Currently its third edition is used. It promotes process focus and process ownership. The framework consists of 34 high-level control objectives (Brand and Boonen 2004) and 318 detailed control objectives; it also contains tools, such as the 'management awareness diagnostics' and the 'IT control diagnostics'. For the 34 high-level control objectives a maturity model has been developed comparable to the capability maturity model of Section 5.4.4. Using COBIT, an IT governance structure can be set up and implemented on the basis of critical success factors, key goal indicators and key performance indicators (COBIT 1998).

In outsourcing relationships the COBIT process, DS2 Managing Third-Party Services, in the management domain Delivery and Support, requires additional clarification. The goal of this process is 'managing third-party services to ensure that the roles and responsibilities of third parties are clearly defined, adhered to and continue to satisfy requirements'. This involves identifying third-party requirements; defining service contracts; organizing supplier interfaces; managing third-party and outsourcing contracts; monitoring contract achievements; reporting service levels; evaluating third-party and outsourcing contracts; and monitoring the process (COBIT, 1998).

5.4.2 ISO17799

British Standard 7799 (BS7799) was first formulated in 1995, and finalized in 1999. On the basis of this standard, ISO[3] issued ISO 17799 in December 2000: the 'information technology code of practice for information security management'. Implementing this standard, which is meant for service providers, requires substantial effort, as does maintaining it (Thorp 2004). But it is a good standard with which to improve IT service delivery (Eloff and von Solms 2000). Since the rise of the Internet, extra attention is paid to security, which has further increased the need for a code of practice (Trcek 2003).

The ISO 17799 standard is organized into ten major sections, each covering a different area: business continuity planning; system access control; system development and maintenance; physical and environmental security; compliance; personnel security; security organization; computer and network management; asset classification; and control and security policy (see www.iso.org).

5.4.3 ITIL and BS15000

The Information Technology Infrastructure Library (ITIL) was developed by the British Central Computer and Telecommunication Agency (CCTA). Since April 2001 it is distributed by another government agency, the Office of Government Commerce (OCG) (see www.ogc.gov.uk). ITIL consists of seven categories: managers; service support; service delivery; software support; networks; computer operations; and environmental issues. Although it covers a number of areas, its main focus is on IT service management (ITSM). This in its turn is subdivided into service support and service delivery, which together encompass ten disciplines that are responsible for the provision and management of effective IT services.

On the basis of ITIL, British Standard 15000 (BS15000) was developed (see www.bs15000.uk.org). This provides a certification programme for service providers. Its formal part, BS15000–1 (which is the actual standard), consists of ten sections: scope; terms and definitions; requirements for a management system; planning and implementing service management; planning and implementing new or changed services; service delivery processes; relationship processes; resolution processes; control processes; and release processes. BS15000–2 then consists of a code of practice, providing support to organizations that are to be audited against BS15000–1 or that are planning service improvements.

5.4.4 The capability maturity model for integration

The Software Engineering Institute (SEI) is a federally funded research and development centre sponsored by the US Department of Defense and operated by the Carnegie Mellon University (see www.sei.cmu.edu/cmmi). In 2000 the capability maturity model (CMM) was used to develop a model that focuses on integration: CMMi. It enables service providers to improve the quality of their product and services development and maintenance processes (SEI 2002). For it to be successful, it is of course important to implement the model properly (Niazi *et al.* 2005). In CMMi much attention is paid to the activities that must be carried out. The model consists of five maturity levels, each of which is coupled to several process areas; it also contains generic goals and practices (SEI 2002).

Indian service providers have very high maturity scores for software development – they have to because the offshore outsourcing in which they operate as service providers means that their clients are spread all over the world. Having good governance processes is therefore even more important to them than to other service providers as geographical distances and cultural barriers have to be bridged and language gaps have to be closed.

5.5 THE INFLUENCE OF LAWS AND REGULATIONS

Financial scandals such as that involving the American utility company Enron have caused authorities everywhere to issue stricter laws and regulations, both on a national scale and internationally. Of course, IT governance is influenced by these developments too, since all these laws and regulations aim to increase companies' financial transparency, and to allow senior managers to be held personally responsible for any transgressions.

Many important new, internationally binding regulations are contained in the International Accounting Standard (IAS) (see www.iasb.org). Accounting standards are authoritative statements of how particular types of transaction and other events should be reflected in financial statements. Accordingly, compliance with accounting standards will normally be necessary for the fair presentation of financial statements. Closely related to the IAS are the International Financial Reporting Standards (IFRS) and the US General Accepted Accounting Principles (US-GAAP), all of which greatly influence IT governance (www. cpa class.com).

A well-known national example of new regulations is the Sarbanes Oxley Act (USA, 2002). One of its sections, for instance, focuses on the continuous improvement and development of a long-term financial architecture, and so directly influences IT governance (Section 404). Other sections, Section 906 and Section 13(a) and 15(d), concern certified reporting, compliance with the country's Exchange Act, and the fair presentation 'in all material respects, [of] the financial condition and results of operations of the company'. Other countries have adopted similar laws.

An overview of the most important of these is presented in Box 5.1; this is not complete, of course, but it gives an idea of which legal standards service recipients and service providers should meet (a fuller description can be found on www.ecgi.org).

BOX 5.1 NATIONAL LAWS AND REGULATIONS CONCERNING CORPORATE AND IT GOVERNANCE

Australia
- Principles of Good Corporate Governance and Best Practice Recommendations, March 2003
- Corporate Governance: A Guide for Fund Managers and Corporations, December 2002
- Horwath 2002, Corporate Governance Report 2002
- Corporate Governance: A Guide for Investment Managers and Corporations, July 1999
- Corporate Governance – Volume One: In Principle, June 1997
- AIMA Guide & Statement of Recommended Practice (Corporate Governance Statements by Major ASX Listed Companies), June 1995
- Bosch Report, 1995

China
- The Code of Corporate Governance for Listed Companies in China, January 2001

European Union

- EASD Principles and Recommendations, May 2000
- Corporate Governance Guidelines 2000, February 2000
- Sound Business Standards and Corporate Practices: A Set of Guidelines, September 1997
- Corporate Governance in Europe, June 1995

France

- Recommandations sur le gouvernement d'entreprise, March 2004
- The Corporate Governance of Listed Corporations, October 2003
- Promoting Better Corporate Governance in Listed Companies, September 2002
- Vienot II Report, July 1999
- Recommendations on Corporate Governance, June 1998
- Vienot I Report, June 1995

Germany

- Amendment to the German Corporate Governance Code (The Cromme Code), May 2003
- The German Corporate Governance Code (The Cromme Code), February 2002
- Baums Commission Report (Bericht der Regierungskommission Corporate Governance), July 2001
- German Code of Corporate Governance (GCCG), June 2000
- Corporate Governance Rules for German Quoted Companies, January 2000
- DSW Guidelines, June 1998
- Gesetz zur Kontrolle und Transparenz im Unternehmensbereich (KonTraG), March 1998

India

- Report of the Kumar Mangalam Birla Committee on Corporate Governance, February 2000
- Draft Report of the Kumar Mangalam Committee on Corporate Governance, September 1999
- Desirable Corporate Governance in India – A Code, April 1998

Japan

- Principles of Corporate Governance for Listed Companies, April 2004
- Revised Corporate Governance Principles, October 2001

- Report of the Pension Fund Corporate Governance Research Committee, Action Guidelines for Exercising Voting Rights, June 1998
- Corporate Governance Principles: A Japanese View, October 1997
- Urgent Recommendations Concerning Corporate Governance, September 1997

The Netherlands

- SCGOP Handbook of Corporate Governance 2004, 2004
- The Dutch Corporate Governance Code, December 2003
- Draft Corporate Governance Code, July 2003
- SCGOP Handbook of Corporate Governance, August 2001
- Government Governance; Corporate Governance in the Public Sector, Why and How? November 2000
- Peters Report & Recommendations, Corporate Governance in the Netherlands, July 1997

Switzerland

- Swiss Code of Best Practice for Corporate Governance, June 2002
- Corporate Governance Directive, June 2002

UK

- Corporate Governance: A Practical Guide, August 2004
- The Combined Code on Corporate Governance, July 2003
- Audit Committees – Combined Code Guidance (the Smith Report), January 2003
- The Responsibilities of Institutional Shareholders and Agents – Statement of Principles, October 2002
- Review of the Role and Effectiveness of Non-executive Directors (Consultation Paper), July 2002
- Code of Good Practice, January 2001
- The Combined Code: Principles of Good Governance and Code of Best Practice, May 2000
- Hermes Statement on International Voting Principles, December 1999
- The KPMG Review Internal Control: A Practical Guide, October 1999
- Internal Control: Guidance for Directors on the Combined Code (Turnbull Report), September 1999
- Hampel Report (Final), January 1998
- Greenbury Report (Study Group on Directors' Remuneration), July 1995
- Cadbury Report (The Financial Aspects of Corporate Governance), December 1992

US

- Asset Manager Code of Professional Conduct, November 2004
- Final NYSE Corporate Governance Rules, November 2003
- Restoring Trust – The Breeden Report on Corporate Governance for the future of MCI, Inc., August 2003
- Commission on Public Trust and Private Enterprise Findings and Recommendations: Part 2: Corporate Governance, January 2003
- Corporate Governance Rule Proposals, August 2002
- Principles of Corporate Governance, May 2002
- Core Policies, General Principles, Positions & Explanatory Notes, March 2002
- Principles of Corporate Governance: Analysis & Recommendations, 2002
- Report of the NACD Blue Ribbon Commission on Director Professionalism, 2001
- TIAA-CREF Policy Statement on Corporate Governance, March 2000
- Global Corporate Governance Principles, 1999
- Statement on Corporate Governance, September 1997

The question that now remains is when will laws be passed that hold corporate managers accountable for their company's IT services as well as for its business management? If such laws are passed, this will have serious consequences for all outsourcing relationships: service providers will then have to meet the requirements set by these laws and their extra efforts and accountability will have to be paid for. For new contracts, the prices will be higher; for existing contracts, the fees will have to be renegotiated. Nevertheless, considering the growing importance of IT services for any company's business, a move toward such higher prices seems inevitable.

5.6 A DESCRIPTIVE FRAMEWORK

The literature on IT outsourcing contains several contributions to the question on how to manage IT outsourcing relationships (McKeen and Smith 2000; Lacity and Willcocks 2001; Beulen and Ribbers 2003; Beulen 2004). According to Lacity and Hirschheim (1993), an IT outsourcing relationship is characterized by the 'service recipient', the 'service provider' and by the existence of a 'relationship'.

The service recipient and the service provider(s) are bound by a (contractual) agreement regarding the provision of IT services.

5.6.1 The companies involved

The service recipient is the company that decides to start a long-term contractual relationship with one or more service providers to provide all or part of its IT services. The service provider is responsible for the delivery of the IT services to the service recipient. In selecting a service provider, the outsourcing organization must choose a service provider with a profile that fits the requested IT services (Willcocks and Fitzgerald 1994; Lacity and Willcocks 2001).

5.6.2 The relationship

Service recipients and service provider(s) engage in a relationship. The characteristics of these relationships may vary considerably, depending on the type and level of responsibilities outsourced to the provider. In particular, the type of outsourcing decisions and the type of services offered (Willcocks and Choi 1995; International Data Corporation 1997) will impact the relationship. Moreover, these relationships may change over time (Kishore *et al.* 2003). As we explained in Chapter 2 with respect to the type of outsourcing decision, two choices must be made. First, between outsourcing the entire IT service and partial outsourcing, also referred to as 'total outsourcing' and 'selective sourcing' respectively (Currie and Willcocks 1998). Next, a choice must be made between outsourcing to a single vendor or to multiple vendors, referred to as 'single sourcing' and 'multiple sourcing' (Currie and Willcocks 1998). Multiple sourcing obviously leads to increased coordination costs. For the type of services, the following distinctions based on the impact of IT outsourcing on the business organization apply (International Data Corporation 1997): Information Systems Outsourcing, Processing Outsourcing, Business Processing Outsourcing.

5.6.3 A descriptive model

The foregoing discussion provides the building blocks for the conceptual model that helps to explain governance of outsourcing relationships (as detailed in Figure 5.2). First the three components of the model that are involved in the governance are the outsourcing company, the service provider(s) and the relationship between them. Next, reference theories we discussed in Chapter 2 help us to distinguish relevant governance factors for each of the three components.

From the competitive strategy theory, the resource-based view and the resource dependency theory, we learn that strategic positioning, which identifies critical internal resources and capabilities and defines external resources on which the firm depends, is critical in governance. Having a clear IS/IT strategy – that includes a sourcing strategy – is obviously a key governance factor for the outsourcing firm, as is having a clear market position for the service provider.

From the economic theories, in particular transaction cost economics and agency theory, we learn that formal arrangements for managing and monitoring the relationship are essential. Formal organizational arrangements are necessary at both the recipient's and the supplier's side of the relationship, and also with respect to the relationship itself. On the one hand, the outsourcing firm has to structure their Information Systems function that represents their demand management. The service provider, on the other hand, has to structure their interface with the supplier, e.g. through Contract and Account Management (CAM) which operates as the counterpart of the recipient's Information Management, and their back office processes, in particular consistent service delivery processes. Formal arrangements regarding the relationship are the existence of adequate contracts, and organizational arrangements that support communication and reporting.

From the social/organizational theories we learn that formal arrangements are necessary but not sufficient conditions for effective governance. Relationships based on shared understanding and commitment between people and organizations are essential. We propose the existence of trust between the parties involved to be an essential governance element. Some authors even see trust as an outcome measure of a successful outsourcing relationship (van der Zee and de Jong 1999; Barthelemy 2003; Langfield-Smith and Smith 2003). The descriptive model that we propose, based on the foregoing discussion, is represented in Figure 5.1.

Service recipients and service providers may use the governance factors presented here to provide substance to their IT outsourcing partnership. While these factors do not constitute a comprehensive inventory of all measures that should be adopted, they do point up specific organizational elements that recipients and providers can implement. This model is thus meant for both parties to outsourcing partnerships, who can use these governance factors to improve their relationships further.

The governance factors for each of these dimensions are summed up in Table 5.2, and discussed more fully in the next three chapters. There, four aspects of each of these factors will be identified and discussed. In this chapter only a brief introduction of the management model's dimensions and governance factors will be presented.

5.6.4 Governance factors for the service recipient

Service recipients must set up the governance of their IT outsourcing partnerships on the basis of those measures and organizational elements that allow them to

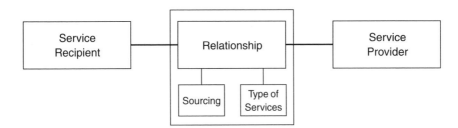

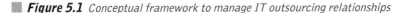 **Figure 5.1** *Conceptual framework to manage IT outsourcing relationships*

Table 5.2 *The IT outsourcing management model's dimensions and governance factors*

Dimensions	Governance factors
The service recipient	• A clear IT strategy • The embedment of IT in the business • A chief information officer (CIO) • Information managers
The service provider	• A clear and consistent market position • A front office • A back office • The availability of IT professionals
The relationship	• Unambiguously defined responsibilities • Contracts • Trust in the partnership • Conferences

control these relationships. These measures and elements are their governance structure's control aspects, which surpass the service levels agreed upon and focus on the organizational structures of their service providers. They define how the service recipient can align its business and IT services, and how it can manage its service providers. Four such governance factors may be distinguished: a clear IS/IT strategy; the embedment of IS/IT in the business; a chief information officer (CIO); and information managers.

By developing and implementing a clear IS/IT strategy, the formulation of which is the responsibility of the company's Information Systems function, service recipients enable themselves to achieve good long-term alignment between their IT and their business processes. This helps focus their outsourcing relationships: external service providers can direct their efforts towards the realization of this IS/IT strategy, for both their offer and their delivery of IT services. Such a strategy need not be completely fixed, however: it can also be used as a starting point for discussions with one's provider, in which it is sharpened further. The provider's input in these discussions contributes to the strategy's effectiveness.

The recipient's senior managers must devote a significant part of their time and attention to the IT services that their company needs. The pressure to do so grows steadily because IT services and business processes are becoming increasingly interdependent – in fact, nowadays IT is often part of the company's products and services. The attention paid will contribute positively to the control achieved over the recipient's IT outsourcing relationships. Since this embedment is important, so is the recipient's internal communication about the objectives of the partnership.

Being at the top of the IT hierarchy, the recipient's chief information officer (CIO) is accountable for all its IT services. In many companies, the CIO is given the impossible mission of controlling the overall IT environment and the company's IT outsourcing relationships in particular – often without getting sufficient time and resources. The CIO's most important task, therefore, is to promote awareness of the importance of IT. The recipient's senior managers and board of directors will have to support him and emphasize this message.

The fourth recipient-side governance factor is their information managers, who must ensure that the information needs of the business are met by the IT services provided by the company's suppliers. These managers thus constitute the organizational link between the company's business units and their service providers.

5.6.5 Governance factors for the service provider

Service providers should also strive to control their relationships with their clients; their governance structure must be set up on the basis of measures and organizational elements that allow them to do so. In the provider's case, however, the emphasis of these control aspects is on the manner in which they can best meet the information needs of their client. Their effectiveness is determined by their organizational structure and the number of IT professionals they have available. The four provider-side governance factors, then, are: a clear and consistent market position; a front office; a back office; and the availability of IT professionals.

For service providers it is important to know the market, what their vision for the future is and which IT services to have in their portfolio. They themselves must also know the sectors and segments of which their market is composed. This includes the geographical scope within which they can deliver their services – although they must realize that being present somewhere does not mean that one's entire portfolio can be marketed there too.

A front office is an important interface between suppliers and their clients. Service recipients use it as their point of contact with the provider's back office. Effectively, this means they use it to control their outsourcing relationships. The provider-side counterpart of this activity is called their contract and account management. It focuses on making sure that the contracted agreements are met, which requires much internal alignment to ensure that the resources needed are really available.

Back offices are responsible for the actual delivery of the IT services contracted. Their managers therefore focus on optimizing manpower capacity and developing new services and products to be offered to the client. The latter task mainly means investigating the applicability of new technology.

Naturally, in order to deliver the required IT services the provider must have IT professionals available. In view of the scarcity on the labour market, service providers must devote particular attention to their human resources – both in a quantitative and in a qualitative sense.

91

5.6.6 Governance factors concerning the relationship

Finally, there are four governance factors that concern the outsourcing relationship as a whole. That is, they are intended to give both recipient and provider control over their partnership. The emphasis of these control aspects is on the manner in which their collaboration and the allocation of responsibilities are defined. Agreements and contracts therefore play an important role here, but they are not sufficient if there is no trust between the parties. And to achieve that, regular conferences are of essential importance.

In IT outsourcing partnerships, both parties' responsibilities should be defined unambiguously. This is even more important if more than one service provider is involved in delivering the IT services that their client needs. Then these providers have responsibilities to one another as well as to the recipient. A distinction can be made, by the way, between responsibilities concerning the recipient's business functions and those concerning their information functions. In all cases, the responsibilities of the service providers need to be clear at all times. When there is more than one service provider, the responsibilities of the service providers with respect to each other must be clear. The responsibilities of each service provider with respect to the service recipient need to be clear as well. A distinction can be made with respect to responsibilities related to the business functions and responsibilities related to the information function within the service recipient. Clear responsibilities prevent service providers from blaming one another or their client should anything go wrong.

Efficient and effective IT outsourcing contracts greatly enhance the clarity and measurability of the agreements made. It is therefore important that the measurements made are expressed in terms that the business functions of the service recipient are able to recognize. Balanced scorecards work well to achieve this, and they are therefore often used. When formulating IT outsourcing contracts, the parties involved should not forget to provide the opportunity for adjusting the terms in order to adapt the contract to changing circumstances. Only then will the services provided remain aligned with the recipient's information needs.

Mutual trust between the service recipient and their providers is important – not only during the selection process but also during the contract period, when the services agreed are delivered. Such trust has to be generated and maintained on a group level as well as between individuals. To do so, people should communicate openly. Should problems arise, they are then immediately discussed with a focus on finding solutions.

Such open communication can be achieved if the recipient's and the provider's staff on all organizational levels – strategic, tactical and operational – regularly confer on the issues at hand. To this end, the authority and responsibilities of every conference must be clearly delineated. One must also define clearly who participates in which conferences, as well as the frequency with which they are to meet. Naturally, these aspects depend to a certain extent on the partnership's dynamics.

5.7 THEORETICAL FOUNDATIONS

We have seen how both business aspects and technological developments affect business models and supplier–buyer relationships. Naturally, much research has been done into the nature of this influence. Many approaches have been discussed in the economics and organization literature and many organization theories have been proposed on the subject (Dibbern *et al.* 2004). The most important of these for our purpose are the theory of competitive strategy, the resource-based view, the theory of transaction costs, the agency theory and two social or organizational theories: the resource dependency theory and the institutional theory. These will be discussed in the following subsections.

5.7.1 The theory of competitive strategy

Strategy is a rather difficult concept to define. One relatively simple way of looking at it is as an attempt to make a fit between one's organization and its environment. This attempt has been considered from many different points of view. Porter's theory on competitive strategy (Porter 1980), which is the subject here, focuses on the influence that external factors have on companies' strategic positions. It represents a school of thought that begins by analysing the company's position in its competitive environment and then considers how it may achieve a sustainable competitive advantage in the context of those external forces. The structural attractiveness of a company is, according to this theory (Porter 1997), determined by five aspects:

1 its customers' bargaining position;
2 its suppliers' bargaining position;
3 the barriers new competitors face when entering the industry;
4 the threat of new, substitute products or services;
5 the competition among current competitors.

Combined, these forces determine how the economic value generated from products, services, technologies and competitive methods is divided between the companies in an industry and their customers, suppliers, distributors and substitutes.

Each of these competitive forces is, of course, itself determined by a number of factors. The bargaining power of one's customers, for instance, depends on the degree of product differentiation, on the size of demand and supply and of the parties involved, but also on how much it will cost customers to change to another supplier. The latter costs, called switching costs, effectively may cause a customer to be locked in. In the area of information technology, this may be the result of

93

proprietary standards. But the improved personalization of one's services, achieved by using modern databases, for example, or the implementation of customer-specific technologies and knowledge, may also make it costly or impractical for the customer to move to another provider. In outsourcing matters, the customer's bargaining position is therefore an important issue to consider. The bargaining power of one's suppliers is a similar subject, but seen from the opposite position. Now it is one's own company that faces the lock-in risk, for example.

Newcomers in an industry face all kinds of barriers, generally of an economic or technological nature, but sometimes also caused by culture or language differences. Entering an industry requires capital and often scale, and one must have the expertise needed to be taken seriously. Likewise, new products or services face the barrier of switching costs. If, however, they can add value without the customer having to make many such costs, they become a serious threat to the industry's current products. Consider the Internet, for example, which cost traditional mail services a significant amount of business by making e-mail accessible to everyone.

Competition is very different in different markets. It may be fierce but sometimes it is relatively relaxed. And it is often influenced by developments outside the company's control. Here, too, the Internet is a good example. Companies and consumers are now directly linked, reducing search costs and increasing market transparency. Companies relying on information asymmetry see their profit positions seriously threatened.

Analysing these five aspects clarifies the fundamental attractiveness of an industry. It exposes the underlying drivers of average industry profitability and provides insight into how profitability evolves in the future. These factors determine the participants' profitability even if the industry's suppliers, channels, substitutes or competitors change (Porter 1980). Achieving success, according to this theory, is thus a matter of choosing the right competitive strategy, for which there are two major possibilities: either you concentrate on being a low-cost producer and your customers will buy from you because your products are the least expensive; or you differentiate from your competitors in terms of the quality you offer, and your customers buy from you because they believe yours are the best products. These strategies can be pursued either overall in the market or by concentrating on a particular niche.

5.7.2 The resource-based view

According to the theory of economic development, innovation is the source of value creation (Schumpeter 1939). Several kinds of innovation have been identified: the introduction of new goods or new production methods, the creation of new markets, the discovery of new supply sources, the reorganization of industries, etc. Effectively, innovation is in this theory considered a matter of using new combinations of resources to provide new products and production methods with which markets and industries are transformed. Economic development is then the result.

To achieve such innovation one must, of course, have the necessary resources. The resource-based view therefore focuses on internal characteristics as factors for companies' competitive success. Enterprises are considered collections of competences and capabilities that must be maintained and developed (Grant 1991; Prahalad and Hamel 1991; Barney 1997; Amit and Zott 2001). Only their 'core' and unique, difficult-to-imitate resources contribute significantly, as they are the foundation of the company's competitive position in their business environment. And even these resources cannot do so on their own; one has to select the right ones and combine them in the right way for the company to be successful. The central idea of the resource-based view is, then, that combining a set of complementary and specialized resources in a unique way may enable a company to generate value from them – if these resources reduce its costs and raise its revenues in comparison with a situation without them (Wernerfelt 1984; Peteraf 1993; Barney 1997).

The resources are of many kinds: capital, equipment, real estate, patents, brands, experience, skills, knowledge, organizational aspects, etc. Some are tangible, others are not. Some are easily bought and sold, but management skills, for example, are not. Consequently, not all resources are equally important. To be the basis of a sustainable competitive advantage, resources must be difficult to buy, difficult to imitate and difficult to substitute – or else your competitor will simply do the same and cannibalize on your profit (Douma and Schreuder 1998). Besides, such resources must have been acquired against reasonable costs, or they will be a burden rather than an asset.

Generally, intangible assets such as knowledge and experience are more difficult to acquire, imitate or substitute than tangibles like equipment or real estate. And unprotected intangibles like organizational routines are in their turn more difficult to trade, replicate or replace than those whose property rights are well defined, such as patents or brand names. After all, trading involves disclosing, which at least partly destroys their value, for even licences and royalties only apply for a limited period. As far as information is concerned, unprotected information is therefore the best basis for a sustainable advantage. For other resources, different arguments may apply: using tankers to transport oil, for instance, may offer a perfectly sustainable competitive advantage if pipelines are impossible or unaffordable to build.

In the field of intangible assets, the concept of core competences has come to play an important role. Core competences are considered the root of the enterprise: its collective knowledge base, skill sets and activities, upon which its competitive position is built (Quinn *et al.* 1990; Prahalad and Hamel 1991). This concept plays an important role in analysing the viability of new business models. If you know what the company's core competences are, then it is clear which resources cannot be outsourced, for example. Outsourcing all other activities may be a good strategic move, because one can then concentrate on the core competences and achieve a leaner, more flexible organization that can respond quickly to the inevitable but unpredictable changes in its environment. Since the resource-based view offers insight into which resources are of critical importance, it helps determine which resources should be kept or acquired. In a similar vein, the resource dependency theory discussed in Section 5.7.5 looks at external resources, and considers ways to cope with the risks of one's dependence on outside providers for them. Resource theories help determine whether one should or should not outsource certain processes and capabilities.

5.7.3 Transaction cost economics

Implementing new business models has implications for companies' strategies. One important question we have already encountered is whether one should produce a certain good or service oneself or buy it from an external supplier. In part, this depends on the efficiency of the transaction involved. According to transaction cost theory (Coase 1937; Williamson 1975, 1983) companies engaging in exchanges with external companies make several kinds of costs, collectively called coordination costs. These include many different kinds of expenditures: for finding and selecting the right trading partner (which includes the costs of information exchange and of determining the client's needs), for negotiations, financing, distribution, monitoring, invoice settlement and the many after-sales aspects that arise from doing business. Also included are operations risk costs, which arise from the possibility that one's partner may misrepresent the situation, withhold information or underperform; and opportunism risk costs (Clemons *et al.* 1993), referring to partners wanting to renegotiate after the other side has already made certain investments, or simply because there are few alternatives. For some products and services, these costs are higher than for others; some circumstances may cause them to rise and others to drop. But companies will always weigh production costs against coordination costs, that is, the advantages of internal management (also called the hierarchy), against those of external procurement governed by a market mechanism.

The central issue addressed by transaction cost economics is why companies internalize transactions that might also be conducted in markets. Analytically, this boils down to two questions that companies facing outsourcing decisions should answer:

1 Which activities should they keep inside their organization and which activities should be outsourced?
2 How should they manage their relationships with their customers, suppliers and other business partners?

Put another way, the main focus is to devise the most efficient governance form for transactions given their specific economic contexts, and the answer is found in the costs associated with these transactions. Essentially, companies will themselves produce the goods and services wanted if the costs of market coordination are greater than the benefits arising from the economies of scale and scope associated with outsourcing to specialists – and vice versa. Later scholars have extended the discussion to include quasi-hierarchical and quasi-market structures as alternative governance forms (Gulati 1995), but the concept remains the same.

Many aspects of inter-business relationships play a role in this field: uncertainty, exchange frequency, the specificity and complexity of the products and services delivered (Williamson 1979; Klein 1996) and even human behaviour (Williamson 1975), in particular bounded rationality and opportunism. These aspects will be discussed in the next two subsections.

Transaction aspects

There are three aspects to transactions that exert a powerful influence over the decision to insource or outsource: asset specificity, product complexity and transaction frequency. The asset specificity of a transaction refers to the degree to which it is supported by assets that are specific to this transaction alone and that cannot be used otherwise or elsewhere without incurring a significant reduction of their value. If you need trained personnel for the transaction, this is called human capital specificity (Douma and Schreuder 1998). If a power station is located close to the coal mines producing its fuel, we speak of site specificity. Likewise, time specificity occurs when the product or service involved must be delivered within a short period (Malone *et al.* 1987), as is the case with some foods, for instance. There are many different kinds of specificity, but they share one characteristic: since the acquisition of the asset involved is generally a long and possibly costly process, asset-specific transactions tend to be performed by the user themselves because that reduces the risk to their continuity and it increases the level of control and coordination. For rather more unspecific transactions, markets usually work well.

Commodity products are simple and often standardized. Buyers choose on the basis of their price, and markets offer a way to compare these. So that is where most commodities are bought (Nooteboom 1999). Complex products, however, involve a significant exchange of information. This is less easily achieved on markets because it increases the transaction costs. As product complexity rises, buyers therefore tend to prefer single-supplier relationships that are more hierarchical.

And finally, even though some circumstances may point to insourcing a certain transaction, setting up transactions hierarchically involves making significant organization costs. Such investments are only recouped if the volume or frequency of the transactions is high enough. If they are low, the goods or services are still better procured from a market (Douma and Schreuder 1998). Companies facing outsourcing decisions must attempt to strike a balance between these conflicting arguments.

Behavioural assumptions

We all try to make our decisions rationally, with a view to optimizing the outcome and turning it to our advantage. The problem is there are often too many variables for us to take them all in. Quite a few questions are simply too complex for human capacity to be able to give the answer, even if we have all the information needed. A famous example is that of the game of chess. The positions of the pieces on the board provide the players with all the information needed, and yet not even the grand masters can think through all possible moves (Douma and Schreuder 1998). This is called bounded rationality: the fact that human beings intend to behave rationally but are simply incapable of doing so to more than a limited degree. This challenge is all the more daunting in complex or uncertain situations. Chess players at least have all the information. A government buying a new fighter plane (another well-known example) cannot be sure of the costs or even of whether all the intended technology will really work. With so many specifications unknown it will be very difficult to reach a decision and lay it down in a contract. The coordination costs of transactions may thus become very high in situations when bounded rationality and complexity or uncertainty reinforce each other.

Another human characteristic is that, regrettably, not all of us are equally honest. Some people try to exploit situations to their own advantage by making what has rather euphemistically been called 'self-disbelieved statements' (Williamson 1975). Not everybody does, of course, and not all of the time. But the problem is that some people do so some of the time, and when you do business you cannot distinguish between honest and dishonest. In business literature, taking advantage of your partner's lack of knowledge and know-how is called opportunism: self-interest seeking with guile (Williamson 1975). Since one can never entirely rule out the possibility that one's partner is less than fully honest, many transactions involve inspections, contracts and the like, even if the partner involved is considered perfectly trustworthy. The occurrence of opportunism may therefore increase transaction costs. This is especially important if there are few potential trading partners. Those partners will then care less about their reputations as there are few alternatives to which their clients might turn if they are not satisfied. Under such circumstances, of what is called small numbers exchange, the possibility of opportunism is very likely to make transaction costs rise.

5.7.4 The agency theory

If one employs or hires another person or company to deliver certain products or services, there is always the problem of making sure this supplier will really act in his client's interests. This issue is the subject of agency theory (Jensen and Meckling 1976; Hancox and Hackney 1999), in which the two parties that in this book are often referred to as recipient and supplier are called principal and agent, respectively. The principal may be a private person, a company acting as employer or a group of shareholders; they are always the party who needs a certain product or service. Agents can be suppliers, employees or the management team of the company involved – the party delivering the products or services. Since the client's profits depend on the actions of the supplier, the principal must try to find ways of making his agent act in accordance with his objectives. But this is difficult, for the principal usually does not have the expertise and information needed, often not even to assess his agent's work properly. Consequently, the recipients meet the monitoring costs. There is always some degree of mistrust between the principal and the agent. Agency theory attempts to explain how such relationships are best organized (Eisenhardt 1985). Its analyses are based on four assumptions (Keill 2005):

- both parties behave rationally and have rational expectations;
- the agent's actions generate the principal's profit and success;
- the parties' interests diverge;
- the principal–agent relationship is characterized by information asymmetry.

Agents are always tempted to serve their own purposes rather than those of the principal. They can do so by hiding their real skills and abilities to do the job properly (hidden characteristics), by being unclear about their own goals (hidden intentions) and by maintaining a certain degree of freedom (hidden actions). The agent's degree of freedom decreases as the principal intensifies his control over his activities in order to decrease his own uncertainty. But doing so costs money. Agency costs essentially are a kind of transaction cost, and they include expenditures for selection, standard-setting, monitoring and possibly residual losses.

We have already, albeit tacitly, introduced the parallel between the subject of the agency theory and the issue at hand in outsourcing decisions. Relationships between principals or recipients on the one hand and agents or suppliers on the other generally fall into three stages (Keill 2005). In the first stage the right supplier must be found; this stage ends when the contract is signed. Then the contract must be executed. Finally, the relationship ends or it is renewed. Each of these stages is characterized by its specific problems.

Outsourcing companies can never fully judge the quality of their potential suppliers, nor their real intentions. It is therefore important that they mitigate the risks of the selection stage by gathering as much independent information about them as possible. Sources for such information are market researchers and current or former clients, who know about the supplier's track record, and sometimes independent authorities or institutes, who may carry out benchmarks. This information need also explains the rise of certification procedures in the past decade or two.

Once the contract has been signed and the products or services are delivered, the recipient must make sure these tasks are carried out in his best interests. The agent, however, has a major information advantage – which is not surprising, as this is probably one of the reasons for outsourcing in the first place – so his actions are difficult to assess. Agents may boost their own profits, for example by spending less time or resources than agreed. Monitoring is one way of countering this risk, but it is costly since one must set performance standards and measure the actual work done or have it audited by independent authorities. Another method is to align the agent's interests with those of the principal, by introducing incentive schemes, for instance. Emotional pressure may also improve the agent's loyalty and prevent them from behaving opportunistically.

At the end of the contract period, both parties run certain risks. We have seen earlier in this section how a client may experience lock-in. But suppliers also may have made investments that have not yet been recovered, a situation called hold-up. The switching costs either party faces in such circumstances may be avoided by minimizing relationship-specific investments which are of little use in relationships with other clients or suppliers, and by limiting one's dependence on the other in terms of exclusive skills and knowledge.

5.7.5 Social or organizational theories

Finally, we can distinguish a category of social or organizational theories that look at the dynamics of decision-making processes between multiple stakeholders. These describe inter-organizational decision-making as a push-and-pull process based on negotiation and coalition building, in which multiple ambiguous goals exist (Cyert and March 1963). Proponents of this approach contend that the experiences and a shared (negotiated) understanding among key stakeholders are essential to effective decision-making processes (Dyer and Singh 1998). According to the social exchange theorists, these interactions are based on trust, collaboration, cooperation and win–win relationships between the participants (Kumar and van Dissel 1996). The notion is that the parties in a relationship share certain risks and rewards, which are reflected in the agreement. Specifically with regard to outsourcing relationships several problems have been identified that may occur, such as hidden costs, the failure to implement new technology innovations, the failure to pass on savings to the client and differences in opinion regarding the interpretation of contract details and performance metrics (Earl 1996). However, the parties in an exchange are in mutual agreement that the resulting outcome of the exchange is greater than what could be obtained through other forms of exchange or from an exchange with a different partner. In this relational view the focus shifts to the continuing strategic relationships between companies in generating value beyond what could be realized independently. This type of relationship is also called a partnership (Rothery and Robertson 1995). However, realizing the benefits from such a partnership is contingent upon mutual trust and organizational complementarity in such things as decision-making processes, control systems, organizational culture, etc. (Dyer and Singh 1998). For the purposes of this book it will suffice to take a closer look at two such social or organizational theories: the resource dependency theory and the institutional theory.

The resource dependency theory

In Section 5.7.2 we have seen how the resource-based view focuses on companies' internal resources with which to achieve a sustainable competitive position. We will now look at external resources. Hence the 'dependence' in the name of the theory discussed here, since that aspect must be managed. Resource dependence theories, first introduced in the 1960s (Thompson 1967) and later elaborated (Pfeffer and Salancik 1978), work from the premise that companies strive for continuity: survival as the fundamental motivation for action. This means that one must attain control over critically important resources. Total autarky cannot be achieved, since no company can own all necessary resources, nor would it be efficient to do so. But one can and therefore must adopt strategies to secure the acquisition of such resources from the environment. The consequent dependence on parties in that environment presents several difficulties. Dependences are multidimensional and the company's social, political and task environments influence them. They cause different degrees of interconnectedness and co-dependence, that is, the number and patterns of relationships and the type of inter-organizational relationships, respectively. As concerns relationship type, the prime question is whether it is reciprocal (involving feedback) or unidirectional. Reciprocal relationships introduce the highest levels of interdependences and consequently require much management effort because they necessitate the involvement of others in one's strategic decision-making processes. In such ways dependences interfere with companies' drive towards continuity: interconnectedness and co-dependence increase their environments' uncertainty and instability (Pfeffer and Salancik 1978).

The resource dependency theory studies the arguments for and against procuring vital resources from external suppliers. The importance or power of a resource is a key issue here. The alternatives available in the market, which are an indication of the freedom left to change suppliers, and the discretion on the part of the supplier with regard to the resource's characteristics and availability, are also important factors to consider (Pfeffer and Salancik 1978). Likewise, if the recipient can control their provider to a certain degree, or if they can easily switch providers, they are more likely to outsource their needs (Grover and Teng 1993); otherwise, they will tend to produce the goods and services themselves. The theory also focuses on how to deal with the dependences that result when such resources are indeed outsourced. The risks involved can be mitigated by several strategies. Coalition building will help reduce the uncertainty in the relationship. Cultivating alternative resources reduces the buyer's dependence on one supplier. Basically the organization will try to reduce its dependence on the environment by constantly balancing two contradictory forces: certainty and autonomy (Davies and Powell 1992).

The institutional theory

The institutional theory is based on the work done by Hughes (1936, 1939), Parsons (1951) and Selznick (1949, 1957), who represent what is called the 'old' institutionalism. The central aspects of their theory included influence, coalitions, competing values, power and informal structures. Their theory focused on finding explanations for the uniformity of many organizations, and it found that the environment played a major role. With respect to outsourcing, the 'old' institutional theory can be applied to recipients as well as providers. It explains why companies opt for outsourcing and why the phenomenon has therefore grown so much. It can also be used to explain the strategic motives of the providers, for example with respect to offshore outsourcing or business process outsourcing. In the IT industry, for instance, mergers and takeovers have led to concentration, which is likely to continue for the next ten years or so.

In reaction to the 'old' institutionalism, a 'new' institutionalism arose (Meyer and Rowan 1977; Zucker 1977; DiMaggio and Powell 1983; Powell and DiMaggio 1991), which made a distinction between coercive, memetic and normative processes leading to conformity, a process also called isomorphic (DiMaggio and Powell 1983). Later (Powell and DiMaggio 1991), cognitive and cultural explanations were also added. Their central question concerned the impact of social choices on institutional arrangements. This includes shaping, mediating and channelling. This issue applies to outsourcing as well – not just with respect to the make-or-buy question, but in the management of outsourcing relationships and the influence on them of institutional arrangements as well. On the basis of the developments of the past decades, it is certainly safe to conclude that outsourcing is institutionalized. It is an important phenomenon, well embedded in every industry.

Institutional theory distinguishes between two kinds of change: revolutionary and evolutionary change (Greenwood and Hinnings 1996). Outsourcing may in this context be considered an evolutionary change. It has grown inexorably but gradually. And institutional theory can explain this: the need to be able to cope with contextual forces that often change dramatically has become a key determinant of competitive advantage and organizational survival (D'Aveni 1994).

☯ CASE STUDY

GOVERNANCE OF OUTSOURCING IN DIFFERENT CULTURES[4]

Summary

The recipient in this case study was an Asian business unit of a company with global activities in discrete manufacturing. Having acquired this business unit, the holding company wished to integrate it into its worldwide organization. This required a business process redesign (BPR) project involving its entire Asian operations, which in turn made it necessary to implement a new IT platform. They then decided to outsource their IT services. The BPR project fell entirely under the business managers' responsibilities, including the consequent IT outsourcing contract.

Provider selection presented no problem in this case, since the holding company had a worldwide relationship with a service provider. An issue that was to be carefully considered, however, was the fact that both parent companies were based in Europe, while their subsidiaries that would now begin a partnership were located in Asia. Cultural differences would thus require attention, an aspect brought more sharply to the fore by the fact that both partners had appointed European expatriates in senior management positions: the recipient's IT director and the provider's service delivery manager. Their roles and responsibilities are detailed in Table 5.3. It was at first unclear whether this would be an advantage or a disadvantage. The central question of this case study, therefore, is how outsourcing partners should handle cultural differences and their inevitable impact on their relationship.

Introduction

The IT outsourcing partnership discussed here was situated in Asia. Two locally managed subsidiaries of European companies began an outsourcing relationship in 1998, on the basis of a five-year contract. The provider belonged to a global service provider employing a staff of more than 1200 in Asia alone. It offered full services

Table 5.3 *Interviewees: case study on governance of outsourcing in different cultures*

The interviewees			
Party	Name and job title	Responsibilities	Remarks
Recipient	Carolien Nijvel, IT director	• IT services at the company's Asian assembly and testing business unit (representing some 30% of the business unit's entire IT budget) • Managing local information management office (eight employees)	• Expatriate (from Europe) • Member of the business unit's management team (plant manager level)
Provider	Claus Hohstadt, Service delivery director	• Maintaining relationships with clients, including contract aspects	• Expatriate (from Europe) • Member of the company's Asian management team (senior manager level)

and ran a regional data centre connected to other regional data centres in order to guarantee worldwide services 24 hours a day. Most of the provider's business was for large multinationals who bought their services elsewhere in the world too. Increasingly, however, local companies and authorities were becoming their clients as well. The recipient was a globally operating discrete manufacturing company that at the time employed more than 3500 people in its Asia region. IT director Carolien Nijvel: 'We had been a big player in this region for several decades.'

There was no specific reason for either of the partners to appoint an expatriate as IT director or service delivery manager. Claus Hohstadt recalls:

> Because of this contract, my company opened a subsidiary in the country, where there hadn't been one before. Staff had to be found for all positions, including the management jobs. I already worked for the company, it seemed like an interesting position, I applied, and there I was.

Indeed, both managers were selected simply because their companies found them the best candidates. But their expatriate status did, of course, pose a few questions. How should they deal with the cultural differences between themselves and their Asian colleagues and staff? Would it be an advantage to have two expatriates to work out the partnership? Would there also be disadvantages? 'We had to take some extra measures in order to have enough qualified IT professionals available to guarantee service delivery to our client', Hohstadt recalls. 'That clearly pointed up some of the cultural differences.' The same happened in the recipient's organization, where changes had to be made in order to let the team function well.

Company and industry profile

The company

The local Asian discrete manufacturing subsidiary that outsourced their IT services belonged to a globally active company quoted on several stock exchanges. As a business unit, it was part of the corporation's division for business-to-business markets, whose products were mainly sold to third parties. The division's value chain consisted of three segments: semi-manufactured products, assembly and testing, and technical marketing. Separate regional business units were set up worldwide for each part of this value chain. Assembly and testing is a labour-intensive process involving high volumes but low added values. The business units in this field were therefore mainly located in low-wage countries. The Asian assembly and testing business unit ran major plants in three countries as well as a large number of offices in various countries.

With 1200 employees, the recipient counted as a medium-sized employer in the region. Its parent company, however, ran many more business units in Asia, and worldwide employed more than 150,000 people in over 50 countries. Its annual turnover exceeded 25 trillion euros.[5] The divisional and corporate management teams did, of course, supervise the business unit, but not very closely. IT director Carolien Nijvel: 'Our parent company gave us much autonomy. We set our own business objectives and formulated our own IT strategy.' This left the IT director much freedom, which was increased still further because the division's IT strategy was not updated frequently.

The market in which this business unit operated was of a highly cyclical nature, but demand was hard to predict. Naturally this influenced the set-up of their IT services, which were expected to play an important role in helping cushion demand fluctuations.

IT services

At first, the contract involved about 20 full-time equivalents (FTEs), all employed in the recipient's largest factory. In addition to 17 employees transferred from elsewhere, three who had previously been assigned to other customers were right from the start allocated to the outsourcing contract, to work on new projects. In time the contract was expanded to 35 FTEs; by then it involved several plants.

The IT outsourcing partnership concerned the transformation of a mainframe platform into a client–server architecture. This project required the provider's full attention, especially since they were also responsible for the maintenance and operation of this infrastructure and its corresponding applications, on a 24/7 basis. The supplier focused on applications (ERP and shop floor control systems). Their activities included new release creation, changes, bug solving and support.

Business process redesign

After the Asian business unit was taken over by a globally active corporation, it became clear how necessary it was to improve its management and governance. The dynamic market in which they operated asked for quick decisions and fast reactions. Its frequently changing demand had to be met with products of the right quality. To enable the business unit to do so, a business process redesign (BPR) project was begun. It focused on the company's business processes, of course, but it also influenced their IT services and so, in turn, had major consequences for the way in which the provider delivered these services. A major modernization was taken in hand. Claus Hohstadt: 'For the plant's employees these new IT services were a move from the Stone Age to the year 2000. They really meant a big change for everyone involved.'

In this specific situation such major investments were justified because the consequent business re-engineering would turn the old-fashioned factory into an up-to-date plant. As a result of these IT investments, the plant would no longer lag behind but instead take a leading position, with short lead times and low stock levels. In their business this was a serious advantage, improving their competitive position significantly. Ultimately, the plan was to use the experience gained here to achieve the same improvements in the business unit's two other plants. Reaching this goal required a large effort from both recipient and provider, for the recipient's business processes had to be adapted in order to raise their organization to a higher maturity level.

Requirements

The recipient's objectives

In 1998, the present owner of the business unit was still in the process of integrating it into their organization, having bought it only a few years before. This integration made it necessary to innovate their business processes, for which a new IT platform was required. Moreover, IT was considered to be of strategic importance. Carolien Nijvel, the recipient's IT director, had no doubt about its value:

> In all industries, including ours, IT services became ever more important. They no longer facilitated our supporting processes only. In my business unit shopfloor applications, for example, were of vital importance.

The company's business and the changing environment in which it operated simply made performance and quality improvements necessary. A transformation was called for. The main argument for contracting out their IT services to an external supplier was the low maturity level of the company's own IT department. Outside support was needed to realize the transition from a mainframe platform to a client–server platform. Therefore, the outsourcing relationship began with an application and infrastructure transformation. Since this transformation involved much business re-engineering it eventually influenced the entire business unit. Service delivery director, Claus Hohstadt: 'Alone, they couldn't pull this off. We, however, could contribute our technical specialists and utilize our global capabilities to meet the changing customer requirements effectively and efficiently.'

Greatly improved IT services require users with more knowledge. Training programmes were therefore set up, acquainting the users with the new applications. This, too, required substantial investments. 'We took on part of those programmes', Hohstadt recalls. 'I consider such training an important element in any successful BPR project.'

The services contracted

The recipient elected to outsource the entire IT services delivery to their new provider. Geographically, the partnership was more limited: it applied only to one of the three countries in which the business unit operated. Service delivery manager Claus Hohstadt, however, from the start aimed to extend his business.'I set my sights on the other two countries, as targets for the following years.'

The recipient's and provider's parent companies, who had already established a global outsourcing relationship, collaborated worldwide on the basis of corporate framework agreements. These provided the general terms and conditions for division-level partnership framework agreements and, finally, service framework agreements at business unit level (Figure 5.2). The recipient's IT director, Carolien Nijvel, explains:

> Since there already was this framework of contracts, it took relatively little time to formulate our service framework agreement and the relevant service level agreements. Most of our partnership's fundamentals had already been agreed on a corporate and divisional level.

Claus Hohstadt agrees: 'We spent much more time talking about how to set up our collaboration than about its contractual aspects.'

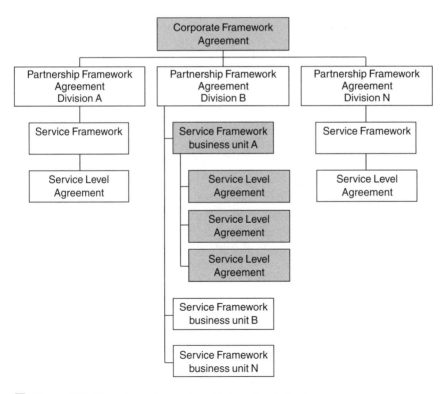

Figure 5.2 *The outsourcing partnership's contract structure.*
Note: Shaded boxes apply to IT.

All individual service contracts were defined as service level agreements (SLAs) fitting within the service framework agreements of their business units. In these SLAs, tasks and responsibilities – in other words, input obligations – were specified. They included the capability levels of the supplier's staff as well as the capacity required, with a guaranteed minimum and an upper limit. The business unit would, of course, inform the supplier in a timely manner if any capacity changes were needed.

Claus Hohstadt, the provider's service delivery manager, mentions the use his company made of global tooling. 'This not only allowed us to deliver our services very efficiently but on a high quality level too. All our staff is trained to use this global tooling.' Another ace up the provider's sleeve was the possibility to assign their top-level consultants to the job for short periods of time. 'They can give a real impulse to our delivery, and meanwhile our other staff learn a tremendous lot from them. A sweet combination of top-level consulting and internal knowledge-sharing.' It was important, however, that such senior consultants were thoroughly aware of the culture differences between their countries of origin or their company as a whole and the local situation in which they had to operate. The provider had to pay much attention to this aspect.

Cultural aspects

For a proper understanding of the cultural aspects involved in the outsourcing partnership discussed here, two matters require some more attention: the business culture of the Asian country in which the outsourcing relationship was set up, and the fact that both the recipient's IT director and the provider's service delivery manager were expatriates of European origin.

Cultural differences between Western and Asian countries can be understood using the *power distance* and *individualism* concepts introduced by Hofstede. The power distance is the extent to which the members of a society accept that power in organizations is distributed unequally. Asian countries are examples of societies with a large power distance. Service delivery director Claus Hohstadt exemplifies: 'Asian employees will usually take over their boss' opinion. That's a lot different where I'm from!' IT director Carolien Nijvel agrees:

> Asian employees don't take the initiative so easily as their Western counterparts. They look up in the organization, to wait and see what happens. That can be a very practical attitude, but it usually isn't. However, if you know this, you are prepared and it needn't be a problem. Especially in the BPR project this was an important element.

Likewise, individualism is defined by Hofstede as 'a preference for a loosely knit social framework in societies wherein individuals are supposed to take care of themselves and their immediate families only'. Its opposite is collectivism: 'a preference for a tightly knit social framework in which individuals can expect their relatives, clan or other in-group to look after them in exchange for unquestioning loyalty.'

On this basis, the USA, the UK, Australia and most Western European countries can be characterized as individualist societies with small power distances. Asian countries, on the other hand, are more collectivist and accept greater power distances. Claus Hohstadt:

> We paid much attention to our employees, trying to generate a one-big-family sense. I must say it worked quite well. We were able to attract good IT professionals. And our labour market image was steadily improving – an important thing, or at least much more important there than it is in the West.

Cultural aspects were also paid much attention within the context of the outsourcing partnership. The provider invested in their relationship by organizing joint workshops with the client's senior business and IT managers. These workshops helped overcome problems related to large power distances. And they contributed to obtaining collective support for the changes – which appealed to the collectivist aspect of local society. In general, in Asia joint workshops really contribute positively to outsourcing relationships.

As we have seen, the choice to appoint Western expatriates as senior managers was not deliberate for either the recipient or the provider. They were simply considered the best candidates. Perhaps there was an unconscious element in the decisions, however. After all, great changes had to be made, for which a BPR project was set up. Sometimes, introducing a culture difference works well in such circumstances. On the other hand, both companies expatriated their employees regularly. Gaining foreign experience was considered an important element in any manager's career. These appointments certainly fitted their companies' policies perfectly.[6]

One advantage of having expatriates on both sides of the partnership was that there were at least no serious culture differences between the two persons with final responsibility for the outsourcing relationship. Carolien Nijvel: 'It was nice to have a counterpart who was a Westerner also. It meant we understood each other easily and so could take decisions quickly.'

The follow-up: how to facilitate cultural differences

The central question of this case study concerns the impact of introducing two Western expatriates as deciding managers in an Asian outsourcing relationship. IT director Carolien Nijvel: 'In this case, I felt there were mostly advantages. But I won't deny there were disadvantages to it as well.' Students should work out these advantages and disadvantages. Be sure to include the consequences of the situation for the IT professionals reporting to these two managers.

To take away or at least lessen the negative consequences of the situation, some extra measures may be taken. Which would they be? Service delivery manager Claus Hohstadt: 'Of course culture and cultural differences have their influence on the way in which such a collaboration effort works out. Describing this influence, however, is not simple. You need many shades and nuances.' Students should describe the answers expected from the recipient's IT director and the provider's service delivery manager.

LECTURERS' NOTES

CASE STUDY: GOVERNANCE OF OUTSOURCING IN DIFFERENT CULTURES

In this case study students work out the positive and negative consequences of the appointment of two Western expatriates in pivotal positions in an Asian outsourcing relationship. They are also asked to give suggestions for solving any problems that might arise from these appointments.

Essentially, there were two positive and two negative effects. Having Western managers in the Asian subsidiaries made their communications with the European parent companies easier, and it relieved the difficulties presented by the traditionally large power distance in Asian business environments. On the other hand, communications with the Asian staff became somewhat more difficult and these newly arrived Westerners could not rely on an established local business relationships network.

The effect of improving the communication between parent companies and subsidiaries is easy to understand. Many Western multinationals control their subsidiaries mostly by holding them accountable financially. This does not match business thinking, especially in Asian countries, where long-term perspectives and (family) relationships are of paramount importance, often overruling short-term financial considerations. Western expatriates in management positions could play a useful role as go-betweens.

The business process redesign project required that the discrete manufacturing subsidiary in Asia develop its own initiatives and then drive the changes. Considering the hierarchical attitude in Asian business culture, it is questionable whether this could have been expected of a locally recruited IT director. The traditionally greater power distance would rather have stimulated a wait-and-see policy, stalling the project. The same holds for the provider's service delivery director: here, too, having a Westerner in that position made for quicker decisions than could probably have been expected of a locally recruited manager.

Communicating with local staff was, of course, more difficult for Westerners than it would have been for nationals of the country involved. English is not the local employees' first language (and in this case it was not that of the Western expatriates either). Much attention therefore had to be paid to knowledge and information transfer, especially since in a context of a large power distance employees will hesitate to ask for more explanation, let alone discuss the matter with their superiors. Efficient and effective communication can be made much more difficult by such culture differences.

Finally, the expatriate managers had no local business relationships when they first arrived. In collectivist countries such networks are very important, not to say essential. Acquiring new business contracts and recruiting new staff can be difficult without them. Therefore, the two Westerners had to put much effort into quickly acquiring such contacts.

To make the partnership work well despite these cultural differences, three approaches may be suggested: pay much attention to one's staff; make sure one's managers include both locals and Western expatriates; and then pay much attention to one's communications.

It is, of course, important to begin by recruiting the right people. First of all, they must be bilingual, in order to be able to do business in English. Highly educated employees are also valuable in such circumstances, because they are usually more receptive to Western business culture. To be able to recruit such highly qualified staff, it is important to build a good image as an employer, since Asians focus much more than Westerners on the collective of the company.[7]

Having only Western managers may at first seem attractive from a competence point of view, but it is probably not a good approach. With locally recruited managers as well, it is much easier to get the intended changes understood and accepted. Employees then see how they can collaborate effectively. Adding expatriate staff can, however, help steepen the learning curve of the organization and its staff.

It is of crucial importance that Western managers try to understand local business traditions and communication styles. Only from that point of departure will they be able to gain acceptance for Western methods, and manage to set up an intermediate approach with which both parties are comfortable. To this end they must make cultural differences explicit, and turn them into something that can be talked about.

NOTES

1 COSO is a voluntary private-sector organization dedicated to improving the quality of financial reporting through business ethics, effective internal controls and corporate governance. The members of COSO are: the American Institute of Certified Public Accountants, the American Accounting Association, Financial Executives International, the Institute of Management Accountants and The Institute of Internal Auditors. COSO was originally formed in 1985 to sponsor the National Commission on Fraudulent Financial Reporting, known as the Treadway Commission, an independent private-sector initiative which studied the causal factors that can lead to fraudulent financial reporting and developed recommendations for public companies and their independent auditors, for the SEC and other regulators, and for educational institutions. COSO then published *Internal Control – Integrated Framework*, also

authored by PricewaterhouseCoopers. Other COSO studies include *Internal Control Issues in Derivatives Usage and Fraudulent Financial Reporting, 1987–1997 – An Analysis of U.S. Public Companies* (www.coso.org).

2 ISACA (the Information Systems Audit and Control Association) was founded in 1967 (www.isaca.org).

3 The International Organization for Standization (www.iso.org).

4 This case study is based on structured interviews with representatives of both recipient and provider, held in 2001 and 2002 and previously published in Beulen and Ribbers (2002, 2003). The material was rewritten for the purposes of this book. All names are fictional.

5 Figures derived from the 2003 annual report.

6 The recent economic downturn, however, has caused both companies to scale down their expatriate programmes for cost reasons, as have many other Western companies.

7 This was more important for the provider than for the recipient. The recipient was an originally local company taken over by a multinational, and still had its local economic ties. The provider, however, had set up a new company and had to start from scratch.

REFERENCES

Amit, R. and Zott, C. (2001) 'Value creation in e-business', *Strategic Management Journal*, 22: 493–520.

Barney, J. (1997) *Gaining and Sustaining Competitive Advantage*, Reading, MA: Addison-Wesley.

Barthelemy, J. (2003) 'The hard and soft sides of IT outsourcing management', *European Management Journal*, 21 (5): 539–548.

Berle, A. and Means, G. (1932) *The Modern Corporation and Private Property*, New York: Macmillan.

Beulen, E. (2004) 'Governance in IT outsourcing partnerships', in W. van Grembergen (ed.) *Strategies for Information Technologies*, Hershey, PA: Idea Group Publishing.

Beulen, E. and Ribbers, P. (2002) 'Lessons Learned: Managing an IT-Partnership in Asia', paper presented at HICSS-35 conference (US), IEEE, 0–7695–1435–9/02, Hawaii.

Beulen, E. and Ribbers, P. (2003) 'A case study of managing IT outsourcing partnerships in Asia', *Communications of the Association for Information Systems*, 11, article 21 (March): 357–376.

Brand, K. and Boonen, H. (2004) *IT Governance – A Pocket Guide, Based on COBIT*, Zaltbommel, the Netherlands: Van Haren Publishing.

Brown, C. and Magill, S. (1994) 'Alignment of the IS functions with the enterprise: toward a model of antecedents', *Management Information Systems Quarterly*, 18 (4): 371–403.

Clemons, E., Reddi, S. and Row, M. (1993) 'The impact of information technology on the organization of economic activity: the "move to the middle" hypothesis', *Journal of Management of Information Systems*, 10 (2): 9–35.

Coase, R. (1937) 'The nature of the firm', *Economica*, 4: 386–405.

COBIT (1998) *Control Objectives for Information and Related Technology (COBIT)*, 3rd edn, Illinois: IT Governance Institute (www.isaca.org/cobit.htm) Accessed 29 August 2005.

Currie, W. and Willcocks, L. (1998) 'Analysing four types of IT-outsourcing decisions in the context of scale, client/server, interdependency and risk migration', *Information Systems Journal*, 8 (2): 119–143.

Cyert, R. and March, J. (1963) *A Behavioural Theory of the Firm*, Englewood Cliffs, NJ: Prentice Hall.

D'Aveni, R. (1994) *Hyper-competition: Managing the Dynamics of Strategic Manoeuvring*, New York: The Free Press.

Davies, G. and Powell, W. (1992) 'Organization–environment relations', in M. Dunnette and L. Hough (eds) *Handbook of Industrial and Organizational Psychology, Volume 3*, Palo Alto, CA: Consulting Psychologists Press.

Dibbern, J., Hirschheim, R. and Jayatilaka, B. (2004) 'Information systems outsourcing: a survey and analysis of the literature', *Databases for Advances in Information Systems*, 35 (4): 6–102.

DiMaggio, P. and Powell, W. (1983) 'The iron cage revisited: institutional isomorphism and collective rationality in organizational fields', *American Sociological Review*, 48: 147–160.

Doh, J. (2005) 'Offshore outsourcing: implications for international business and strategic management theory and practice', *Journal of Management Studies*, 42 (3): 695–704.

Douma, S. and Schreuder, H. (1998) *Economic Approaches to Organizations*, 2nd edn, Hertfordshire: Prentice Hall Europe.

Dyer, J. and Singh, H. (1998) 'The relational view: cooperative strategy and sources of interorganizational competitive advantage', *The Academy of Management Review*, 23 (4): 660–679.

Earl, M. (1996) 'The risks of outsourcing IT', *Sloan Management Review*, 37 (3): 26–32.

Eisenhardt, K. (1985) 'Control: organizational and economic approaches', *Management Science*, 31 (2): 134–149.

El Sawy, O., Malhotra, A., Gosain, S. and Young, K. (1999) 'IT-intensive value innovation in the electronic economy: insights from Marshall industries', *Management Information Systems Quarterly*, 23 (3): 305–335.

Eloff, M. and von Solms, S. (2000) 'Information security management: a hierarchical framework for various approaches', *Computers & Security*, 19 (3): 243–256.

Fama, E. and Jensen, M. (1983) 'Separation of ownership and control', *Journal of Law and Economics*, 26: 301–326.

Galbraith, J. (1993) *Organizing for the Future, the New Logic for Managing Complex Organizations*, San Francisco, CA: Jossey-Bass.

Galbraith, M. and Cohen, N. (1998) *Tomorrow's Organization: Crafting Winning Capabilities*, San Francisco, CA: Jossey-Bass.

Grant, R. (1991) 'The resource-based theory of competitive advantage: implications for strategy formulation', *California Management Review*, 33 (3): 114–135.

Greenwood, R. and Hinnings, C. (1996) 'Understanding radical organizational change: bringing together the old and the new institutionalism', *The Academy of Management Review*, 21 (4): 1022–1054.

Grover, V. and Teng, J. (1993) 'The decision to outsource information systems functions', *Journal of Systems Management*, 44 (11): 34–37.

Gugler, K., Mueller, D. and Yurtoglu, B. (2004) 'Corporate governance and globalization', *Oxford Review of Economic Policy*, 20 (1): 129–156.

Gulati, R. (1995) 'Does familiarity breed trust? The implications of repeated ties for contractual choice in alliances', *The Academy of Management Journal*, 38 (1): 85–112.

Hancox, M. and Hackney, R. (1999) 'Information technology outsourcing: conceptualizing practice in the public and private sector', Paper presented at 32nd HICSS conference, Hawaii, January.

Henderson, J. and Venkatraman, N. (1993) 'Strategic alignment: leveraging information technology for transforming organisations', *IBM Systems Journal*, 32 (1): 4–16.

Hughes, E. (1936) 'The ecological aspects of institutions', *American Sociological Review*, 1: 180–189.

Hughes, E. (1939) 'Institutions', in R. Park (ed.) *An Outline of the Principles of Sociology*, New York: Barnes and Noble.

International Data Corporation (1997) 'European consulting and management services: riding the wave: an analysis of outsourcing market leaders in Western Europe', research report, International Data Corporation.

IT Governance Institute (2004) *Board Briefing on IT Governance*, 2nd edn, Illinois: ISACA.

Jensen, M. and Meckling, R. (1976) 'The theory of the firm: managerial behaviour, agency costs and ownership structure', *Journal of Financial Economics*, 2 (October): pages.

Keill, P. (2005) 'Principal agent theory and its application to analyze outsourcing of software development', Paper presented at EDSER conference, St Louis, MO, 15 May.

King, W. (2005) 'IT strategy and innovation – outsourcing becomes more complex', *Information Systems Management*, 22 (2): 89–90.

Kishore, R., Rao, H., Nam, K., Rajagopalan, S. and Chaudhury, A. (2003) 'A relationship perspective on IT outsourcing', *Communications of the Association for Computing Machinery*, 46 (12): 87–92.

Klein, S. (1996) 'The configuration of inter-organizational relationships', *European Journal of Information Systems*, 5 (2): 75–84.

Kumar, K. and van Dissel, H. (1996) 'Sustainable collaboration: managing conflict and cooperation in interorganizational systems', *Management Information Systems Quarterly*, 20 (3): 279–300.

Lacity, M. and Hirschheim, R. (1993) *Information Systems Outsourcing*, Chichester: Wiley & Sons.

Lacity, M. and Willcocks, L. (2001) *Global Information Technology Outsourcing: In Search of Business Advantage*, New York: John Wiley & Sons.

Langfield-Smith, K. and Smith, D. (2003) 'Management control systems and trust in outsourcing relationships', *Management Accounting Research*, 14 (3): 281–307.

Luftman, J. (1996) *Competing in the Information Age*, Oxford: Oxford University Press.

McKeen, J. and Smith, H. (2000) 'Managing external relationships in IS: trends in outsourcing of information systems', paper presented at HICSS conference, Hawaii.

Malone, T., Yates, J. and Benjamin, R. (1987) 'Electronic markets and electronic hierarchies', *Communications of the Association for Computing Machinery*, 30 (6): 484–497.

Meyer, J. and Rowan, B. (1977) 'Institutionalized organizations: formal structure as myth and ceremony', *American Journal of Sociology*, 83 (2): 340–363.

Niazi, M., Wilson, D. and Zowghi, D. (2005) 'A maturity model for the implementation of software process improvement: an empirical study', *Journal of Systems and Software*, 74 (2): 155–172.

Nooteboom, B. (1999) *Inter-firm Alliances: Analysis and Design*, London: Routledge.

OECD (2004) *Principles of Corporate Governance*, Paris: OECD (www.oecd.org/dataoecd/32/18/31557724.pdf) Accessed 29 August 2005.

Parsons, T. (1951) *The Social System*, New York: Free Press.

Peteraf, M. (1993) 'The cornerstones of competitive advantage: a resource-based view', *Strategic Management Journal*, 14 (3): 179–191.

Pfeffer, J. and Salancik, G. (1978) *The External Control of Organizations*, San Francisco, CA: Harper Collins.

Porter, M. (1980) *Competitive Strategy*, New York: The Free Press.

Porter, M. (1997) 'Creating tomorrow's advantages' in R. Gibson (ed.) *Rethinking the Future*, London: Nicholas Brealey.

Powell, W. and DiMaggio, P. (eds) (1991) *The New Institutionalism in Organizational Analysis*, Chicago, IL: University of Chicago Press.

Prahalad, C. and Hamel, G. (1991) 'The core competence of the corporation' in C. Montgomery and M. Porter (eds) *Strategy: 'Seeking and Securing Competitive Advantage'*, Boston, MA: Harvard Business School Press.

Quinn, J., Doorely, T. and Paquette, P. (1990) 'Beyond products: services based strategy', *Harvard Business Review*, 68 (2): 58–60.

Rothery, B. and Robertson, I. (1995) *The Truth About Outsourcing*, Aldershot: Gower.

Sambamurthy, V. and Zmud, R. (1999) 'Arrangements for information technology governance: a theory of multiple contingencies', *Management Information Systems Quarterly*, 23 (2): 261–290.

Schumpeter, J. (1939) *Business Cycles: A Theoretical and Statistical Analysis of the Capitalist Process*, New York: McGraw-Hill.

Schwarz, A. and Hirschheim, R. (2003) 'An extended platform logic perspective of IT governance: managing perceptions and activities of IT', *Journal of Strategic Information Systems*, 12 (2): 129–166.

SEI (2002) 'Capability Maturity Model Integration (CMMISM)', Version 1.1. SEI, CMU/SEI-2002-TR-029.

Selznick, P. (1949) *TVA and the Grass Roots*, Berkeley, CA: University of California Press.

Selznick, P. (1957) *Leadership in Administration*, New York: Harper and Row.

Shleifer, A. and Vishny, R. (1997) 'A survey of corporate governance', *The Journal of Finance*, 52 (2): 737–783.

Thompson, J. (1967) *Organizations in Action: Social Sciences Bases of Administrative Theory*, New York: McGraw-Hill.

Thorp, C. (2004) 'Implementing ISO17799: pleasure or pain?', *The Information Systems Control Journal*, 4: 25–26.

Trcek, D. (2003) 'An integral framework for information systems security management', *Computers & Security*, 22 (4): 337–360.

van der Zee, J. and de Jong, B. (1999) 'Alignment is not enough: integrating business and information technology management with the balanced business scorecard', *Journal of Management Information Systems*, 16 (2): 137–156.

van Grembergen, W. (2002) 'Introduction to the minitrack: IT governance and its mechanisms', Proceedings of the 35th Hawaii International Conference on System Science (HICSS) Hawaii.

Weill, P. and Ross, J. (2004) *IT Governance, How Top Performers Manage IT Decision Rights for Superior Results*, Boston, MA: Harvard Business School Press.

Weill, P. and Vitale, M. (2002) *Place to Space, Migrating to eBusiness Models*, Boston, MA: Harvard Business School Press.

Wernerfelt, B. (1984) 'A resource-based view of the firm', *Strategic Management Journal*, 5 (2): 171–180.

Willcocks, L. and Choi, C. (1995) 'Co-operative partnerships and "total" IT-outsourcing:

from contractual obligation to strategic alliance?', *European Management Journal*, 13 (1): 67–78.

Willcocks, L. and Fitzgerald, G. (1994) *A Business Guide to Outsourcing IT*, London: Business Intelligence.

Williamson, O. (1975) *Markets and Hierarchies*, New York: Free Press.

Williamson, O. (1979) 'Transaction cost economics: the governance of contractual relations', *Journal of Law and Economics*, 22 (2): 233–261.

Williamson, O. (1983) 'Organizational innovation: the transaction cost approach', in J. Ronen (ed.) *Entrepreneurship*, Lexington, MA: Lexington Books.

Zucker, L. (1977) 'The role of institutionalization in cultural persistence', *American Sociological Review*, 42 (5): 726–743.

Chapter 6

Governance factors – the recipient

This chapter offers a detailed discussion of the four recipient-side governance factors identified in Chapter 5:

- A clear IT strategy, which is needed for the governance of partnerships.
- The embedment of IT in the business, to ensure IT is well supported.
- A chief information officer (CIO), whose tasks include attaining the alignment of IT and the business.
- Information managers, who contribute to the management of the outsourcing activities.

6.1 INTRODUCTION

Outsourcing IT services does not mean that the recipient is no longer responsible or can stop paying attention to them (Lacity and Hirschheim 1993). We have seen in Chapter 3 how the responsibilities should be distributed over the organizational levels involved. Our conclusion there was that only operational responsibilities for IT services delivery can be outsourced. And even then, the recipients must still manage their delivery (Rockart *et al.* 1996; Feeny and Willcocks 1998). This point was elaborated in Chapter 5, in which four recipient-side governance factors were identified: a clear IT strategy, the embedment of IT in the business, a chief information officer (CIO) and information managers.

These governance factors are embedded in the theories, as detailed in Section 5.7. The first governance factor 'a clear IT strategy' is linked to the competitive strategy of Porter (1980). The service recipient has to determine the competitive strategy first. The second governance factor is 'then embedment of IT in the business'. The business managers and IT managers have to collaborate. The resource dependency theory provides insights into the fundamental motivations for actions

(Thompson 1967; Pfeffer and Salancik 1978). For service providers it is very difficult to recruit a qualified chief information officer and qualified information officers. The third and fourth governance factors, a clear demand management structure on the strategic and tactical levels, are linked to the resource-based view because they relate to competencies the service recipient must possess (Barney 1997; Prahalad and Hamel 1991). These governance factors are linked to the core competences of the service provider.

These factors will now be discussed in detail. To get a grip on the subject, for each factor four aspects are defined that are important to achieve the desired results. In Table 6.1 these factors and aspects are listed in the order in which they will be discussed in the following sections.

Table 6.1 *Governance factors and aspects – IT outsourcing (recipient)*

Governance factors	Governance aspects
A clear IT strategy	• Aligning the IT and business strategies • Aligning the IT strategy with that of the parent company • Preparing for the company's business dynamics • Involving external experts
The embedment of IT in the business	• Appointing IT portfolio managers in the business • Changing from a cost perspective to an added-value perspective • Involving the provider in product development • Involving the business in the management of the partnership
Clear demand management structure on strategic level: Chief Information Officer (CIO)	• Developing the IT strategy • Maintaining good relationships with the business • Knowledge of both the business and technology • Reporting to the board of directors
Clear demand management structure on tactical level: Information Managers	• Implementing the IT strategy • Maintaining good relationships with the business • Knowledge of both the business and technology • Reporting to both the CIO and the business

6.2 A CLEAR IT STRATEGY

A service recipient's IT strategy may be defined as their strategy with respect to IT, IT services and the role these play in their company. For such a strategy to be any good, it must be well aligned with the business. Therefore, the contribution of the business, and especially that of the chief executive officer (CEO), is indispensable. CEOs may display several different attitudes towards the company's IT services. The most effective is that of 'believer'. This is where the CEO believes in the strategic advantages offered by good IT services, and demonstrates this belief in his daily behaviour (Earl and Feeny 2000). Achieving good alignment between business and IT strategy is usually easier for small companies than it is for large multinationals, simply because they are more flexible and their communication processes are less complicated (Cragg *et al.* 2002).

Clear IT strategies show service providers the direction in which their clients intend to move. Providers must therefore know and understand their client's IT strategies very well, for only then will they be able to deliver the services needed and anticipate future developments. Service providers who are not given proper insight into their client's IT needs cannot do their job well. An example of such a situation is given by the managing director of a service provider:

> At one time, we received a request for proposal from a prospective client. The market in which this company worked was very dynamic, but nothing of these dynamics could be found in their IT strategy as presented to us in the request. I had no idea what to propose. Apparently, this company could not define where they were going. So I decided not to try to win the contract, for you could see trouble coming. Their chief information officer, lacking a clearly defined course, would zigzag. Their business units would not hesitate and start trying to influence the process too. There would be no way to satisfy both parties, so I decided to give it a miss. I expect my clients to know what they want. Of course, I'll gladly help them figure this out, but without clear objectives there is nothing but trouble ahead. My response to their request for proposal was a no-bid answer.

Having a clear IT strategy is not enough, however. It must also be implemented. To assess the extent to which this is successfully done, a balanced scorecard may be used (van der Zee and de Jong 1999). Balanced scorecards allow input from both the IT and the business sides, with which to keep the IT outsourcing partnership on the right track. Depending on the nature of the partnership they may include a number of key performance indicators, such as customer satisfaction, innovativeness and total cost of ownership. An example of a balanced scorecard is presented in Figure 6.1.

6.2.1 Aligning the IT and business strategies

Aligning the IT and business strategies is of essential importance (Henderson and Venkatraman 1993). Although the IT strategy is derived from the business strategy, the influence is not just one-way. New technologies, for example, will also have their effect on the company's business strategy. The increasing interaction between business and IT renders a proper alignment increasingly important (Pollalis 2003). IS executives can no longer afford to focus on IT only; they must also be involved in corporate planning. Likewise, outsourcing contracts also must be used to promote organizational systems integration, and internal coordination mechanisms should facilitate systems consistency as well as a decrease of transaction costs.

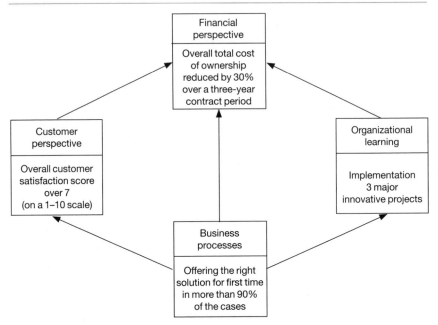

Figure 6.1 *An example of a balanced scorecard for IT outsourcing partnerships (based on Kaplan and Nolan 1992)*

These are complicated objectives. To attain them, outsourcing companies may set up an IT board (Drury 1984). These bring IS officers together with representatives from the company's business units, to exchange thoughts and opinions on how IT should be used to the company's advantage. IT boards do not take decisions but serve to facilitate information exchange. They are chaired by the chief information officer. As an example will show, it is important to have the right business people on such a board: 'What you need, really, is subject experts who understand how their department functions, what is its purpose and role, and how it fits in with the rest of the business' (Beulen 2000: 190).

6.2.2 Aligning the IT strategy with that of the parent company

In large companies all organizational levels (business units, divisions and the parent company) have their own IT strategies. There is then a hierarchy between these strategies, which are sometimes organized into an IT implementation matrix (Gottschalk 1999). Since the parent company's IT strategy influences those of its subsidiaries, aligning the upper and lower hierarchy levels is important. The increasing consolidation of financial information in large corporations renders this alignment even more essential, especially in listed companies, as these must be able to offer insight into their finances at any time.

120

Aligning the IT strategies across organizational levels enables companies to attain procurement advantages for hardware platforms, software licences, etc. The real cost advantages, however, are to be gained in maintenance. Standard interfaces make this much cheaper to do than when there is an array of different, customized links between the information systems of several divisions and business units. In strongly diversified companies alignment is difficult to achieve, however. Forcing subsidiaries to accept corporate standards may have less than optimum results. Nevertheless, increasing alignment is the trend. Says an account manager whose client is a truck manufacturer (Case IV; see Appendix, p. 268, for all Case details): 'Since they were bought by [. . .] two years ago, their IT strategy is partly determined by the parent company. The parent's influence increases all the time' (Beulen 2000: 194).

6.2.3 Preparing for the company's business dynamics

Mergers, acquisitions, divestments and the rise of network organizations cause ever-increasing business dynamics. These, in their turn, influence IT services delivery and IT strategies (Johnston and Yetton 1996). When companies merge or when they are bought, their information systems must be coupled and realigned with those of their new colleagues. Divestments, on the other hand, require that they be disentangled. And such changes usually come unexpectedly, with very little time between the announcement and their becoming effective. Therefore, it is wise for service recipients to organize their IT services such that their constituent parts can be disconnected easily from one another or integrated with those of other companies. This implies strategic choices for proven technology and limited IT services integration. Also, the interfaces between information systems preferably should be standard products (King and Aisthorpe 2000).

The information manager of a Dutch energy company (Case XV) explains:

The liberalization of the energy market in our country has brought a shower of mergers and acquisitions. Flexibility has therefore become a prime objective as defined in our IT strategy. And we have included a clause in our outsourcing contract specifying that we can terminate the contract when we become involved in a merger or acquisition ourselves. This 'termination for convenience clause' gives us maximum flexibility in that respect.

6.2.4 Involving external experts

Defining and implementing an IT strategy is quite a challenge. It takes highly qualified personnel to do so – staff which not all service recipients have. Nevertheless, hiring experts on a permanent basis is not a wise choice. It does not improve continuity and is very expensive. Also, hired help will always find it difficult to get a thorough grasp of the company's business processes, so they are less effective than one's own employees. On the other hand, external experts can be involved temporarily, in times of peak activity or when some very specialized expertise is required. Even in large companies, the CIO's and his information managers' work volume fluctuates intensely. Temporarily hiring experts is then a fitting solution.

To prevent conflicts of interests arising, service recipients would do well to hire independent experts rather than consultants working for service providers who deliver IT services or may do so in the future. This explains why freelancers and specialized firms are well represented in this field. In all cases, the service recipient retains final responsibility for the decisions taken, however many external experts they hire. The managing director of a truck manufacturer (Case IV) explains:

> What happens is this. You let people investigate and do research to find you answers to your questions. In some cases consultants appoint a project manager to run this process. You then use the answers to refine your own views on the matter. But in the end it is you who decide the information policy, not any external consultant – not even partly.
>
> (Beulen 2000: 193)

6.3 THE EMBEDMENT OF IT IN THE BUSINESS

As we have seen several times now, aligning the IT and business strategies is a necessary condition to success (King 1978; Henderson and Venkatraman 1993). Companies who pay attention to embedding IT in the business perform better with respect to growth and profitability than companies who do not (Bergeron *et al.* 2004). And the need to do so grows as information technology is increasingly inter-woven with both primary and supportive business processes. Embedded software is now often part of the product, and information supply plays an important role in customer retention. MaxFactor for example, a Procter & Gamble trademark in cosmetic products such as lipstick and eyeshadow,[1] uses its website to support its products with extensive consumer information. Customers and potential custo-mers are invited to join the MaxFactor Club. They get information and free samples of new products, and to make it even more attractive they have a chance of winning tickets to movie premieres.

The importance of the company's IT strategy in such cases is clear. But there are many more aspects in which alignment can be attained: the service recipient's organizational set-up and the distribution of responsibilities, among other things. There should be a dialogue between the company's business people and their IT staff. The CIO of a major manufacturer in the electronics supplies business (Case XVI) tells us how he tries to achieves this:

> My company figures prominently in the design and manufacture of industrial batteries. Much of our IT services is outsourced to external providers. Their

contracts and therefore our contacts with them are part of my responsibilities. So far, so good. Our relations and agreements with them are fine. But the company's previous CIO focused entirely on optimizing IT services delivery and neglected his relations with our company's business units. So when I came, I sought out the most IT-savvy business managers, and together we are trying to optimize not IT services delivery but the business results of IT services delivery. To do so, IT must be anchored firmly in the business. Unfortunately, to most business managers IT is something very remote. This will have to change. The business units, too, must be involved in how IT service delivery is used to improve our business processes. So that was my main message when I went around the company to introduce myself.

6.3.1 Appointing IT portfolio managers in the business

All companies of some size have IS departments, which include their CIOs and other information officers. Since the 1980s, however, researchers have pointed out the need to make business managers responsible for IT as well (Gerrity and Rockart 1986). This is increasingly done, but so far their involvement and commitment are not nearly enough (Croteau and Raymond 2004). An effective way to change this is by appointing IT portfolio managers in the company's business units. These are business managers and members of their units' management teams, but they are also the IS department's contacts. Being an IT portfolio manager is not a full-time job, but a task added to their other responsibilities. In practice it is often the younger management team members who assume this role, since they have more affinity with IT than do their older colleagues. By formally appointing IT portfolio managers, clear communication lines between the IS department and the business are established. The attention these business managers pay to information technology also has positive effects on IT outsourcing relationships (Quinn and Hilmer 1994), since IT portfolio managers can be contacted directly by the company's providers.

The information manager of a Dutch energy company (Case XV) tells us about his experience with IT portfolio managers:

We are one of the smaller independent energy companies in the market. To guarantee efficiency and delivery continuity as well as a good price I must be in constant contact with both our service providers and our business managers. I therefore have permanent contact persons in the business units, most of whom I talk to every day.

6.3.2 Changing from a cost perspective to an added-value perspective

The role of information technology changes, and the way to look at it should therefore also be changed. After all, IT can enable companies to achieve competitive advantages (Earl 1987). In this respect there is a remarkable difference between American and European companies. Americans focus much more on the value that may be added by using IT than do Europeans (Kakabadse and Kakabadse 2002), for whom saving costs is still the dominant outsourcing motive (Lacity and Willcocks 1998; Hirschheim and Lacity 2000). Perhaps some of the difference can be attributed to the performance of their respective economies. Fortunately, it does not mean that service providers in Europe can get away with providing services without added value (Kotabe and Murray 2004).

The most important value that suppliers can provide in outsourcing relationships is introducing new technologies. Since they work for multiple clients, they can invest in research into new developments and their potential much more effectively and efficiently than internal IT departments. Listen to the information manager of another Dutch energy company (Case XVII):

> About a year ago we decided to outsource our IT department. But which of the many suppliers in the market could really provide added value? They were all capable of running several hundred servers and managing several thousand desktop computers. Real added value, however, is provided by projects that are outside our scope, like equipping our sales representatives with mobile communication hardware.

6.3.3 Involving the provider in product development

Outsourcing product and service development is a subject that receives attention much more broadly than from an IT perspective alone (Quinn 2000; Wynstra *et al.* 2003). In good outsourcing relationships service providers can contribute in an early phase of their clients' development processes. IT providers can delegate specialists to their customers' development teams. And this is done more frequently, since marketing a new product or service makes increasing demands on the information provision processes involved: applications must be adapted or even set up from scratch, and extra hardware may have to be bought. Unless this is done properly, it may unnecessarily increase the time-to-market.

A service recipient's (Case XVIII) business development manager tells about his experience developing new insurance products:

> The speed with which we get our new products on the market is an important factor in their success. So we involve both our internal IT department and our

service providers in the product development process. In the past we often lost a lot of time because we couldn't get the right IT support when we needed it. Now we have IT experts with us from the start.

Confidentiality may be an argument for outsourcing companies not to include external IT specialists in their product development teams. The question is, however: is confidentiality fully assured when only the company's own staff are involved?

6.3.4 Involving the business in the management of the IT partnership

Business embedment can be improved by appointing IT portfolio managers among the business managers, as we have seen in Section 6.3.1. This is not only important during the IT strategy development process. Once IT services have been outsourced, the business should also be involved in the management of the outsourcing partnership (Klepper 1995) and in assessing the quality of the services provided. Again, this task lies primarily with the IS department, but this does not relieve the business managers of their responsibility for it (Grover *et al*. 1993).

In many companies, several managers are involved in running IT outsourcing relationships. First of all, the CIO, of course. Since the costs and investments associated with IT outsourcing are substantial, the chief financial officer (CFO) is often also involved.[2] Then there is the procurement department, who generally support their company's IS department in the management of the outsourcing relationship. Care must be taken during negotiations, however, since their lack of IT knowledge may cause them to focus too much on cost decreases, instead of on increasing the value added by the provider.

The CIO of a Dutch telecom company (Case XI) explains the involvement of his CFO:

We have outsourced our IT services to a number of providers rather than to one. This, we feel, helps us keep them sharp. When I report to my CFO, I always indicate the share provided by each supplier. None of these should become too great.

6.4 CLEAR DEMAND MANAGEMENT STRUCTURE ON STRATEGIC LEVEL: CHIEF INFORMATION OFFICER

The chief information officer (CIO) is the highest-ranking employee in the company who spends 100 per cent of his time on information systems (Earl and Feeny 2000). All other information managers report to the CIO. Chief information officers are responsible for the development of their company's IT strategy (Grover *et al*. 1993) and for optimizing the use it has of the IT services delivered – the recipient's side of IT services delivery. This means, among other things, that if the company also has an internal IT department the CIO cannot be its manager, for such a manager is responsible for the execution of IT services delivery – that is, the supplier side. Combining the two functions would cause a conflict of interests, so companies with internal IT departments must appoint a separate IT director. IT directors focus on maximizing the use made of their department's services production capacity, in terms of IT professionals, hardware and software. For CIOs, internal capacity is of less interest. New technologies, for example, will therefore more usually be introduced on the initiative of CIOs than of IT directors, for doing so may make it more difficult to recoup the costs of previous investments. Of course, their generally stronger technical background means that IT directors can and therefore will advise their company's CIOs about such new technologies. They are better able to judge the effects on IT services delivery. CIOs and IT directors must therefore collaborate closely, certainly when new technologies are introduced.

For chief information officers to be effective and develop a robust IT strategy, they must keep their position for a relatively long period. Unfortunately, this is not always the case. CIOs can be hard to find, and companies sometimes resort to hiring external experts for the meantime. This does not improve continuity, nor provide the profound insight in the company's business that is needed for a good IT strategy. Another problem is that CIOs are often let go when service delivery is imperfect or too expensive. Business managers tend to think that firing the CIO will solve such problems. But a new chief information officer can only improve matters after he has got to know the company well, and this takes time. Certainly during the first six months, companies should not expect much from a new CIO. As the general manager of a large chemicals company (Case III) told us:

> Recent research in the US showed that the average CIO holds his position for about 18 months. That is way too short to achieve anything. Before you really know what's going on in the company and can launch well-thought-through proposals those 18 months are over. In such a short period, you get nowhere. I must confess that these statistics worry me.
>
> (Beulen 2002: 118)

For a real positive contribution, CIOs should stay in their post for five years at least.

6.4.1 Developing the IT strategy

Chief information officers working on their company's IT strategy must take care to ensure support for it in the organization. This means they must collaborate with the company's business managers to decide on how information technology is to be used (Karimi *et al.* 1996). Considering the business dynamics most companies are involved in, their IT strategy will have to be updated every year. This can be done using a 'rolling period' method: every year decisions are made or adjusted for the next five years. By doing so the IT strategy is kept up to date while still allowing room for long-term views on the use of information technology. In practice, it can be difficult to give enough attention to the long term: 'Quite often, IT strategy has little to do with real strategic thinking. Then they are just yearly budgets. People do little more than try to save a few dollars and off they go' (Beulen 2000: 189).

With respect to long-term views, CIOs must often perform a balancing act between standardization, which reduces total costs of ownership, and flexibility, which contributes to the optimum match with the information needs of the business. This requires substantial analytic acumen. The CIO of a Dutch labour market intermediary (Case XIX) recalls:

> The board of directors hired me to clear up what had become something of a mess. My information managers and I began by identifying the commonalities with respect to IT services. We found that even in office automation and such common areas there was no standard. Everybody just did their own thing. So we set up a change plan and, in collaboration with an IT supplier, standardized things.
>
> (Beulen 2002: 119)

6.4.2 Maintaining good relationships with the business

For service recipients it is very important that their general business strategy and their IT strategy are well aligned. CIOs play an important role here. They must therefore prove their own added value to the business, by lowering the IT services costs for example, or by showing the advantages of new technologies. Such 'lateral influence behaviour' (Enns *et al.* 2003) will help gain acceptance by the business, something that will always take some time. To speed this up, CIOs may associate themselves with a few high-visibility, short-term projects right when they start their job. When these are successfully completed, their reputation is quickly enhanced. From then on, the CIO must spend a lot of time and attention on his relationships with his company's business managers, in order to strengthen these further. Says the CIO of a major chemicals producer (Case III):

> I think I spend about 50 per cent of my time tuning my work with our business managers. Another 30 per cent is used to align with my information managers, and some 10 per cent to do so with my provider. And the final 10 per cent, too, is spent on tuning – with our management board.

6.4.3 Knowledge of both the business and technology

There is much discussion on the degree of technological knowledge chief information officers should have. If they have too much, they may lose themselves in the details and neglect setting and guarding long-term policies. But the advantage of profound knowledge is that it renders the CIO capable of judging the technical possibilities and their implications. It is obvious, therefore, that CIOs must have thorough technological knowledge (Enns *et al.* 2003). This is all the more important in those many companies where CIOs have rather few staff and resources to do research – they must simply be able to do that themselves.

The need to have business knowledge is much less disputed. Only profound insight into the company's business processes and the difficulties involved will enable a CIO to arrange IT services to match those needs (Vedder *et al.* 1999). To keep their business knowledge up to date, CIOs must keep close contact with their company's business managers. The CIO of a car leaser (Case VIII) explains:

> In my contacts with the company's business managers I profit greatly from the fact that I have worked on their side also. I understand their issues and can translate these into IT services needs. This also makes me a good partner for the information managers and our service providers.

6.4.4 Reporting to the board of directors

To enable the chief information officer to function properly the CIO position must be located at the proper organizational level. A few years ago some CIOs were made board members because major problems were expected with the millennium bug and (in Europe) the introduction of the euro. In such cases, positioning the CIO on the board can be justified temporarily. Generally, however, IT services provisioning is the responsibility of the board as a whole.

> Anyone who'd like to be an entrepreneur – and this should include all board members – simply must have IT knowledge. Maybe the service aspects can be left to the CIO, but the understanding of what information technology can do for the business should become an integral part of entrepreneurship.
>
> (Beulen 2004: 323)

Positioning CIOs outside the board also prevents them from being used as a scapegoat for anything in the field of IT that does not go as planned. CIOs should report to one of the board of directors' members (Earl and Feeny 2000). The trend seems to be in the direction of reporting to the general manager, and away from reporting to the director of finances or the chief operations manager. But whomever they report to, the unpredictability of many IT projects means that it is very important for them to manage their boss's expectations. Good communication here is essential to survival (Potter 2003).

6.5 CLEAR DEMAND MANAGEMENT STRUCTURE ON TACTICAL LEVEL: INFORMATION MANAGERS

Information managers are responsible for linking the IS function with the business in order to implement their company's IT strategy. Theirs is mostly a bridging task involving relationships at the tactical level (Ragu-Nathan *et al.* 2001); they report to the chief information officer and the business managers. Information managers have a difficult job, since the resources with which to do it are not part of their own organization but of the company's internal IT department or the external service providers, or both. Thus they depend on others for the ability to carry out their tasks. Keeping the internal IT department and the external service providers on track requires much consultation and coordination, especially with respect to aligning the delivery of the diverse services needed. In fact, internal and external providers often depend on one another too. Upgrading an ERP application, for instance, may have consequences for the hardware needed and may influence the delivery of other IT services. All these consequences and interdependencies must be managed by the recipient company's information managers.

Like the CIO, information managers must be permanent staff. The continuity needed requires that they do their job for several years, with little personnel or job rotation. Implementing an IT strategy is not a matter of a few months but a continuous activity (Ward and Peppard 2002). The information manager of a global niche food company (Case XX) agrees with this advice:

> My company used to have difficulty hiring qualified information managers. For years my colleagues were freelancers hired on a temporary basis. They were qualified and had good insight in what was needed. And yet it didn't work – even apart from the salary differences between them and me. Being freelancers, they did not identify with the company. It wasn't reasonable to expect them to care about a five-year strategy, since they'd be working somewhere else by then. This convinced me that strategy implementation and external staff do not go together. I'm glad our new CIO realizes this too and has changed the situation. Two new information managers were recently appointed. Now we've got the right people working on the right things.

6.5.1 Implementing the IT strategy

While the CIO is responsible for developing the company's IT strategy, it is the information managers who implement it (Ward and Peppard 2002). This is often made harder by there being very few of them. It is difficult to put exact numbers to it, but most companies have no more than one information manager per organizational unit: every division will have one and so will every business unit, but that's all.

129

Apart from their strategy implementation task, information managers must keep an eye on changes in the business and the company's business processes. Business dynamics may profoundly influence the IT strategy (Peppard 1999) and even cause it to be changed. If this happens, information managers can provide their CIO with bottom-up assistance. It follows that information managers must frequently exchange information and experience, to keep informed and to learn from each other's successes and mistakes. Says the CIO of a major electronics manufacturer's East-Asian subsidiary (Case VII): 'We stimulate information exchange between our factories. Being spread over three different countries could present a problem so our Information Managers Group facilitates discussion and internal learning.'

6.5.2 Maintaining good relationships with the business

Today's business is very dynamic. Companies who can handle these dynamics well, sometimes called adaptive enterprises (Evgeniou 2002), are more successful than those who cannot. Doing so, however, makes major demands on their IT services. Information managers contribute to the flexibility of these services. By maintaining good relationships with the business, they can react quickly and ensure adequate and up-to-date service delivery.

It goes without saying that information managers must have excellent communication skills. They have to generate support for the IT strategy, which is much more effective than forcing decisions on people. Information managers must sell their proposals to the business, so for long-term success acceptance by the business cannot be overlooked. An information manager working for a chemicals producer (Case XXI) says:

> One of the aspects included in my bonus scorecard is the satisfaction of the business with the IT contribution to their processes. Another is the attention I pay to my company's business managers. At first, I considered this a bit of a joke – I felt almost like one of our service provider's account managers. But I realize now that selling is actually an essential part of my work.

6.5.3 Knowledge of both the business and technology

To be able to bridge between the IS department and the company's business management, information managers must have knowledge of both the business and technology (Heckman 1999). For many information managers keeping both kinds of knowledge up to date is difficult. They do not work daily with technology anymore, so their knowledge slowly becomes outdated, making it difficult to follow and assess new technological developments. Attending seminars and regularly inviting experts are ways to stay up to date, but it requires constant attention.

 130

With respect to business knowledge, information managers of course have their contacts with their company's business managers. This is not enough, however. A good idea is for companies to include information managers in their management development programmes, rotating them with business managers and so stimulating some cross-fertilization. But so far, few companies see the value of this approach. Information managers usually are technical experts promoted from their original positions in the IT department. They have much knowledge and know-how in technical matters, but when it comes to the business their knowledge and experience are usually limited. This seriously weakens their position and performance. A contract manager working for a service recipient in the energy business (Case XIII) corroborates this analysis:

> We have excellent people who have held all kinds of positions – system programming, UNIX environments, mainframes – and who for several years now have been working with Windows NT. [...] So if you're talking about technical expertise, yes, they've got it.
>
> (Beulen 2000: 200)

But because his people are technical experts, they have little business experience. It is important to strike a balance.

6.5.4 Reporting to both the CIO and the business

Positioning information managers in the organization proves to be a difficult matter for many outsourcing companies (Peppard 1999). They can have the information manager report to the CIO or to their business managers. Each has its advantages and disadvantages. A frequently chosen solution is to let information managers report to the CIO *and* the business. This contributes to the alignment between the business and IT that is to be achieved. An important question to answer in such cases is to whom they will report hierarchically and to whom functionally. Centrally organized companies will position their information managers hierarchically as the CIO's staff, with functional accountability to the business managers. Less centralized companies will include information managers in their business management teams hierarchically and let them report functionally to the CIO. Many companies even seek an intermediate position between these two possibilities and opt for a small central staff of information managers reporting directly to the CIO plus a number of information managers who are members of the business management teams. This secures a strong position for the CIO and yet stimulates maximum alignment with the business.

An information manager working for a telecom company (Case XXIII) states:

Hierarchically, I report to a business manager, but functionally, to the CIO. The developments in our business move so fast and the interaction between IT and our products and services is so great that only through hierarchic links to our business management can we make sure the right priorities are set. My functional reporting to our CIO ensures that I stay within the larger company framework.

CASE STUDY

CHANGING SUPPLIERS – VIRGIN MOBILE UK

Summary

This case study is based on structured interviews with UK executives of both Virgin Mobile and Atos Origin, held in April 2004, approximately a year after Virgin Mobile switched suppliers and signed a new contract with Atos Origin. The case study focuses on Virgin Mobile's arguments for and against switching providers as well as on Atos Origin's arguments for and against taking the opportunity to join the bidding. The decisions were taken early in 2003.

Interviewees Virgin Mobile UK:

- Jon Kandiah: Chief Information Officer, member of the Management Board (at the time of the interview, Kandiah was the board's Technical Services Director).
- John Melton (contractor): Head of the Technical Services Department, responsible for the implementation of the company's billing system.

Interviewees Atos Origin UK:

- Steve Smith: Customer Development Director, Client Executive Virgin Mobile; executive sponsor of the opportunity to quote.
- Nigel Freeth: Senior Contract Manager Virgin Mobile.

Management summary

Virgin Mobile UK, a 100 per cent subsidiary of the Virgin Group, is a young, rapidly expanding company in the mobile telecommunication market. Its basic strategy includes outsourcing all business processes, or parts of them, that can be outsourced. IT strategy development and implementation are of course carried out by the company itself, but its IT infrastructure services have been provided from the start by external suppliers. These services include a service desk, distributed computing services (Unix systems), enterprise operations services and Oracle DBA services. In early 2003, a decision had to be made either to renew the current contract or to find a new IT supplier.

In 2003, as today, the company's business was very dynamic. And although Virgin Mobile was not entirely satisfied with its supplier, combining a change of IT service provider with its many other projects might have threatened business continuation. The risks involved in a transfer of responsibilities to another supplier therefore needed to be carefully assessed.

The company's potential new suppliers had to decide whether or not to make the substantial pre-sales investments needed to have a chance of getting the contract. After all, its current supplier would certainly offer a quotation too – did other suppliers stand a real chance or was Virgin Mobile just using them for benchmarking purposes?

Introduction

Autumn 2002. Jon Kandiah, Virgin Mobile UK's Chief Information Officer, was looking out the window. The weather was terrible: windy and torrential rain. Being inside did not keep him out of the storm, though. He had a major decision to take. Virgin Mobile was preparing to tender out its IT infrastructure services and Jon had just had a meeting with Steve Smith, Atos Origin UK's client executive for Virgin Mobile, who had again told him of his company's capability to execute the services needed effectively and cost-efficiently.

It was not that Jon did not believe him. In fact, Atos Origin's offer was better than that of his current supplier and it radiated the kind of confidence he liked. Besides, he was not completely satisfied with the current provider's performance over the past three years. In order to make the important steps in its development that Virgin Mobile was facing, it had to improve the structure of its business processes, and he doubted whether his current supplier would be able to contribute as he wished. So far, then, the matter was clear enough. The trouble was, could Jon be certain that the risks of changing suppliers could be controlled? Would he be able to convince his CEO, Tom Alexander? Which extra measures should he take in order to guarantee the IT service levels needed, considering the dynamics of his company's market? And he had only one week left to decide and make his case before the executive board.

Meanwhile, in his car, Steve Smith was not much happier. Of course, he was pleased that Atos Origin was one of only two IT services providers still in the race, as Jon Kandiah had just told him. But he had also learned that his competitor was in a very strong position, being Virgin Mobile's current supplier. How would he tell his fellow executive board members about this? Which arguments would make them agree to let him continue to pursue this opportunity? Sometime halfway during his drive back to the office, he called his country manager. Then he, too, concluded it was stormy weather indeed.

133

Company and industry profile

The company

Virgin Mobile is a young, rapidly growing company that offers mobile telephone services on the telecommunication market. It was established in 1999 as a joint venture by Virgin and One 2 One; currently it is a 100 per cent subsidiary of the Virgin Group. Its customers can shop in Virgin's Megastores, in Virgin Atlantic's airplanes and in other retail businesses – a total of some 6,000 outlets in the UK. They can also use their telephones and the Internet to buy the company's services. In 2000 Virgin Mobile entered the Australian market, and in 2002 the American market; there are now plans for an introduction in Canada.

Virgin Mobile's aim is to offer maximum service at a reasonable price. There are no subscriptions; customers pay only for the actual use of their telephones. Virgin Mobile is a mass-market, consumer-focused organization. It is a market taker rather than a market leader, which means it does not introduce new services but tries to outbid the services offered already. Currently, Virgin Mobile has four million customers in the UK, making it the fastest growing mobile telephone provider in the world.

In order to stay in business in this dynamic and fast-expanding market, Virgin Mobile has adopted the basic strategy of its parent, which is to outsource all business processes and parts of business processes that can be left to partners and external suppliers. This allows the company to focus on its core business. A large number of contractors enable it to react to market fluctuations. This in turn buys it time to find and recruit the extra staff needed.

Virgin Mobile's headquarters and customer service department are located in Trowbridge, Wiltshire; another call centre is located in Middlesbrough. Its brand and marketing departments were established in London, and it has a warehouse in Daventry. To render its services, Virgin Mobile uses the network owned by T-Mobile, which makes it the first virtual mobile operator in the UK.

The market

The mobile telephone market is very dynamic. When Virgin Mobile was founded, only 25 per cent of the British owned mobile telephones. Since then, this figure has grown and it is still growing: between September 2001 and September 2003, seven million new connections were established in the UK. In the meantime, the services offered were expanded, from only speech and text messaging to information services and images.

Virgin Mobile's most important competitors are O2, Vodafone, Orange and T-Mobile. They compete primarily on the basis of price, services offered and customer service quality. Virgin Mobile has, over the last three years, won both the Mobile Choice Best Prepay Package and the Best Customer Service Awards.

Market saturation, however, is at hand. Mobile telephone providers must therefore begin focusing on keeping their customers. To do so, Virgin Mobile has introduced several incentives:

- 3p texts, Virgin to Virgin;
- £5 airtime vouchers: these were launched when other networks raised the minimum voucher denomination in a bid to move people onto contracts;
- Glue: a loyalty scheme which rewards current customers with £10 airtime for every person they connect, with a maximum of eight per year;
- Flash it! £1 free airtime for every £10 spent in Virgin Megastores, obtained simply by showing a Virgin Mobile at the till.

Richard Branson's reaction to Virgin Mobile's 2003 performance:

> This is a glittering result for Virgin Mobile. In the run-up to Christmas, more than half a million new customers chose us in the belief that we have the best tariff, the best value, the best marketing and the best customer service in the industry – and they are right! We have grown faster than any of our rivals over the past two years, and we have absolutely no intention of slowing down.[3]

Business dynamics

The immense growth of the mobile telephone market during the past few years has had its consequences, and so does the slow-down to less astronomical figures. Says John Melton, head of Virgin Mobile's technical service department:

> Two years ago we grew some 200 per cent per year. This meant our department could simply provide capacity and then wait for it to be used. The worst that could happen was that some of it might be provided a bit too early. Now our yearly growth is around 25 per cent, so we have to stop and think before we make major IT services investments: perhaps we can meet the demand with the capacity available. Nevertheless, 25 per cent growth is still a lot. It requires dynamic management and we as a technical department must make sure to keep up.

It is these dynamics that stimulated Virgin Mobile to outsource parts of its business processes.

In addition to business process outsourcing, Virgin Mobile hires the services of many contractors. One reason for doing so is the flexibility this offers. Another is the fact that qualified staff are often hard to find at short notice. In its first year, for example, Virgin Mobile created 500 new positions, which were impossible to fill with permanent staff only. Now that business growth percentages are gradually returning to normal, the number of contractors is growing smaller.

135

IT services

The IT services Virgin Mobile requires are provided through its technical services department, on the basis of contractual agreements with the company's business units. Not all services are actually supplied by the department itself: since Virgin Mobile's aim is to operate as a virtual organization, there is no intention to run large internal teams or make major investments. All business processes and parts of business processes that can be outsourced are therefore, indeed, performed by external providers and partners.

IT strategy development and implementation are carried out by Virgin Mobile itself, of course. Likewise, all application design, application maintenance, architecture design and change implementation tasks are performed by the company's own staff, and those FTEs that are provided by contractors are directly managed by Virgin Mobile. The reason is that these tasks are too close to the company's primary business processes to be left to others. Virgin Mobile also retains responsibility for the integration of its IT services, in order better to manage them. Finally, Virgin Mobile owns all the hardware needed. This is made possible by the company's cashflow, which is sufficient not to have to lease hardware or procure it by letting the IT supplier buy it.

The main field of cooperation with external suppliers is IT infrastructure services. These include a 24/7 service desk, distributed computing services (Unix systems), enterprise operations services and Oracle DBA services; they support the company's primary processes and are largely delivered during office hours. Until 2003, these services were provided on the basis of a 36-month outsourcing contract, although here, too, Virgin Mobile did retain their management. When this contract expired, the decision-making processes discussed here came into view.

The technical services department also maintains relationships with other service providers, such as Hitachi Data Services, Veritas and Sun. Since these people know so much about Virgin Mobile's management and the technological developments involved, their services are managed by Virgin Mobile itself as well. They enable it to assess and manage the proposals and performance of its IT suppliers.

In order to guarantee the continuous supply of these services, the technical services department uses a medium-term planning system that is based on the company's annual operating plan and is adapted for every three-month rolling period. John Melton: 'As IT has the longest lead times to produce, the annual operating plan is driven by IT.' Consequently, 80 per cent of the IT services needed are always known 12 months in advance.

Virgin Mobile's previous supplier

When Virgin Mobile was first established, one of the Virgin Group's suppliers was contracted for a three-year period to provide the new company's IT services.

 136

The company's Chief Information Officer, Jon Kandiah, and his technical services department were reasonably satisfied with this supplier; the service levels agreed were met. Nevertheless, Kandiah was not entirely happy: he felt his supplier 'required considerable coaching. Instead of them telling us what to do, we had to tell them what they should do'. Obviously, this is not what outsourcing should be like; you might as well do it yourself.

Secondly, the process of delivering the IT services contracted was insufficiently structured, an important omission considering Virgin Mobile's immature and rapidly growing organization. An IT supplier working with well-structured processes might have helped the company ahead. And finally there was not a fully coordinated, predictable and authorized stream of invoices. The contractor continually offered consulting services to support Virgin Mobile's management, and since the company's authorization procedures had not yet been well regulated, its Chief Information Officer was sometimes getting invoices for consulting services rendered.

Requirements

Virgin Mobile's objectives

The expiration of the original service provision contract meant that Virgin Mobile's IT infrastructure services would be tendered out for a new contract period, this time for five years. The company therefore had to define its objectives for the new period. The first of these was achieving a cost decrease while maintaining the quality level. In a margin business such as that in which Virgin Mobile operates, having low costs is of prime importance for survival. Therefore, it expects its suppliers to have structured their delivery processes with a view to optimum cost efficiency.

Jon Kandiah also wanted his supplier to be a partner, a company able to provide support in more fields than IT services alone: 'We wanted to be able to use their service delivery processes to improve our own business processes. Thus, our suppliers would contribute to the growth of Virgin Mobile into a mature organization.' Well-structured processes would reinforce the effort to use the available resources as efficiently as possible.

Then there was flexibility. The requirements of Virgin Mobile's business units were anything but stable, and the company was still growing fast. Any provider of IT services involved had to be able to handle these dynamics.

The final objective was of a different nature, but nevertheless of crucial importance: preventing service delivery disruptions. The risk of such disruptions is greater if the responsibility for delivery is transferred to a new supplier than when the old contract is renewed or modified. Therefore, it had to be thoroughly taken stock of and managed with the utmost care.

The scope of the services contracted

The services contracted would consist of infrastructure management services, also called baseline services. These included a 24/7 service desk logging all calls, offering first-line problem solutions and passing on the more difficult questions to the second line or third parties. They also included distributed computing services (Unix systems), enterprise operations services and Oracle DBA services.

Many other services would also have to be provided, probably by the same supplier, but Virgin Mobile could not specify their character or scale for the projected five-year contract period. Said Jon Kandiah: 'In our market it is very difficult to predict what will happen, which is why I refuse to commit the company to future projects.' Virgin Mobile's IT service projects would therefore still have to be planned on the basis of its 12-month operational IT planning and its three-month rolling periods.

Virgin Mobile also maintained relationships with other service providers, who supplied services related to those provided by its main IT service provider. Sun and Hitachi Data Systems, for example, supplied software and the consulting services required for their implementation. It was an open question whether the main provider should also be Virgin Mobile's system integrator. This would save much work, but would also make it more difficult for the company to manage its service providers.

Interference with other projects

While all this was being discussed, three other matters were straining the organization's personnel resources. On the marketing side of things, three new products were being introduced, all of them new subscription forms. Doing so required adapting and extending IT service delivery and so took up much of the attention of the company's business and IT managers. Second, it was the September through November period, in which a huge effort is always required to get all stores supplied for the December sales rush.

Third, Virgin Mobile was implementing a new billing system. Billing is a mobile operator's most critical task, so this was perhaps the most important of the three. The new billing system to be implemented was a customized version of a standard solution supplied by ADC, a billing system provider for the telecommunication market whose employees collaborated with Virgin Mobile staff in the application development teams. Thus, the new system perfectly met Virgin Mobile's needs. But while billing systems have no direct relationship to infrastructure services, their information must be processed on the company's servers and in its databases. Changes in the company's IT systems would therefore affect the implementation of the new system too, and might lower its performance. Again, much management attention was required.

Clearly, switching IT service suppliers would involve delivery disruption risks, which in their turn might endanger any of these three major efforts. The consequences for Virgin Mobile could be immense.

Governance implementation

As mentioned above, Virgin Mobile had no full control over the flow of invoices from its IT supplier. In order to improve its control, it set up a governance structure consisting of a partnership board, a commercial forum, a service liaison group and a centre of excellence. Generally, the provider's performance was discussed in the service liaison group. The invoices then had to be authorized by the commercial forum, after which the provider formally sent them to Virgin Mobile. If any matters remained undecided, they were discussed in the partnership board, whose authorization was also needed for any contract changes proposed. Meanwhile, the centre of excellence focused on infrastructure capacity planning. Detailed reporting enabled the service provider, for example, to anticipate hard disk or network overloads; investment proposals could then be prepared in order to guarantee continued IT service provision.

This governance structure was discussed in all meetings with potential service providers. Virgin Mobile could thus be sure it would not face any difficulties in this respect during the contract negotiations. What remained to be decided was whether it should share its business and IT strategies with its future service provider. Although the services to be delivered were not directly related to the company's business management, all potential providers said they would very much like to help Virgin Mobile think out its IT strategy, thus becoming partners rather than just suppliers.

The bidding process

The bidding process was set up as a collaborative project by the technical services and procurement departments. Thus, both technical and commercial expertise were available. To be able to assess the many potential service providers' qualities, the project organization invited eight of them to answer a 'request for information' (RFI), containing general questions about the provider's service delivery capacity, organizational structure and track record. On the basis of their answers, Virgin Mobile's current supplier, Atos Origin and one other company were then selected to answer a 'request for proposal' (RFP). From the concrete tenders it received, Virgin Mobile selected those of Atos Origin and its current supplier for further discussion: the 'beauty contest'.

Initially, Atos Origin had no business relationships with Virgin Mobile. Steve Smith: 'This put us well behind our competitors at the start.' Fortunately KPMG UK, which Atos Origin was at the time in the process of buying, did have relations with Virgin Mobile. Thus, Atos Origin got its first chance to meet Chief Information

139

Officer Jon Kandiah. Doing business with Virgin Mobile would offer Atos Origin a great opportunity to realize its growth targets in the IT outsourcing market in the UK. And the immense growth and dynamics in Virgin Mobile's business would also provide Atos Origin with an excellent reference for future acquisitions. Having been invited to the 'beauty contest', however, it was important to assess the risk that it was only being used for benchmarking purposes, before any further investments in this opportunity would be made.

Changing suppliers? Joining the beauty contest?

Virgin Mobile now had to answer the question whether it should switch suppliers. Which arguments should Jon Kandiah use to convince his fellow board members? Should he set any extra conditions for the contract, concerning the governance structure for example? It would certainly improve his position in the board if this aspect could first be worked out in more detail. And should he perhaps include some extra projects in the contract, thereby widening its scope so that he could obtain a better price? He preferred not to have his hands tied, but it might make it easier to get the procurement department to cooperate.

Steve Smith, too, had to report to his board colleagues. He had made substantial investments going after this contract, but entering the 'beauty contest' would entail spending a lot more. And focusing attention on Virgin Mobile would mean spending less time on other opportunities, some of which might offer a better chance of success. Was there a way he could get Virgin Mobile to be a little clearer about his chances? What certainly could help would be building a close and personal relationship with Jon Kandiah. Was there a personal match between them? Was it possible in the next phase to really understand each other from a personal perspective? 'Personal trust is a huge factor when there are so many uncertainties and I know we both have to spend time getting to know and understand each other.'

Besides, he had to think about a contract manager: which qualities was he looking for here? Perhaps Nigel Freeth would be the man for the job – he did have the right contract management experience.

So both companies had to decide which course to steer. There were opportunities, but there were risks as well. If the risks could somehow be made even a little smaller, it would be very attractive to take the chance. Virgin Mobile and Atos Origin would certainly make a good team!

LECTURERS' NOTES

CASE STUDY: CHANGING SUPPLIERS – VIRGIN MOBILE UK

Students should propose solutions, from both Virgin Mobile's and Atos Origin's perspective, as if the issues of late 2002 were still undecided. Below, these issues are therefore broken down into individual questions and arguments.

The Virgin Mobile perspective

Virgin Mobile's current supplier vs Atos Origin

Virgin Mobile has to consider the following issues:

- Can Virgin Mobile manage a change of suppliers, considering the dynamic business it is in? A thorough inventory has to be made of all current and future projects and the impact the transition would have on them.
- Atos Origin has qualified for the job of providing the services needed; there is no doubt about its capabilities in this respect. But do both the current supplier and Atos Origin have the transition capabilities needed?
- Identify and calculate the costs Virgin Mobile has to make to switch providers, plus the effort needed in terms of personnel resources. Are these financial and staff resources available?
- Do the advantages of saving costs and obtaining a better service delivery out-weigh the risks involved?
- What are Virgin Mobile's interests? Are these better served by continuing its relationship with its current supplier or by switching to Atos Origin?

Contract scope

Virgin Mobile has decided to contract out the so-called 'baseline services' only. Further services will certainly be needed, but market dynamics make it impossible to predict which and in what quantity. Therefore, the contract has to allow for extensions of its scope into application management and projects. These are the arguments in favour of extending the contract's scope:

- A greater service provision scope would allow for a better integration of these services (end-to-end responsibility).

- Virgin Mobile would have to spend less effort on coordinating the services delivered, since there are then fewer suppliers.
- A greater scope affords advantages of scale, thus saving the company costs.

Service provider = system integrator?

The greatest advantage of letting the service provider also function as system integrator has already been mentioned: it would save Virgin Mobile much trouble in coordinating the services delivered. Another advantage is that the greater service provision scope allows for a better integration of these services (end-to-end responsibility). Finally, Virgin Mobile would find it easier to manage and control the IT service delivery's 'total costs of ownership' (TCO).

Governance extras

The governance measures that Virgin Mobile can implement are well outlined in the 'governance implementation' section of the case study. However, some extra attention may be paid to two possible extras:

- Can Virgin Mobile use the IT outsourcing relationship for the purpose of implementing innovation?
- What are the advantages and disadvantages of including penalty clauses in the contracts, and of asking bank guarantees in case the IT provider's performance does not meet the standards set? (Such measures would not contribute to the realization of Virgin Mobile's objectives; they may only help reduce the damage connected with the risks involved.)

Should Virgin Mobile share its business and IT strategies?

IT suppliers always like to be involved in their clients' IT strategy processes, since that enables them to anticipate the developments their clients foresee. This also presents a risk, though, since suppliers are ultimately out to maximize their turnover and profit.

So far, Virgin Mobile has not involved its IT services provider in its primary business processes. Sharing its business and IT strategies with them therefore has not been necessary. In this respect ADC's position, for example, is different because it is responsible for Virgin Mobile's billing system. Should the IT services provider also become the company's system integrator, the need to share business and IT strategy with them will become greater.

Account must also be taken of the fact that Virgin Mobile is still a subsidiary of a listed company. (Remember: for the purposes of these questions, it is late 2002. At the actual time of writing Virgin Mobile is listed independently.) Therefore, extra care with the company's business and IT strategies is required.

The Atos Origin perspective

Stay in the bidding process?

The most important argument here is Steve Smith's commercial gut-feeling: does Jon Kandiah consider Atos Origin a serious alternative to his current supplier? But the number of alternative opportunities open to Atos Origin counts as well, as does the degree to which Virgin Mobile is willing to offer extra certainty. These issues will be treated below. First let us list the arguments for and against continuing the bidding process.

Arguments in favour:

- Virgin Mobile is an attractive client to use as a reference (for its image and the dynamics of its business and growth – 'if they can keep a customer like Virgin Mobile happy, they can do a good job for us too').
- Virgin Mobile's market and financial position are excellent; there is little or no risk of them going bankrupt.
- This contract may offer openings for doing business with the company's parent, the Virgin Group, as well as with other telecom companies.
- There is agreement about the governance structure to be used. (An important point for Virgin Mobile on which Atos Origin can well agree, which reduces the risks to Atos Origin's reputation.)
- Atos Origin does not have to invest in hardware, since Virgin Mobile buys it itself; this means fewer capital expenses.
- A substantial amount of money and effort has already been spent on this opportunity (sunk costs), which must be written off and made all over again for any other opportunity.

Arguments against continuing the bidding:

- The contract offers only a limited relationship with the client, in terms of the management level involved, the duration of the collaboration and the interaction with the client's management.
- The dynamics of Virgin Mobile's business make it impossible for them to switch suppliers because of the risks involved; Atos Origin will therefore never really get the contract.
- The dynamics of Virgin Mobile's business also present a risk to Atos Origin: should the results not be satisfactory, its reputation will suffer.
- The large number of other contractors increases the difficulty of structuring the governance required; and again Atos Origin's reputation may suffer if the results are not satisfactory.
- Virgin Mobile's current supplier may have relationships within the Virgin Group, tilting the balance in its favour and reducing Atos Origin's chances.

Alternatives

In order to choose between one business opportunity and its alternatives, the following questions have to be answered:

- What are the chances of success and the costs involved in the alternatives?
- How is the opportunity's market visibility compared to that of the alternatives?
- What are Atos Origin's interests? How would they be served by deciding in favour of the alternatives (extending the contract scope elsewhere; gaining good references for future growth)?
- What would the consequences be with respect to timing? (Atos Origin being a listed company, promises to analysts are sacrosanct. Does the company need the Virgin Mobile contract to fulfil these promises?)

Extra certainty

There are several ways in which Virgin Mobile can make Atos Origin feel more secure of its chances, which may be used singly or in combination:

- Organizing a bidding conference with both its current supplier and Atos Origin at the table; both would then receive extra information with which to prepare the next steps.
- Having the chief information officer send a letter explaining and thus objectifying the selection procedure.
- Having the chief information officer send a letter stating that Virgin Mobile would use objective criteria to select its supplier and stressing that Atos Origin was not simply being used as the current supplier's benchmark.

Contract management

Atos Origin will, if the deal is made, need a contract manager for the Virgin Mobile contract. The following demands have to be met:

- The contract manager has to have experience with the management of outsourcing contracts of a similar scale.
- The contract manager has to be experienced in managing and maintaining relationships with subcontractors (in this case, Sun and Hitachi Data Systems and Veritas) independent of Virgin Mobile's decision concerning the systems integration management role.
- The contract manager must know the telecommunication industry.
- The contract manager must be familiar with Atos Origin's service delivery processes and procedures.
- The contract manager has to have an internal Atos Origin network to fall back on.

 144

NOTES

1 See www.maxfactor.com
2 In fact, CIOs often report to their company's CFO for just this reason.
3 Press release financial results Q4 2003 (www.virginmobile.com).

REFERENCES

Barney, J. (1997) *Gaining and Sustaining Competitive Advantage*, Reading, MA: Addison-Wesley.

Bergeron, F., Raymond, L. and Rivard, S. (2004) 'Ideal patterns of strategic alignment and business performance', *Information & Management*, 41 (8): 1003–1020.

Beulen, E. (2000) 'Beheersing van IT-outsourcingsrelaties: een beheersingsmodel voor uitbestedende bedrijven en IT-leveranciers', PhD thesis, Tilburg University (in Dutch).

Beulen, E. (2002) *Uitbesteding van IT-dienstverlening*, Den Haag: Ten Hagen en Stam (in Dutch).

Beulen, E. (2004) 'Governance in IT outsourcing partnerships', in W. van Grembergen (ed.) *Strategies for Information Technologies*, Hershey, PA: Idea Group Publishing.

Cragg, P., King, M. and Hussin, H. (2002) 'IT alignment and firm performance in small manufacturing firms', *The Journal of Strategic Information Systems*, 11 (2): 109–132.

Croteau, A. and Raymond, L. (2004) 'Performance outcomes of strategic and IT competencies alignment', *Journal of Information Technology*, 19 (3): 178–190.

Drury, D. (1984) 'An evaluation of data processing steering committees', *Management Information Systems Quarterly*, 8 (4): 257–265.

Earl, M. (1987) 'Information systems strategy formulation', in R. Boland and R. Hirschheim (eds) *Critical Issues in Information Systems Research*, Chichester: Wiley & Sons.

Earl, M. and Feeny, D. (2000) 'Opinion: how to be a CEO for the information age – as many CEOs struggle to understand their role in IT strategy, their careers and companies hang in the balance', *Sloan Management Review*, 41 (2): 11–24.

Enns, H., Huff, S. and Higgins, C. (2003) 'CIO lateral influence behaviors: gaining peers' commitment to strategic information systems', *Management Information Systems Quarterly*, 27 (1): 155–176.

Evgeniou, T. (2002) 'Information integration and information strategies for adaptive enterprises', *European Management Journal*, 20 (5): 486–494.

Feeny, D. and Willcocks, L. (1998) 'Re-designing the IS function around core capabilities', *Long Range Planning*, 31 (3): 354–367.

Gerrity, T. and Rockart, J. (1986) 'End-user computing: are you a leader or a laggard?' *Sloan Management Review*, 27 (4): 25–34.

Gottschalk, P. (1999) 'Strategic information systems planning: the IT strategy implementation matrix', *European Journal of Information Systems*, 8 (2): 107–118.

Grover, V., Jeong, S.-R., Kettinger, W.J. and Lee, C.C. (1993) 'The Chief Information Officer: a study of managerial roles', *Journal of Management Information Systems*, 10 (2): 107–130.

Heckman, R. (1999) 'Organizing and managing supplier relationships in information technology procurement', *International Journal of Information Management*, 19 (2): 141–155.

Henderson, J. and Venkatraman, N. (1993) 'Strategic alignment: leveraging information technology for transforming organisations', *IBM Systems Journal*, 32 (1): 4–16.

Hirschheim, R. and Lacity, M. (2000) 'The myths and realities of information technology insourcing', *Communications of the Association for Computing Machinery*, 43 (2): 99–107.

Johnston, K. and Yetton, P. (1996) 'Integrating information technology divisions in a bank merger: fit, compatibility and models of change', *The Journal of Strategic Information Systems*, 5 (3): 189–211.

Kakabadse, A. and Kakabadse, N. (2002) 'Trends in outsourcing: contrasting USA and Europe', *European Management Journal*, 20 (2): 189–198.

Kaplan, R. and Nolan, D. (1992) 'The balanced scorecard measures that drive performance', *Harvard Business Review*, 1: 71–79.

Karimi, J., Gupta, Y. and Somers, T. (1996) 'The congruence between a firm's competitive strategy and information technology leader's rank and role', *Journal of Management Information Systems*, 13 (1): 63–88.

King, S. and Aisthorpe, P. (2000) 'Re-engineering in the face of a merger: soft systems and concurrent dynamics', *Journal of Information Technology*, 15 (2): 165–179.

King, W. (1978) 'Strategic planning for management information systems', *Management Information Systems Quarterly*, 2 (1): 27–37.

Klepper, R. (1995) 'The management of partnering development in I/S outsourcing', *Journal of Technology*, 10 (4): 249–258.

Kotabe, M. and Murray, J. (2004) 'Global sourcing strategy and sustainable competitive advantage', *Industrial Marketing Management*, 33 (1): 7–14.

Lacity, M. and Hirschheim, R. (1993) *Information Systems Outsourcing*, Chichester: Wiley & Sons.

Lacity, M. and Willcocks, L. (1998) 'An empirical investigation of information technology sourcing practices: lessons from experience', *Management Information Systems Quarterly*, 22 (3): 363–408.

Peppard, J. (1999) 'Information management in the global enterprise: an organising framework', *European Journal of Information Systems*, 8 (2): 77–94.

Pfeffer, J. and Salancik, G. (1978) *The External Control of Organizations*, San Francisco, CA: HarperCollins.

Pollalis, Y. (2003) 'Patterns of co-alignment in information-intensive organizations: business performance through integration strategies', *International Journal of Information Management*, 23 (6): 469–492.

Porter, M. (1980) *Competitive Strategy*, New York: The Free Press.

Potter, R. (2003) 'How CIOs manage their superiors' expectations', *Communications of the Association for Computing Machinery*, 46 (8): 74–79.

Prahalad, C. and Hamel, G. (1991) 'The core competence of the corporation' in C. Montgomery and M. Porter (eds) *Strategy: 'Seeking and Securing Competitive Advantage'*, Boston, MA: Harvard Business School Press.

Quinn, J. (2000) 'Innovation – outsourcing innovation: the new engine of growth', *Sloan Management Review*, 41 (4): 13–28.

Quinn, J. and Hilmer, F. (1994) 'Strategic outsourcing', *Sloan Management Review*, 35 (4): 43–55.

Ragu-Nathan, B., Ragu-Nathan, T.S., Tu, Q. and Shi, Z. (2001) 'Information management (IM) strategy: the construct and its measurement', *The Journal of Strategic Information Systems*, 10 (4): 265–289.

Rockart, J., Earl, M. and Ross, J. (1996) 'Eight imperatives for the new IT organization', *Sloan Management Review*, 38 (1): 43–55.

Thompson, J. (1967) *Organizations in Action: Social Sciences Bases of Administrative Theory*, New York: McGraw-Hill.

van der Zee, J. and de Jong, B. (1999) 'Alignment is not enough: integrating business and information technology management with the balanced business scorecard', *Journal of Management Information Systems*, 16 (2): 137–156.

Vedder, R.G., Vanecek, M.T., Guynes, C.S. and Cappel, J.J. (1999) 'CEO and CIO perspectives on competitive intelligence', *Communications of the Association for Computing Machinery*, 42 (8): 109–116.

Ward, J. and Peppard, J. (2002) *Strategic Planning for Information Systems*, Chichester: Wiley & Sons.

Wynstra, F., Weggeman, M. and van Weele, A. (2003) 'Exploring purchasing integration in product development', *Industrial Marketing Management*, 32 (1): 69–83.

Chapter 7

Governance factors – the provider

In this chapter the four provider-side governance factors identified in Chapter 5, as important for IT outsourcing partnerships, will be discussed in further detail:

- A clear and consistent market position.
- A front office.
- A back office.
- The availability of IT professionals.

Also included in this chapter is a case study describing a partnership in which both an internal IT department and external companies are involved as service providers.

7.1 INTRODUCTION

Within the context of an outsourcing partnership it is the provider who must take care of the actual delivery of the IT services contracted for. This provider can be either an internal IT department or an external company, or both. For governance purposes this makes no difference in principle, since all providers must pay governance thorough attention in order to be able to guarantee proper service delivery (Lacity and Hirschheim 1995). This includes developments facing the service recipient (the external focus, from the provider's point of view) and the manner in which the services will be delivered (the internal focus) (Cullen and Willcocks 2003). In Chapter 5, four provider-side governance factors were identified: a clear and consistent market position; a front office; a back office; and the availability of IT professionals.

These governance factors are embedded in the detailed theories, as detailed in Section 5.7. The first governance factor 'A clear and consistent market position' is linked to the institutional theory (DiMaggio and Powell 1983). What is the strategy of the service provider towards the market? The implementation of the front and back offices are related to the organizational theories. The effectiveness of the decision-making process is key (Dyer and Singh 1998).

The resource-based view supports the fourth governance factor 'the availability of IT professionals'. What core competence do the IT professionals need?

We will now take a closer look at these factors. And as we did with the recipient-side governance factors in Chapter 6, each will be subdivided into several aspects, as listed in Table 7.1.

Table 7.1 *Governance factors and aspects – IT outsourcing (provider)*

Governance factors	Governance aspects
A clear and consistent market position	• A vision on the future • Product portfolios • Market segmentation • Geographical scope
A front office	• Senior management embedment of the partnership • Account management • Contract management • Innovation management
A back office	• The organizational embedment of the back office • Service delivery management • Process-based service delivery • Audit processes
The availability of IT professionals	• Sourcing portfolios • Embedding transferred employees • Attention for individual employees • A planned approach

7.2 A CLEAR AND CONSISTENT MARKET POSITION

Service providers must be able to show their clients and potential clients what IT services they can deliver and how. This includes their plans for the future, which form the basis of any IT outsourcing partnership. Naturally, communication about such a vision on the future is a two-way process: service providers must be receptive to developments and opinions in their markets, and must adapt their strategies and product portfolios as needed (Gadde and Snehota 2000). Service recipients include the assessments made of service providers by financial analysts in their outsourcing decisions. The degree to which providers manage to realize their financial plans, after all, are an indication of their capability to perform in the longer run. And recipients are interested in financial prognoses and strategies as well. It is therefore

149

important for service providers to maintain good contacts with financial analysts and provide them with the information they need.

A first selection of service providers is often made on the basis of their profiles, derived from such information as their vision on the future, their product portfolio and the market segments in which they operate. Only providers who make the selection shortlist are sent a request for information or a proposal. Service recipients often hire external consultants to help them make such shortlists. Providers must therefore also maintain good relationships with these consulting firms and keep them informed of their strategy and the IT services they can deliver, in order to be placed on a shortlist.

An information manager working for a major telecom company (Case XXII; see Appendix, p. 268, for all Case details) explains how this works:

> We are used to dealing with many different parties. Collaborating with service providers on IT services delivery is therefore nothing special to us. We assess potential providers by the solutions they offer to specific requests, of course. But before we ask them anything, they must first get on our shortlist, and we allow only mature providers with a broad product scope and a clear vision on the future on it. It is a matter of principle not to work with small, local parties. They need too much management attention and constitute a continuity risk we are not willing to take.

7.2.1 A vision on the future

IT outsourcing partnerships may be defined as collaboration efforts between service recipients and providers that last several years. The provider's strategy is therefore important to the recipient. Having a clear vision on the future helps a provider to keep tuned to their client's needs. Companies who lack such a vision will have as much difficulty getting or renewing contracts as do companies with bad financial results, for many chief information officers (CIOs) and other senior managers will hesitate to let their IT services be provided by unstable partners. And their fear is understandable. A service provider in a tight spot will spend much management attention on internal matters, which leaves less time for their clients. The consequences of a service provider going bankrupt are even more disastrous. It entails making significant contracting costs to find a new provider plus a serious continuity risk to one's business processes. Most service recipients cannot afford to take such risks.

The chief information officer of a company in agricultural products recalls (Case XXIII):

> We needed a service provider who could supply us with worldwide IT services for our office automation. After a long selection process there were two

candidates left. A short time before, however, one of these had almost gone bankrupt. One of the options they had to improve their situation was selling some of their subsidiaries. But this would also remove some of their IT services from their product portfolio. Fortunately, it didn't come to that. Their financial position improved quickly and they could give extra guarantees. But if it hadn't, and without those extra guarantees, I would never have done business with them.

7.2.2 Product portfolios

Service providers use product portfolios to show which services they can deliver. Such a portfolio is not a static collection. The changes in the needs of their clients and potential clients force them to keep their portfolios up to date, as do technological developments. Interestingly, service providers must manage their own IT needs as portfolios too, and must decide which of them to insource and which to outsource (Peppard 1999).

Most service providers offer integrated product portfolios, which means they are capable of fulfilling most of their clients' information needs. This is especially true of commodity services such as desktop, server and network management. The differences between service providers are generally found in the additional services they provide. These extras are often specific to certain industries and require specific knowledge and experience on the part of the provider. They offer them a chance to distinguish themselves from their competitors.

Another important difference between service providers is whether they provide only services or hardware and hardware-related software too. The so-called system integrators, such as CSC, EDS and Atos Origin offer only services, which means they can choose the hardware platform to be used on the basis of the situation's specific needs and thus achieve a close match with their clients' wishes. And since they are not the ones selling the hardware, they often manage to get good hardware prices for their clients. On the other hand, providers who also offer hardware and the software going with it, such as IBM and Hewlett-Packard, can make fully integrated offers. Companies doing business with them rarely get into hardware performance discussions, since these providers take responsibility for both application and hardware. But the prices of their services and hardware are not always clear, so that their offers are less transparent. And service recipients have no choice in the hardware used.

An information manager working for the Dutch national government describes the situation in his department (Case XXIII):

We have mostly HP equipment. In view of the European rules for tendering we have to tender out our IT services publicly. Nevertheless, a provider like IBM can hardly win the contract, since doing business with them would involve major divestments. Replacing all HP hardware by IBM products would never be cost-effective. When the time came to renew or change the contract, it was therefore obvious that the winner would be either HP itself or a system integrator. And indeed it was.

7.2.3 Market segmentation

Since many IT services are commodities, such as desktop, server and network management, price is the most important sales argument. Nevertheless, the provider's knowledge of their client's industry and the market developments in it can be used to offer extra added value and achieve a competitive advantage. Therefore, having such knowledge is essential. The supplier has to have both sector and domain knowledge and experience (Willcocks *et al.* 2004).

Large service providers are well represented in all major industries. This does not suffice, however, for delivering real added value in IT outsourcing relationships, which requires clear market positioning. The providers' market managers must use their knowledge of their client's industry to convince service recipients they can be of real help.

The CIO of a global niche food producer (Case XX) was impressed by the extent of some of the providers' knowledge: 'The industry knowledge of their market manager for consumer packaged goods gave them an advantage over many competitors. We want suppliers who can help us ahead. Branch knowledge is therefore indispensable.'

7.2.4 Geographical scope

IT outsourcing partnerships increasingly have an international scope. Service providers must therefore also deliver outside their own countries. To do so they have a choice between relaying the work to subsidiaries or collaborating with other providers. Nowadays, many of the services to be delivered need not be executed on the spot. Remote service provisioning has been a serious possibility for decades now, causing the rise of offshore outsourcing. This used to be a matter of transferring only software development to developing countries (Carmel 1999), but the transfer increasingly includes infrastructure management as well (Beulen *et al.* 2005).

Subcontracting part of the IT services to local parties increases the risks for the service recipient. The primary contractors must therefore assume end-to-end responsibility. Many service providers therefore collaborate with subcontractors on the basis of framework agreements. This enables them to call in 'trusted' subcontractors quickly and cost-effectively. Without such framework agreements it will be much more difficult to arrange ad hoc solutions, which will increase the service recipients' risks.

The CIO of a chemical products producer (Case XXI) tells of his experience:

For our desktop services we chose to install a central desktop architecture and use it as a basis for partnerships with several service providers. For every country in which we operate we selected the provider offering the best price–performance ratio. Thus we prevented service providers having to subcontract some of the work. That would only bring extra risks.

7.3 A FRONT OFFICE

A front office is the interface between a service recipient and a service provider. They are also called customer interfaces (McFarlan and Nolan 1995) or client relationship management (Levina and Ross 2003) and they strongly influence the effectiveness of the provider and thereby the whole of the partnership's governance. Front offices include account management (which is responsible for relationship aspects) as well as contract and innovation management. These must be executed on all three organizational levels – strategic, tactical and operational – and the people doing so are the hands and feet of the outsourcing partnership. For a successful operation these responsibilities must be tightly aligned, to ensure a quick and adequate reaction to questions and delivery problems. Of course, the partnership must be well anchored in the provider's senior management efforts. This, too, will improve the provider's agility and effectiveness.

An information manager with a chemicals producer (Case XXIV) tells us about the outsourcing of their desktop, server and network management: 'None of this is really exciting. Nevertheless, it is nice to always have the ear of the provider's contract or account manager. Nothing is such a bother as facing a problem and having nowhere to go with it.'

7.3.1 Senior management embedment of the partnership

For the success of an IT outsourcing partnership it is essential that the senior managers of both provider and recipient can easily contact one another. This does not involve the CIO only; the recipient's business managers must also have a direct line to their provider's senior managers. In case of trouble or otherwise, response times must be short.

Both parties must also be aware of one another's position. The service provider, for instance, usually has more information than the recipient. Sharing it openly with their client is a good means of taking away any distrust (Aubert et al. 2003). And while many service providers' senior managers only pay attention during the selection phase, they would do better to stay in touch regularly during the whole of the contract period, even when everything is going fine. This generates trust and contributes to the good governance of the partnership. Besides, they may well be rewarded with an increase of their contract scope when new or extra work is to be done.

153

The chief information officer of a major Dutch telecom company KPN (Case XXV), P. Buijs, has experienced how this works:

> The senior managers of our provider (AtosOrigin) displayed unswerving commitment to this deal from the start. They were at every meeting, building relations and encouraging the sort of swift decision-taking that made it all happen so quickly and so well.
>
> (Beulen *et al*. 2004: 9)

7.3.2 Account management

Account management is about maintaining and building one's relationships with the client. This involves building a network of relationships in the recipient's company as well as staying ahead of the developments in their industry (Verra 2003). The relationships to be built should include preferably not just the client's CIO and his information managers, but also their business managers. Unfortunately, not all service recipients allow their suppliers to do so. Some are afraid that direct contacts between their providers and their business managers might influence the business managers' information needs. They generally believe that their CIO and information managers are quite capable of translating the needs of the business into terms providers can work with. In such cases, getting permission to contact the client's business managers takes time – time to gain the CIO's and information managers' trust. It is often useful to let the CIO or the information managers be present when you meet their business managers; they will then consider these contacts much less of a threat.

The trouble with account managers is that they tend to exaggerate their company's capabilities. This is not in their client's interest, however, and therefore not in their own longer-term interest either. A distinction must be made between account management and public relations. It has been said that service providers should unbridle account management and bridle public relations (Lacity and Willcocks 2003).

Apart from their knowledge of the client's industry and market, account managers must obviously know their own company's product portfolio very well. If they do not, their partnership can experience severe stress. In order to present their company's product portfolio well, account managers often bring along their service delivery managers, who are responsible for the actual delivery of the services contracted. An account manager, whose client is a Dutch energy distributor (Case XV), does so frequently:

> My client's information manager has much knowledge of the technologies involved, since he started as a database administrator. Our discussions are therefore often of a highly technical nature. Fortunately, I have quite some

technical expertise myself, but whenever necessary I bring along our service delivery managers or other technical experts. Just recently we were discussing an upgrade of their ERP system. I was glad our service delivery manager was with me, because I cannot really estimate the impact an upgrade will have. What I *can* estimate, however, is the amount of extra business I will get out of implementing this project!

7.3.3 Contract management

In outsourcing partnerships, the provider's contract managers represent the second major contact for the recipient, next to their account managers. Contract management means optimizing the contractual agreements between supplier and client. It involves managing the IT professionals who execute the work as well as taking care of the administrative aspects of the partnership, including reporting. With respect to invoicing, it is always wise to align with one's client – thus avoiding discussions and ensuring quick payment. These broad responsibilities have the consequence that service providers make allowances for substantial costs for contract management (Cullen and Willcocks 2003).

Whereas contract management is a front office task, service delivery managers are part of their company's back office. Contract managers act to increase customer satisfaction, service delivery managers focus on efficiency and effectivity.

The information manager of a large financial corporation (Case XXVI) explains:

> Availability is of prime importance in our business. We have made clear agreements with our IT provider about it. To give us insight into their performance they include graphs summarizing their work in their invoice. One look at the graphs tells us whether they have met the service level agreed. And if they haven't, our contracts include penalty clauses allowing us to pay less. Fortunately, that rarely happens. But our accountants must have insight in the services delivered. Also, the graphs are used for our monthly talks with our provider, when they explain any details we might have questions about.
>
> (Beulen 2002: 109)

7.3.4 Innovation management

Many service providers have a chief technology officer, who represents their innovative efforts. This is not enough, however, to ensure that their clients always get true state-of-the-art technology. Service providers should therefore set up innovation management teams, allocating innovation managers to their clients. Those clients then have someone with whom they can discuss the potential offered by new technological developments, and who are thus important links to the recipient's business managers.

155

Innovation managers draw the business managers' attention to new technologies. The discussions that follow often cause changes in the IT services to be delivered. They can even cause changes in the client's business: business process redesign (BPR). Another of the innovation manager's tasks is ascertaining the proper alignment (Broadbent and Weill 1997) between provider and recipient. They provide their account managers with essential support, enabling them to deepen the partnership with the client. Innovation managers offer their clients concrete proposals, often focused on value propositions rather than on technological products or services and frequently made in alliance with the provider's partners. This allows the provider to distinguish themselves from their competitors and to add real value for their client.

The marketing vice president of a global consumer packaged goods manufacturer (Case XXVII) has seen this for himself:

In the late nineties I was offered the support of location-based services for my marketing efforts, delivered by a consortium of four parties: a mobile devices manufacturer, a mobile services provider, a communications network provider and a systems integrator. They were way ahead of their time – so far, in fact, that the market wasn't ready for them yet. So I didn't participate in their pilot project and later heard that it never really took off. But their innovativeness had certainly qualified them for future projects. And they are now the parties with which I do business, even if it is not what they proposed at the time.

7.4 A BACK OFFICE

Back offices take care of the actual delivery of the IT services agreed upon in the contracts between the recipient and the provider. Since these delivery processes are the heart of the outsourcing partnership, service recipients must feel confident that their supplier's back office is up to the task. During the selection process it is very difficult, however, for recipients to get a good idea of the capabilities of the providers making them offers. It is therefore important that both client and supplier carry out due diligence assessments before any contracts are signed (Willcocks et al. 2004).

In practice, service providers often set up a 'pursue team' during the selection process, composed of senior IT professionals who must try to win the contract. Once successful, they tend to replace such seniors by more junior staff. It is therefore important that service recipients watch their interests closely and include their demands with respect to the team that will execute the services needed in the contract.

An information manager working for a Dutch government department (Case XXIII):

Our consultants advised us to include in our request for proposal a question concerning the staff that would carry out the service delivery, both during the intended transition and afterwards. They were required to enclose employee profiles with résumés, and we wanted to meet these people before making our choice. To prevent our service provider from putting other people on the job once the deal was done, the contract included penalty clauses specifying penalties of up to fifty thousand euros.

Another advantage of such contract clauses is that you are then more certain the provider will really be capable of delivering the services agreed.

7.4.1 The organizational embedment of the back office

Service providers must make choices with respect to the execution of their IT service delivery. Efficiency and effectiveness are the objectives. The arrangement should also leave room for new technologies and the time to gain experience with them (Benamati and Lederer 2001). Their back office must be set up such that it matches their service portfolio.

One of the choices to be made is between dedicated and non-dedicated resources. Allocating dedicated resources means that a close alignment can be achieved with the client's wishes because the available knowledge of their business can be solidly anchored in the team of professionals carrying out the service delivery. On the other hand, dedicated resources allow little room for advantages of scale, while non-dedicated resources do. Generally speaking, the deciding factor is the character of the services rendered. For commodity services non-dedicated resources are usually the right solution. They also enable the service provider to contribute industry knowledge by allocating IT professionals with experience in the field.

Another choice concerns employees transferred from the service recipient to the service provider. Should they be directly integrated into the provider's back office, or be maintained in a separate unit as a part of the recipient's organization? Since recipients usually outsource their IT services because they need a change, integration seems the best option. Social obligations may point both ways, however.

The personnel manager of a Dutch telecom company (Case XXV) has experienced such a transfer:

> When we transferred our people it was important to them that they would continue to work for us for some time. This gave them the peace of mind that was needed to guarantee service delivery continuity – not an unimportant aspect, I should think. The agreement with our provider also specified that they would maintain the conditions of our personnel contracts for two more years.

7.4.2 Service delivery management

Service delivery managers face many developments, both in the business and in technology. They must be able to act on all of these (Edberg et al. 2001). Another aspect of their work is people management. Service delivery managers constantly face challenges in identifying, recruiting and retaining competent IT staff in order to possess the necessary skills to manage the service recipient's IT needs. Human resources is key in the success of a service delivery manager (Agarwal and Ferratt 2002).

A major focus of the job of service delivery manager is efficiency. But resources must also be made available for innovation. Most service providers allocate a set percentage of their budget to innovation, and by using that money to best effect service delivery managers can ensure that the services delivered will in the future be valuable too. Thus they help secure their company's continuity.

As one service delivery manager, working for a consulting firm's server management group, says:

> I have a group of almost one hundred server experts working for me. They manage a great number of servers for many clients. Using scripts describing the specifics of server infrastructure set-ups, they can work for several clients at once. This enables me to use my personnel resources to optimum effect, and to guarantee to my clients the continuity of our services delivery.

7.4.3 Process-based service delivery

To deliver services effectively and efficiently, providers must define and implement standard processes: methodology development and dissemination (Levina and Ross 2003). Having such standards shows clients and potential clients that one can really deliver as promised. Many service recipients have therefore begun to demand process certification as part of their selection processes. The first step to such a process orientation is acquiring ISO-9000 and BS7799 certificates. Implementing the Capability Maturity Model (CMM) for application development and maintenance (Paulk et al. 1993) and ITIL/BS15000 for infrastructure management (CCTA 1993) is also important for process-based service delivery. Finally, Six Sigma (originally developed by Motorola) may be implemented, with the aim of achieving focused improvements (Peña 1990; Linderman et al. 2003).

An expert in the field claims:

> The process-oriented delivery of services is no longer a differentiating factor for IT suppliers. It is a necessity. Even so, it is important for outsourcing organizations to keep a close watch. Furthermore, many outsourcing organizations must regularly audit their suppliers as a consequence of their own procedures or certification.

(Beulen 2004: 327)

7.4.4 Audit processes

It is essential that service providers implement audit processes (Scott 1996; Aldhizer and Cashell 2003). They can use these to show their clients how their IT service delivery processes have been set up. Also, some service recipients have legal obligations that are transferred to their service providers. These obligations usually involve information security (in the financial services industry, for example) or data reliability (as in the pharmaceutical industry). Setting up audit processes helps cover the most important risks involved (Caplan and Kirschenheiter 2000). Audit processes receive increasing attention, therefore. In the United States, the main audit processes are those of Sarbanes Oxley, HIPPA, Gramm-Leach-Billey, the DB Breach Security Notification Act (CA) and the USA Patriot Act. In the UK, the most important is the Companies Bill, in Germany, the Cramme Code and in Switzerland, the Swiss Code of Best Practice. All other EU countries have their regulations (McDonald 2004).

Auditing processes involve three major matters: internal controls, compliance and calculations (Cullen and Willcocks 2003). The US Statement of Auditing Standards (SAS) 70 is the *de facto* global standard regarding service providers' special purpose reports on internal controls. Compliance with the provisions of contracts and service level agreements (SLAs) include a broad range of subjects. And, finally, there are similar benchmarks for contractual agreements on the calculation of charges and performance levels by the service providers.

The corporate auditor of a discrete manufacturing company (Case VII) recently had a discussion with his service provider:

> The question was whether the services were delivered according to the standards set. There had been many disruptions during the last several months, of which there wouldn't have been quite so many if the provider had followed the processes agreed upon. So they had an independent auditor investigate the situation. Our agreements were the basis for that investigation. I am now in the process of studying their report.

7.5 THE AVAILABILITY OF IT PROFESSIONALS

In the 1990s there was an enormous shortage of qualified IT professionals (Agarwal and Ferratt 2001). Graduating students as well as people re-entering the job market were offered brilliant terms by service providers who desperately needed their skills. The general economic boost, the millennium scare and – in Europe – the introduction of the euro caused much of this effect. Now that the economic tide is out, attracting IT professionals is less difficult. And they stay longer too, which further reduces the demand. Offshore outsourcing has also greatly increased the supply of IT professionals, since many developing countries have a great number of highly educated professionals who are available for work in the IT sector. The IT professionals' labour market in the developed world is therefore under a lot less pressure than before.

Nevertheless, keeping IT professionals for longer periods is still difficult. There remains a shortage of those who have the right training and experience. This situation is caused by the rapidity of the technological developments in the field. IT professionals must keep up to date, which involves much training and a steady hand to guide careers: IT professional career development (Levina and Ross 2003).

A service delivery manager working for a major IT provider explains:

> My group of almost one hundred IT professionals consists mostly of SAP experts. The developments in their profession move so fast – new modules, new releases even – that they must constantly be trained in order not to lose touch. Not only does this involve great costs, it also means that while they're training they cannot work. In effect, it's costing me money twice. But there just isn't any alternative.

7.5.1 Sourcing portfolios

For the execution of their IT services delivery providers have a choice between onshore and offshore outsourcing, a special case of the latter being near-shore outsourcing (Lowson 2002). Onshore outsourcing means that the services are delivered from the recipient's country of residence; offshore and near-shore indicate that they are delivered from abroad – usually countries with lower wages such as India, Brazil, Poland or China, the greatest advantage of course being a cost decrease. The difference between offshore and near-shore outsourcing is the distance between recipient and provider. There are no hard and fast rules here, but for a North American service recipient delivery from Central America would be near-shore; from India, offshore (Carmel and Agarwal 2002).

As not all services are equally suited to all three options, providers must give their distribution over their portfolio good thought. Near-shore and offshore outsourcing are usually only included in provider's offers if their clients specifically ask for it. This is caused by the allocation of profit and loss accountability: generally speaking, each country's operating company is held accountable for its results, and management teams in developed countries will therefore not like to see their turnover move to other countries even if it saves their clients costs. The sub-optimum tenders that are the consequence turn service providers operating out of developing countries into dangerous competitors.

An information manager of a discrete manufacturing company (Case VII) remarks:

> Our requests for proposal challenge service providers to include offshore outsourcing in their offers. We too would like to profit from the cost advantages that can be attained. On the other hand I understand one cannot do everything from

India. I don't know how to decide between onshore and offshore, but I guess that's the providers' problem. I'll just wait and see what they offer.

7.5.2 Embedding transferred employees

Outsourcing involves divestments on the part of the service recipient. If this includes the transfer of employees to a service provider, extra care must be taken with staff who are no longer young (Lyon *et al.* 1998). They are very vulnerable and when fired may not easily be able to find new jobs. Nevertheless, outsourcing often has change as its objective, so service providers will make the necessary changes to the IT delivery processes, making it difficult for older employees to keep up. It may be necessary to deploy other people than the original staff now transferred to the service provider.

A contract manager whose client is in the utilities industry (Case XIII) has witnessed such changes:

> For the change from a mainframe environment to a client server environment, I needed IT professionals with a completely different skill set from the people that were originally their own staff. So the mainframe experts were phased out on the basis of a staff disposition plan, and now work for those of our customers who still use mainframe technology. To provide the new services, I was given a new team that had worked for another customer. I complemented this team with three newly recruited trainees and an experienced service manager from the unit responsible.
>
> (Beulen 2004: 329)

The changes in the way services are delivered frequently cause older employees who have been transferred to the service provider to leave there also, before reaching normal retirement age. This situation requires much attention and effort, in the shape of training and coaching, for example, to try and keep such staff employable.

7.5.3 Attention for individual employees

It is very important to pay attention to individual employees. They must feel at home with their company (Pfeffer 1998). The service delivery director of a discrete manufacturing company in East Asia (Case VII) remarks: 'We run our company as one big family. We pay a lot of attention to the individual employees and the team spirit. We regularly organize events in the evenings and the weekends. Partners of our employees are also invited to some of these meetings.'

But service providers must also offer career perspectives, of course. This includes training possibilities (Pfeffer 1998) and is closely related to salary matters. The company's financial policies in this respect must therefore be flexible. Non-recurring bonuses may be given, or temporary labour market surcharges – all to prevent the salaries of IT professionals rising permanently as a result of temporary conditions, which would make it difficult to readjust them once those conditions are normalized. Many examples of the latter problem were seen in the late 1990s, when IT salaries had to be paid that were no longer commensurate to the skills hired. To ensure flexibility and yet not be ruled by temporary conditions, service providers must be able to refer to their salary policies.

The personnel manager of a major service provider recently discussed the salary of a dissatisfied programmer:

> He felt he was paid much too little. A friend of his working with a competitor made much more. So we sat down to evaluate his knowledge and experience, and to see if he still fitted the job description of a programmer. To be senior programmer he needed a minimum of three years' experience, including twelve months of independent work. He had been employed by us for no more than two years, of which he had only served two short, two-month periods independently. That was a quick end to that discussion. Because I could show him the demands for senior programmers he at least understood my point of view.
>
> (Beulen 2002: 145)

7.5.4 A planned approach

The predictability of the resources needed for the mid-term and long-term future are an issue service providers must pay serious attention to. This is not easy and therefore requires a planned approach (Anderson 2001), including a so-called staff disposition plan. Such plans are based on the current capacity in terms of recognized (technical) competences, but also include the changes expected. For example: is the number of senior project managers and COBOL programmers available now also sufficient for next year's service delivery? The three kinds of change that are likely to influence the company's capacity are employee turnover (people resigning, being fired or retiring), training (increasing the depth or breadth of their knowledge) and recruitment.

Service providers must realize that the continuity of their IT services delivery may be jeopardized if 20 per cent or more of their IT professionals are replaced within 12 months. Such rapid changes cause a loss of tacit knowledge (Nonaka and Takeuchi 1995). A similar problem is that of service providers' internal dynamics. Quite contrary to their staff disposition plans, it often happens that their best professionals are moved from one client to another to solve the problem of meeting the agreements contracted. Again, continuity may be jeopardized. This is a difficult subject, as one service manager we talked to told us:

> I often just don't know where to send my people first. There are only a few among my staff who can really do anything and everything, and all clients want them for

their service delivery. But I need them for troubleshooting, and once that's done I move them elsewhere. Indirectly, this serves my clients' interests too: if I leave them in one place for too long, they get bored. Before you know they've found another job, which is no good to me or my clients.

 **CASE STUDY**

SELECTIVE MULTIPLE OUTSOURCING

Summary

On the basis of their sourcing strategy a truck manufacturer had, since the early 1990s, procured their IT services partly from their internal IT department and partly from an external provider. The roles and responsibilities of interviewees for this case study are detailed in Table 7.2. The internal department provided application development services; the external provider, infrastructure management services. Later, when the company was bought by an international truck manufacturing concern, a second external provider was added. It supplied WAN services, which the new parent company already sourced from them. Finally, the internal IT department regularly hired external staff on a project basis, to increase its capacity temporarily and meet the demands of specific activities while still remaining flexible and cost effective. The consequence of this selective multiple outsourcing approach was a very complicated governance situation. The matter under discussion in this case study, therefore, is how the service providers involved should deal with this complicated partnership. How should they maintain their relationships with all parties, how should they collaborate and deliver effective IT services? Students will focus on several specific issues arising from the complexity of this situation.

Introduction

The recipient of this case study was a truck manufacturer. The truck market being very competitive and of a cyclical nature, they decided to outsource part of their IT services in order to keep costs down and increase flexibility. From the early 1990s, infrastructure management – including both hardware and software maintenance and support – was therefore procured from an external party. At the same time, some IT services were still provided by the company's own IT department: the relationship especially between application development and the company's primary business processes was considered too close for outsourcing. This internal department, however, was confronted with the ups and downs of the market as much as the rest of the company, and could not afford to employ a large number of experts permanently.

163

Table 7.2 *Interviewees: case study on selective multiple outsourcing*

The interviewees[1]

Party	Name and job title	Responsibilities
Recipient	Carel Greve, Director of Business Logistics	• Managing the business logistics department (an important user of IT services) • Purchasing (a process of critical importance to the company's business processes, and one for which EDI processing is used)
	Hajo Sietszma, IT Manager	• Developing and implementing the company's IT strategy • Managing his department (20 FTEs) • Managing the company's internal IT department • Managing two service providers and their performance
Infrastructure management service provider	Knut Sandringson, Account Manager Alia Broer, Contract manager	• Maintaining the relationship with the client • Delivering the IT services contracted to the client

An average of 30 FTE external staff were therefore hired and allocated on a project basis. To complicate matters further, after a few years the recipient was bought by an international truck manufacturing concern. This new parent company sourced its WAN services from still another provider. The logical thing for the recipient to do was to join the parent company's contract. As a result of these developments and decisions, the recipient company's IT outsourcing situation was very complex.

Alia Broer, contract manager for the infrastructure management service provider, remarks that there were no problems as long as service delivery ran smoothly. 'Together with our client's information managers we had worked hard to streamline our service delivery and to optimize our communication. Everybody knew what to do.' Of course Knut Sandringson, the provider's account manager, realized this did not mean that nothing would ever go wrong. 'But if it did, we knew how to find one another quickly and do something about it.' This was of essential importance to the continuity of the service delivery – and therefore to the recipient's business continuity.

A situation with several service providers meant that they must all operate in a competitive environment. Sandringson:

> Other providers were always trying to get a piece of the action too, for every activity that was tendered out. Fortunately, we could work on the basis of preferred supplier agreements, coupled to the scope of our work for this client.

Generally speaking, then, this was a healthy, competitive market situation. But it did require the collaboration of several suppliers. This complicated matter of effectively delivering a fragmented set of IT services meant that the providers involved had to meet special requirements. The recipient's IT manager, Hajo Sietszma, recalls: 'During the selection of our providers, their partnering capabilities were an important criterion. It was extensively discussed during our reference visits to their other clients.'

Company, market and industry profile

The company and its market

The truck manufacturer that is the subject of this case study had a complicated history. It had bought several of its competitors before facing bankruptcy in the early 1990s. With government support, a new start was made, partly in order not to have to fire its more than 6,000 employees. Then, in the mid-1990s, the company was bought by an even larger, internationally active concern. The recipient's more than 40,000 trucks per year came to represent about half of the parent company's annual production, whose turnover in 2003 exceeded US$8 billion. Carel Greve, the recipient's business logistics director, remarked: 'And we're still growing, both in terms of turnover and market share.' Considering the economic slack of the past several years this was quite a good performance. Many transport companies, after all, had postponed the replacement of their trucks. Indeed, Greve felt, 'Not many of our competitors can claim to do so well. High operating costs and reorganizations cause them much difficulty to keep their financial balance positive.'

Heavy and medium-heavy trucks were the recipient's main products, which were manufactured on the basis of their client's specific demands. This had two main consequences. Considering the non-commodity character of their products, customer loyalty was of prime importance. And because of the market's fierce competition client demands did not include only product price and quality, but after-sales services too. Should a truck break down, its driver should be able to count on the manufacturer's service organization to help him back on the road as quickly as possible. Transport contracts usually include penalty clauses for delayed delivery, so this aspect was essential for customer loyalty. The manufacturer therefore needed to have an extensive dealer network, and had to be able to get spares on location quickly. This in turn required fast communication between the manufacturer and their dealers – communication that had to be supported by information technology. To achieve this, an electronic dealership was set up and an e-portal made available. Greve:

> Communication with our dealers is important because they have direct contact with our clients and must be enabled to transfer specifications to us quickly and

accurately. On the basis of this information we can make our price calculations and, after the deal is made, start production.

IT services

The IT services involved were of three kinds: application development, infrastructure management and WAN services. The first of these were procured from the company's internal IT department. Hajo Sietszma, the company's IT manager, explained:

> Applications are so close to our primary business processes, we cannot afford to outsource them. However, considering the scale of our company we cannot afford to employ all the experts we need on a permanent basis either. So we hire an average of 30 FTE external staff who are allocated to specific projects, to keep us abreast of the technological developments. Like this we have both capacity and flexibility.

Likewise, the company's Baan package was implemented by their internal IT department too, since doing so required more business knowledge than could be expected of external service providers. A final argument not to outsource all IT services was that if the people involved in these implementations remained company employees, they would be available for trouble-shooting later, helping both the company itself and their customers. This would ensure the continuity of the recipient's business processes and of customer service delivery.

Infrastructure management was outsourced to the provider discussed in this case study. This partnership, which at the time the interviews were held had already run for a decade, included hardware and software maintenance and support: managing mainframe data centres, network connections and infrastructure, and supplying middleware support and database administration. The infrastructure management provider also supplied EDI processes, which were used to handle some 80 per cent of the recipient's purchasing processes. Obviously, these IT services were of prime importance to the truck manufacturer: without them, their business processes would be seriously at risk. Occasionally, this provider would also supply consulting services, especially in connection with projects involving infrastructure management services (such as the implementation of firewalls). These services were invoiced on the basis of hourly rates.

In the late 1990s the recipient decided to outsource its WAN services too, which had hitherto been provided by the internal IT department. As with infrastructure management this meant setting up a long-term IT outsourcing partnership. Hajo Sietszma:

> You have to realize what an increasingly international business we are in. Having been taken over by a large concern, WAN services had become much

more important. Our parent company had already outsourced them and a straightforward cost–benefit analysis showed that we had best join their contract. Apart from the advantages of scale involved, this would also improve our connectivity.

Knut Sandringson, the infrastructure management provider's account manager, remarked:

> We ourselves buy WAN services from third parties too, and were therefore not the one to supply them to our client. Nevertheless, the introduction of an extra provider had me worried: how would this influence the delivery of *our* services?

Processes

For the service delivery of the recipient's providers the processes developed by the IT Infrastructure Library (ITIL) were used. Both for infrastructure and WAN services these processes were certified. Organizing service delivery in this way was necessary because the character of the WAN and infrastructure services meant they were rather alien to the manufacturer's regular production staff. Unlike these employees, however, Hajo Sietszma's IT department did, of course, have much contact with the service provider's employees. 'Setting service delivery up on the basis of these processes made it easier and more manageable to control and monitor the services delivered.'

The most important aspects concerning service delivery continuity were change and incident management. Alia Broer, the provider's contract manager, remembered:

> At one time there was a severity one.[2] A disruption in the WAN services locked several hundred employees of one of our client's sites out of their central applications. Imagine the commotion – even though the problem only lasted a few minutes!

Close collaboration between the infrastructure management supplier and the WAN services provider made it possible to have all systems running again on short notice. Said Carel Greve: 'Only when something goes wrong do you realize how important these processes are. That is why we pay so much attention to them in our business. And I'm glad our IT providers understand the importance too.'

ITIL processes also played a role in the three-party conferences between the recipient's information managers and their service providers. Said Hajo Sietszma: 'The processes help us speak the same language.' This is how it worked. Every project the truck manufacturer initiated was given a unique number by their service providers. This number was used to monitor the project's progress – both by the recipient's information manager and the provider's contract manager. Progress and project costs could then be discussed in their regular operational conferences. Meanwhile, the actual services involved were delivered by those of the provider's staff working on the recipient's location – who in the case of infrastructure management were generally former recipient staff transferred to the provider as part of the partnership. All those interviewed showed themselves happy with this arrangement. Knut Sandringson, account manager: 'They have much knowledge that is important to a proper delivery of the IT services.' By using strict definitions of the processes involved, the parties were able to prevent their staff from using their informal contacts to let provider staff solve the problems experienced by their former colleagues at the recipient. Carel Greve was happy, however, to note that after some time new employees were added to those originally transferred:

> IT professionals with experience elsewhere can help us very well, certainly in the way of innovation. And we must keep innovating to maintain our competitive position. Personally, I think that to achieve innovation we need IT professionals with a different profile from those of our transferred staff.

Roles, responsibilities and governance

Since the service delivery to the recipient was carried out by several parties, a clear definition of each provider's responsibilities was needed. Application development was the responsibility of the recipient's internal IT department, but their activities were closely intertwined with those of the infrastructure management provider, who would, after all, have to manage the applications once they were developed. Therefore, the infrastructure management provider would have to carry out acceptance tests. Alia Broer, the provider's contract manager: 'Fortunately, our technical experts are involved right from the moment specifications for new applications are formulated. This prevents surprises when the applications are implemented.' Hajo Sietszma: 'Such a pro-active involvement is needed, too, because new applications often replace current ones. This means that data must be converted. To prepare for this, the provider's technical specialists must be involved.'

Once new applications were implemented and had to be maintained and serviced, collaboration between the internal IT department who had developed them and the external provider responsible for their upkeep was needed as well. Knut Sandringson, the infrastructure management provider's account manager: 'There is always some commercial arguing about such efforts. At least we both agree they are substantial, but it isn't always clear whether they are part of the deal or not.' Hajo Sietszma: 'Should they not be included, I consider them pre-sales efforts. The successful implementation of new applications is in our provider's interest too.' The usual way of solving any differences of opinion was to set up a project, from the budget of which part of the provider's efforts could be paid.

As with application development, WAN services delivery was intertwined with infrastructure management activities. In a geographically widespread company, WAN services are a very important part of the IT services, since they connect the infrastructure management provider's data centre with the recipient's locations. Alia Broer:

> Look, once we implement a new application, we must align our activities with those of the WAN services supplier because the WAN infrastructure must be equipped to handle our data communication. Implementing the Baan package, for example, required much adaptations to the WAN infrastructure since a much bigger bandwidth was required.

Contracts

Despite the fact that IT was of strategic importance to the company's business management, Carel Greve was not inclined to oversee every detail himself. 'I'm perfectly happy to let our internal IT department maintain our relations with IT service providers. After all, IT costs represent only a few percent of our total business management costs.' Consequently, the recipient's IT department managed the contracts with their external providers. Hajo Sietszma: 'I run both the infrastructure management contract and the WAN services contract.' This implied, too, that his department was responsible for the whole of the services needed, end-to-end. These services were delivered to the recipient's divisions and operating companies on the basis of service level agreements (SLAs) detailing both the content of the services and their prices. To meet the SLAs, which were reviewed every year, the contracts specified that the providers would conform their services to these internal agreements.

Considering the scale of the WAN and infrastructure management services to be delivered, the contracts drawn up consisted of two levels: general issues laid down in framework agreements and operational issues defined in service level agreements. The framework agreements also contained specific matters concerning the collaboration between the internal IT department and the company's providers. Hajo Sietszma:

> One of the things we specified in the contract with our WAN service supplier was that if a difference of opinion should arise over the bandwidth required, they would make sure always to be on the safe side. Often, decisions concerning such matters must be taken under considerable pressure, with no time to calculate things precisely. We like to be pragmatic about such issues, and prefer to pay a little too much over risking the continuity of our IT services delivery.

The framework agreement on WAN services was managed by the corporate IT department of the truck manufacturer's parent company, because they had been outsourcing these services to this provider since before the recipient was bought. The autonomy of the recipient's internal IT department was therefore limited to the service level agreements. However, Hajo Sietszma felt:

169

We shouldn't dramatize this aspect. The framework agreement contains no clauses directly related to service delivery. All we have to do is ensure connectivity with our parent company, which is important to the financial reporting of a listed company. This is a condition we can work with easily, even though it requires much effort by both my staff and the providers' people.

The follow-up: challenges

Three issues requiring attention arose from the collaboration between the recipient and their two service providers. The first of these is the allocation of the recipient's internal IT department staff to the tasks at hand. Hajo Sietszma: 'Sometimes I have difficult choices to make. If I have people available but they lack some of the skills and capabilities needed, do I let them do the job anyway or should I ask our service providers to take care of these activities?' This problem is typical for service recipients who have outsourced part of their IT services.

The second issue is related to the collaboration between the recipient's internal IT department and the service providers, especially when changes must be implemented. Knut Sandringson:

> Changes are often substantial matters with respect to their size and the time needed. They also often cause major changes in the delivery of current services. So both we as service providers and our client's IT department must be closely involved.

The question is: how does one organize this? And should not the truck manufacturer's business managers also play a role in such implementations?

And finally, there is the added value of the recipient's internal IT department as intermediary between their company's business processes and their service providers. Hajo Sietszma does not like his providers to be in too close contact with the company's business managers. What might be his arguments? And are there any arguments in favour of allowing the service providers to maintain direct relationships with the company's business managers?

 **LECTURERS' NOTES**

CASE STUDY: SELECTIVE MULTIPLE OUTSOURCING

In working out this case study, students should address all three issues outlined above. Some pointers will now be discussed.

Internal or external sourcing

Should service recipients hire external staff if their own employees lack some of the skills needed? This is always a difficult matter. The costs for internal staff have already been made, while hiring external experts will give rise to extra out-of-pocket costs. Most companies will therefore be inclined to allocate their own employees rather than hiring externals, even if their own employees cannot fulfil all requirements.

In this case study the issue is a little less important than usual, because of the task division between the internal IT department and the company's service providers. If the problem arises, it will therefore be in the field of project management. Good project managers, however, are of essential importance to achieve the objectives set, and many projects are essential to the company's business continuity. The question must, therefore, still be answered.

As a rule of thumb, 75–85 per cent of the personnel resources of internal IT departments should be their own employees. The last 15–25 per cent is best hired externally, that is, from their service providers. Such an arrangement guarantees the flexibility required, is cost efficient and ensures innovative input.

Implementing changes

Change implementation and incident management usually require the involvement of both the internal IT department and the company's service providers. This involvement is then organized along the lines of the ITIL change management processes. Much conferencing and a proactive attitude are required, and the activities are generally best organized on a project basis, which means that it is made clear to everyone what people are responsible and what the project's deliverables and time horizons are. A project office may stand the project organization in good stead, to improve and maintain the communication between all parties and people involved. Such communication is especially important if the original project objectives are changed at some point. In large-scale projects management tools such as planning packages and collaborative software may be of advantage.

Project team reporting also must be well-anchored in all parties' organizations. This enables those involved to take decisions quickly when necessary. In this case study Hajo Sietszma would be the reports' addressee for the recipient, and Alia Broer for the infrastructure management provider. If the changes planned are to have a substantial impact on the recipient's business processes, it may be a good idea to involve their business managers in the project too.

The internal IT department as intermediary

For many companies, IT is very important – sometimes even of strategic value. Nevertheless, in comparison with their general business management expenses, IT costs are usually limited. Most business managers will therefore not be inclined to pay much attention to their IT services. And yet there are several distinct advantages to direct relationships between business managers and the company's IT service providers:

- Direct contact ensures a better alignment of the services supplied with the needs of the business. There is no internal IT department filtering the requirements of the business, and business managers can tell what they want directly to those who are hired to deliver it. As a result, they have much more direct influence, certainly under changing circumstances.
- Business innovation based on IT is much easier to realize when business managers also talk to IT service providers. In many outsourcing relationships without such direct contacts, innovation remains limited to technology. Only in direct relationships do providers get a chance to add value by joining the client's deliberations on how IT might help optimize the company's business processes.
- And, obviously, but often ignored, direct relationships save overhead costs because the communication between client and supplier is simpler without intermediaries.

Nevertheless, there are also good arguments against direct relationships between the business and the company's service providers:

- Business managers know their own needs but do not usually have the whole view of all the company's IT needs. Their decisions, if not supported by a central IT department, often lead to sub-optimum solutions.
- Most business managers have insufficient IT knowledge to be able to direct the course of their providers' efforts.
- Considering the relatively low expenses made for IT services, they and their providers will frequently be given low priority, even though IT services are of essential importance.

Our truck manufacturer's business managers did not have direct relationships with their company's IT service providers. Partly, this was for historic reasons: as is usually the case, it was originally the internal IT department that maintained all contacts with external IT service providers. Besides, in this case the staff responsible for infrastructure services consisted of the company's own former employees, who had been transferred to the provider as part of the outsourcing deal. For these employees it would be a major change to suddenly have to talk to the company's business managers. Even though they originally worked for the same company as their clients, the culture differences would be a serious obstacle.

NOTES

1 This case study is based on structured interviews with executives of the infrastructure service provider and their client, which were held in 2000. They were previously published in Beulen (2000), and supplemented with information from the recipient's annual reports of 1999 and 2003. All material was rewritten for the purpose of this book; all names are fictional.

2 Severity one: a serious disruption of the IT services delivery.

REFERENCES

Agarwal, R. and Ferratt, T. (2001) 'Crafting an HR strategy to meet the need for IT workers', *Communications of the Association for Computing Machinery*, 44 (7): 59–64.

Agarwal, R. and Ferratt, T. (2002) 'Enduring practices for managing IT professionals', *Communications of the Association for Computing Machinery*, 45 (9): 73–79.

Aldhizer III, G. and Cashell, J. (2003) 'Internal audit outsourcing', *CPA Journal*, 73 (8): 38–43.

Anderson Jr, E. (2001) 'The nonstationary staff-planning problem with business cycle and learning effects', *Management Science*, 47 (6): 817–832.

Aubert, B., Patry, M. and Rivard, S. (2003) 'A tale of two outsourcing contracts: an agency-theoretical perspective', *Wirtschaftsinformatik*, 45 (2): 181–190.

Benamati, J. and Lederer, A. (2001) 'Rapid information technology change, coping mechanisms, and the emerging technologies group', *Journal of Management Information Systems*, 17 (4): 183–202.

Beulen, E. (2000) 'Beheersing van IT-outsourcingsrelaties: een beheersingsmodel voor uitbestedende bedrijven en IT-leveranciers', PhD thesis, Tilburg University (in Dutch).

Beulen, E. (2002) *Uitbesteding van IT-dienstverlening*, Den Haag: Ten Hagen en Stam (in Dutch).

Beulen, E. (2004) 'Governance in IT outsourcing partnerships', in W. van Grembergen (ed.) *Strategies for Information Technologies*, Hershey, PA: Idea Group Publishing.

Beulen, E., Baas, R., Dain, J., Hudson, J., Reitsma, E., Symonds, M. and van der Zee, H. (2004) 'Outsourcing: the Atos Origin outsourcing life cycle – building successful outsourcing relationships', White Paper (www.atosorigin.com/corporate/viewpoint/vp_270104.htm) Accessed 29 August 2004.

Beulen, E., van Fenema, P. and Currie, W. (2005) 'From application outsourcing to infrastructure management: extending the offshore outsourcing service portfolio', *European Management Journal*, 23 (2): 133–144.

Broadbent, M. and Weill, P. (1997) 'Management by maxim: how business and IT managers can create IT infrastructures', *Sloan Management Review*, 38 (3): 77–92.

Caplan, D. and Kirschenheiter, M. (2000) 'Outsourcing and audit risk for internal audit services', *Contemporary Accounting Research*, 17 (3): 387–428.

Carmel, E. (1999) *Global software teams, collaboration across borders and time zones*, Englewood Cliffs, NJ: Prentice Hall.

Carmel, E. and Agarwal, R. (2002) 'The maturation of offshore sourcing of Information Technology work', *Management Information Systems Quarterly Executive*, 1 (2): 65–76.

CCTA (1993) *The Infrastructure Library: An Introduction,* London: CCTA.

Cullen, S. and Willcocks, L. (2003) *Intelligent IT Outsourcing: Eight Building Blocks to Success,* Oxford: Butterworth-Heinemann.

DiMaggio, P. and Powell, W. (1983) 'The iron cage revisited: institutional isomorphism and collective rationality in organizational fields', *American Sociological Review,* 48: 147–160.

Dyer, J. and Singh, H. (1998) 'The relational view: cooperative strategy and sources of interorganizational competitive advantage', *The Academy of Management Review,* 23 (4): 660–679.

Edberg, D., Grupe, F.H. and Kuechler, W. (2001) 'Practical issues in global IT management: many problems, a few solutions', *Information Systems Management,* 18 (1): 34–46.

Gadde, L. and Snehota, I. (2000) 'Making the most of supplier relationships', *Industrial Marketing Management,* 29 (4): 305–316.

Lacity, M. and Hirschheim, R. (1995) *Beyond the Information Systems Outsourcing Bandwagon,* Chichester: Wiley & Sons.

Lacity, M. and Willcocks, L. (2003) 'IT sourcing reflections: lessons for customer and suppliers', *Wirtschaftsinformatik,* 45 (2): 115–125.

Levina, N. and Ross, J. (2003) 'The vendor's value proposition in IT outsourcing', *Management Information Systems Quarterly,* 27 (3): 331–346.

Linderman, K., Schroeder, R.G., Zahee, S. and Choo, A.S. (2003) 'Six Sigma: a goal-theoretic perspective', *Journal of Operations Management,* 21 (2): 193–203.

Lowson, R. (2002) 'Assessing the true operational costs of offshore sourcing strategies', *International Journal of Logistics Management,* 4 (3): 97–108.

Lyon, P., Hallier, J. and Glover, I. (1998) 'Divestment or investment? The contradictions of HRM in relation to older employees', *Human Resource Management Journal,* 8 (1): 56–67.

McDonald, M. (2004) 'IT risk management: strategizing the operational profile', Gartner conference, 31 October–4 November, Cannes, France.

McFarlan, F. and Nolan, R. (1995) 'How to manage an IT outsourcing alliance', *Sloan Management Review,* 36 (2): 9–24.

Nonaka, I. and Takeuchi, H. (1995) *The Knowledge Creating Company: How Japanese Companies Create the Dynasties of Innovation,* Oxford: Oxford University Press.

Paulk, M., Curtis, W., Chrissis, M.B. and Weber, C.V. (1993) 'Capability Maturity Model, version 1.1', *IEEE Software,* 10 (4): 18–27.

Peña, E. (1990) 'Motorola's secret to total quality control', *Quality Progress,* 23 (10): 43–45.

Peppard, J. (1999) 'Managing IT as a portfolio of services', *European Management Journal,* 21 (4): 467–483.

Pfeffer, J. (1998) 'Seven practices of successful organizations', *California Management Review,* 40 (2): 96–124.

Scott, S. (1996) 'Audit and control of information services outsourcing', *IS Audit & Control Journal,* 6: 46–51.

Verra, G. (2003) *International Account Management,* Deventer: Kluwer.

Willcocks, L., Hindle, J., Feeny, D. and Lacity, M. (2004) 'IT and business process outsourcing: the knowledge potential', *Information Systems Management,* 21 (3): 7–15.

Chapter 8

Governance factors –
the relationship

In Chapter 5, four governance factors were identified that concern the whole of the partnership relations between the outsourcing company and their IT providers:

- Unambiguously defined responsibilities, for both the service recipient and their providers.
- Contracts, in which such responsibilities (as well as other aspects) are captured.
- Trust in the partnership, well embedded in both organizations.
- Steering organizations, set up to ensure the regular exchange of information and opinions.

These governance factors will now be discussed in further detail, divided – as in the previous chapters – into four governance aspects each for extra clarity.

8.1 INTRODUCTION

Apart from the governance factors relating to the service recipient and their providers individually, attention must also be paid to the governance of their relationship as a whole. Since such relations are the nucleus of IT partnerships (Willcocks and Fitzgerald 1994), this is an important issue, requiring a breakdown into several governance factors.

First of all, the responsibilities of each of the partnership's participants must be clear, without any ambiguity. The outsourcing contract plays an important role here, sometimes referred to as the 'centrality of the contract' (Lacity and Hirschheim 1993). Having a contract, however, is not enough. Participants to a partnership must continuously keep each other's interests in mind: trust is an important factor in realizing IT partnership governance (Barthelemy 2003). Finally, steering organizations are needed in order to generate such trust.

These governance factors are embedded in the detailed theories, as discussed in Section 5.7. Most of the governance factors are linked to the agency theory, as there is information asymmetry between the service provider and the service recipient (Fama and Jensen 1983). The insights of the resource-based view contribute to the implementation of the responsibilities and steering organizations (Barney 1991; Prahalad and Hamel 1991). The insights of the transaction cost theory contribute to the governance 'contracts' (Coase 1937; Williamson 1975). The coordination costs of outsourcing contracts are substantial and the fourth governance factor, 'steering organizations', is part of the coordination costs.

These four governance factors – clearly defined responsibilities, well set-up contracts, trust in the partnership and steering organizations – are listed in Table 8.1.

Table 8.1 *Governance factors and governance aspects of IT outsourcing relationships*

Governance factors	Governance aspects
Unambiguously defined responsibilities	• Defining client–supplier interfaces • Defining organizational responsibility interfaces • Optimizing and updating organizational responsibility interfaces • Setting up procedures for responsibility transfer
Contracts	• Defining the IT services unambiguously • Defining a procedure for situations not described in the contract • Structuring the contract into layers • Defining a procedure for price changes
Trust in the partnership	• Arranging for trust to be built continuously • Ensuring personal trust between key staff members on both sides • Measuring trust regularly • Aligning frames of reference
Steering organizations	• Steering organizations on the strategic organizational level • Steering organizations on the tactical organizational level • Steering organizations on the operational organizational level • Ensuring coherence between the several steering organizations

8.2 UNAMBIGUOUSLY DEFINED RESPONSIBILITIES

Even in IT partnerships that involve little complexity, it is important that everyone's responsibilities are completely clear. In reality, IT outsourcing partnerships often involve many participants, especially since most service recipients prefer having multiple suppliers (Cullen and Willcocks 2003). Coordinating all these service providers then falls to the service recipient's IS department. But how can they guarantee optimum collaboration between all providers? For one, it is essential that the IT services are managed as a portfolio (Peppard 1999).

Another issue that must be considered here is service providers who subcontract some of their activities to third parties. This generally improves the flexibility of the set-up, but it requires much more of the provider's management attention (Mouritsen 1999), and attention must also be paid from a partnership governance point of view. The most important matter is to have all parties work together smoothly – only this will lay the basis for a successful IT outsourcing partnership.

A contract manager working for a Dutch aeroplane builder (Case XXVIII; see Appendix, p. 268, for all Case details) recalls:

> A few years ago we outsourced our ERP services, which involved transferring several responsibilities. While I feel it shouldn't matter whether you outsource activities or carry them out yourself, in practice, communicating with a service provider is just a little more difficult than with your own IT department. Now that we're a few years along, we're getting the hang of it, though.

8.2.1   Defining client–supplier interfaces

Service recipients must themselves define their information needs. This responsibility is shared between business managers, who must decide which information needs they have, and the company's information managers and CIO, who must decide how these needs are to be fulfilled. The actual delivery of the services is then the responsibility of the service providers – one of whom may be the outsourcing company's internal IT department.

Service providers often attempt to support their clients' CIOs and information managers in their task of identifying information provisioning solutions. By involving their suppliers, CIOs and information managers may achieve advantages of scale. An important disadvantage of doing so, however, is that some control over service delivery may be lost to those providers. Shifting such responsibilities may lessen the recipient's grip on their providers. Recipients would do well to prevent this by setting up client–supplier interfaces, limiting their providers' responsibilities to the actual delivery of the services needed (Gadrey and Gallouj 1998).

A business manager of a large financial corporation (Case XXVI) relates how he tackles this problem:

> We are considering how we should set up the IT services we need. So I regularly discuss my information needs with our IT professionals. They have allocated part of the delivery of these services to external providers. I am aware of this,

but since I'm a business manager this is not so important to me – as long as my information needs are fulfilled, it matters little to me by whom.

8.2.2 Defining organizational responsibility interfaces

When responsibilities are defined, the lines between service recipient and service providers are usually pretty clear. But determining the boundaries between individual providers' responsibilities is quite a bit less straightforward (Kishore 2003). Therefore, organizational responsibility interfaces must be defined. These describe the situations in which the activities of different providers connect with one another. A good rule is to ensure as little interdependence between providers as possible. If one supplier provides network management services, for example, including the on-site services involved, it is best not to have another provider, who works on server management, carry out on-site server tasks as well. The network management services supplier is in a better position to handle these activities too, since network disturbances and server disturbances are often directly related.

An information manager working for a telecommunications company (Case XI) told us:

> We consciously chose to outsource our IT services to multiple suppliers. In the contracts we set up much attention is paid to delineating every individual provider's responsibilities. Only once in several years now have I had to reprimand a provider who tried to pass off the responsibility for a disturbance to someone else.

8.2.3 Optimizing and updating organizational responsibility interfaces

The nature and scope of IT service delivery change with time, as do the company's information needs. Organizational responsibility interfaces must therefore be updated regularly (Kern and Willcocks 2000). If a standard desktop environment is introduced, for example, it may be wise to let a single provider manage it entirely. One or more organizational responsibility interfaces are then removed. Likewise, if a new server management system is introduced, a new provider may be needed to implement it; then, an extra organizational responsibility interface is added. In another vein, it is sometimes necessary to update one's organizational responsibility interfaces because the service providers involved do not perform as they should. Then the responsibility for delivering the IT services needed may be transferred to another supplier, thus again causing changes in the organizational responsibility interfaces. Situations such as the ones described here turn the updating of one's organizational responsibility interfaces into a continuous process.

An information manager working for a large financial conglomerate (Case XXVI), who has many large service providers, remarks:

I watch their performance very closely. Sometimes they pay a little less attention, for example, and while it's not that they fail to meet their service level requirements, they are just a little less sharp. That's when I have to do something, because outsourcing only works if you're right on top of things. Imagine the trouble of having to change providers, for instance! A new supplier would have to be integrated into a well-tuned business machine. Getting synchronized costs time and money. I'd rather spend my energy on keeping our current providers focused than on replacing underperformers – that's such a waste.

8.2.4 Setting up procedures for responsibility transfer

Many outsourcing contracts are repeatedly renewed, which sometimes makes them seem almost permanent. Nevertheless, all contracts end at some point, so it is a good idea to be prepared for the transfer of responsibilities that must then take place. Transfer procedures should be set up, the main objective of which being to eliminate continuity risks to the service delivery. One of the aspects of such procedures is the thorough documentation of all activities that are to be carried out by the new provider. They need this information in order to be able to carry out their tasks properly.

Maintaining such procedures costs money, of course. A service provider will for instance easily spend two weeks per year on them for a US$10 million per annum contract. These costs must be considered part of the necessary coordination costs made for the partnership. An even closer look into this subject will be taken in Chapter 10.

The CEO of a chemicals producer (Case XXI) has experienced a good transfer:

All our IT services used to be outsourced to one single provider. As we reached the end of the contract period, I felt there should be a little more variation. So we contracted two new IT suppliers. Meanwhile, our relations with our old provider remained very good. They acted very professionally and helped us with advice on our two new providers' transition plans. A company with such an attitude may count on being included in the selection process when we next have outsourcing decisions to make. This time their offer wasn't competitive enough, but who knows what it will be like next time.

(Beulen 2002: 153)

8.3 CONTRACTS

In IT outsourcing partnerships contracts are important instruments for both service recipients and service providers (Willcocks and Fitzgerald 1994; Klepper 1995). In them the agreements on the services to be delivered, the service levels expected and the consequent prices are laid down. Contracts will be more fully discussed in

Chapter 10, but we can focus on a few aspects here. For instance, service recipients should never simply accept their suppliers' general terms and conditions. Especially considering payments, liability and intellectual property the rule is: avoid the vendor's standard contract (Lacity and Hirschheim 1995). These three matters must therefore be thoroughly discussed before an agreement is reached.

Another important aspect of contract writing is the balance between business and technology perspectives. Too many technical details cloud the issue since only a few people are then able to understand what the contract specifies – and these are usually not the business managers whose information needs the contract is supposed to cater to. Business managers must be enabled to play their part in the contract discussions. This is confirmed by an expert in the field:

> All-over outsourcing deals usually involve loads and loads of – very technical – details. Most of these are largely irrelevant to the average businessman. Keeping track of all those details may be necessary to ensure proper service delivery, but business managers only want to get the information they need for their business. Contracts should therefore contain something like a simple scorecard listing the seven or so most important information items needed, plus an agreement on how to keep track of their delivery.
>
> (Beulen 2000: 225)

8.3.1 Defining the IT services unambiguously

A first objective when writing outsourcing contracts is to define the IT services unambiguously. This includes both the provider's and the recipient's tasks and responsibilities, which must be described in some detail. The service levels required must also be defined (Domberger *et al.* 2000).

Many service providers use sets of definitions to describe their work. Service recipients doing business with several providers may be confronted with a number of such sets, all of which are slightly different from the rest. They would do well to make their own set and require all providers to work on its basis rather than accepting any of their providers' definition sets. An added advantage of doing so is that the recipient then has more control over their suppliers.

Since many services of the total delivery package are interrelated and inter-dependent, such relationships must also be laid down in the contract. Defining these interfaces will establish better understanding among the several parties of the interdependencies in the partnership as a whole. A contract manager whose client is a discrete manufacturing company (Case VII) approached this issue by setting up framework agreements:

> Our contract with this client includes simple and clear definitions of all kinds of services, such as storage facilities, extra capacity and the like. The moment

that any of its divisions needs such a service, we can deliver it quickly, since the framework agreement means that the contracts needed are easily and quickly set up – a matter of copy-and-paste, really, and then of filling in the right numbers.

8.3.2 Defining a procedure for situations not described in the contract

It is obvious that one should not agree with anything before the negotiations are finished: do not sign incomplete contracts (Tirole 1989). While you can never foresee every possible situation, the IT outsourcing market is now so mature that both recipients and providers are generally capable of addressing the most important issues in their contracts. However, business dynamics and the developments in the field of technology are such that there will always be unexpected situations (Tirole 1989; Segal 1999). These may cause friction or even disputes between recipients and their providers. All parties should then try to solve such matters in concert, and avoid having to go to court over them (Beulen 2000: 230). To facilitate such discussions, contract parties can include agreements on how to deal with situations not described in the contract. These agreements must define which people will contact one another; financial pointers may be included as well. The goal is always to prevent a situation getting in the way of service delivery.

One possible solution must be kept in mind and should preferably be included in the contract: independent, binding arbitration. This means that a third party decides when the recipient and their providers cannot themselves find a solution to which all parties agree. Taking a decision is always better than letting the problem exist unresolved. If arbitration has been included in the contract before the partnership begins, a solution is all the more quickly found when a problem arises.

An account manager whose client is an energy company (Case XVII) has practical experience with the unexpected:

> We had long-term contracts, but the economic situation forced our client to introduce cost-cutting programmes. We, too, were involved and had to do the same work for less money. We accepted, on condition that the contract period was lengthened and its scope widened. This solution was in both our and our client's interests.

8.3.3 Structure the contract into layers

Business dynamics and technological developments do not influence all contractual agreements equally. Structuring the contract in several layers will accommodate the differences between the relatively stable aspects and those components that are more likely to need a change. Aspects that are unlikely to change much, like payment, jurisdiction and liabilities, may be laid down in framework agreements. Service

181

agreements can then be used to define the IT services involved. And finally, service level agreements (SLAs) contain the service levels and quantities to be delivered, as well as their price. Many service providers work with service catalogues. These contain descriptions of the services they can deliver – a kind of menu from which to choose. These catalogues are used to set up service agreements and SLAs.

The chief information officer of a multinational in chemical products (Case III) tells of his approach:

> Our contract with our main supplier is a framework agreement. It contains the conditions, general terms and tariffs of our relation, but not the actual volume of our business. So it does not represent any contracted revenue for our supplier. This matches our decentralized organization structure: even for infrastructure services the local organization units have full responsibility. My corporate department has a say, of course, but the final decisions are taken locally. I'll give you an example. We have outsourced our network to two external suppliers, on the basis of a framework agreement, which allows our local units to settle service level agreements themselves as long as they meet the framework's conditions. The local organizations are thus the suppliers' final contract partners. This has resulted in differences between local companies, with respect to both price and service offerings for network services. So you see: the needs of our organizational units differ, and these differences are reflected in their SLAs.

8.3.4 Defining a procedure for price changes

Cost saving is one of the prime arguments for outsourcing. Establishing the right price level is therefore important, not only as a part of the selection and agreement process, but also during the rest of the contract period. This is not as easy as it perhaps seems. During the selection and agreement phase, providers compete for the contract, thus effectively setting the price together (Kern *et al*. 2002). But once the contract is signed, there is no more competition. Contracts must therefore contain clauses that ensure market conformity during their running time.

To this end, the initial price is often combined with an indexing mechanism, the advantage of which – from the recipient's point of view – is that the costs of the services are highly predictable. But this set-up does not allow for adaptations as a result of price-level changes in the IT outsourcing industry as a whole. Another possibility is the open-book approach. The service provider shows his client the costs made for the delivery of his services; should these costs rise, the increase may be included in their prices. The disadvantage here is the lack of incentive for cost effectiveness. This approach therefore only works well for innovative projects. Finally, the contract may include a benchmarking agreement. A yearly benchmark then provides input for setting next year's prices. The recipient can be sure always to pay a market-conform fee – no more, but no less either. To increase the benchmarking efficiency (and thus decrease its costs), the services delivered should be in accordance with the benchmarking bureau's definitions. For commodity services this is usually no problem, since most providers use almost the same definitions for them anyway. Nevertheless, benchmarking is always an expensive process.

Many companies devise a combination of indexing mechanisms and bench-marking: in principle the prices of the services delivered are indexed every year, but if the fees in the industry as a whole deviate too much from the index a benchmark is carried out and used as the basis for next year's prices. An information manager working for a large financial corporation (Case XXVI) does exactly that:

> Most of our outsourcing partnerships have contract times of 36 to 60 months. Consequently, we must regularly investigate whether the prices set originally are still realistic. Usually, we work on the basis of an initial price level plus an indexing mechanism, with benchmarking as a fall-back option. In practice, I invite those providers whose prices I feel are too high. Then I try, in all fairness, to reach a new agreement. Only if that doesn't work do we resort to benchmarking, but I've only had to do that twice so far. And a good thing too, because benchmarking is not only expensive. It also takes up a lot of management time – mine and my provider's – and that's not something I'm keen on.

8.4 TRUST IN THE PARTNERSHIP

Managing IT outsourcing partnerships is not a matter of the 'hard side' only. Much attention must be paid to the 'soft side', especially trust, which is of essential importance (Barthelemy 2003). Several kinds of trust may be defined: organizational trust, group trust and personal trust, among others (Fukuyama 1995). They all require attention if the partnership is to be a success.

The major difficulties with trust are that it takes time to generate and that it is very hard to measure. To give trust time to grow, providers and recipients must begin by clearly expressing to one another that they will put effort into it. Then trust building is on the programme explicitly.

8.4.1 Arranging for trust to be built continuously

A first step towards generating trust is being open in one's communication. Service suppliers must provide clear and understandable reports on the services they have delivered; service recipients should give clear feedback on their supplier's perform-ance (Langfield-Smith and Smith 2003). Essentially, this is a matter of communi-cation hygiene, and it applies especially to the parties' formal communication.

With respect to their informal communication, much trust may be generated by consultation: before any formal communication takes place, the partners discuss matters informally. If new ideas and solutions can be tested and discussed first, before they are laid down and everybody reads about them in their formal communication, mishaps can be prevented. Care must still be taken, of course, but informal consultation generally brings the parties closer together.

A contract manager whose client (Case XXV) operates in the telecommunication industry really values these informal contacts:

> If I have an idea about a solution for some problem, I don't have to wait until the next formal meeting. I just pop in at my counterpart's office and we talk about it. We exchange views. At the next formal meeting these matters then require very little time, just a formal decision. Informal consultation beforehand makes the whole process so much smoother.

8.4.2 Ensuring personal trust between key staff members on both sides

Trust between organizations and groups is important but not enough. For collaboration efforts to work, personal trust is needed too (Fukuyama 1995). The process of generating personal trust begins during the contract negotiation process. Both provider and recipient must get a feel for which personal profiles best fit the management of their partnership. Some researchers even advise recipients to select the account manager they feel the most comfortable with (Lacity and Hirschheim 1995). Then, after the contract has been signed, the key people on both sides[1] must take time to get to know each other. Sports and cultural outings are excellent opportunities to do so. Should the match be less than comfortable, it may at this point still be necessary to replace one or two individuals. Both parties must realize, however, that frequent personnel changes do not help generate personal trust; and personal relationships should always remain professional.

A contract manager who has an energy company as a client (Case XIII) considers personal trust very important:

> Their IT manager must trust me personally as his contract manager. He must be able to rely on what I say as the truth. Without such trust you're in deep trouble. And that doesn't go for me only; all staff who maintain contacts with their client or supplier must be able to trust one another.

(Beulen 2000: 216)

8.4.3 Measuring trust regularly

IT outsourcing partnerships involve much reporting. These reports should not only concern the services delivered but also the degree of trust between the partners. This has long been a difficult subject to discuss, especially since most recipients thought of their outsourcing relations in terms of client–customer relationships rather than partnerships. But for IT outsourcing to work well, relationships must go much beyond that. To measure trust, objective instruments should be used. Several consulting companies, such as Gartner and TPI, offer tools with which such a measurement can be facilitated. These tools generally resemble balanced scorecards (Purser 2001). Once the degree of trust between the partners has been measured, the results must be used to increase it further. To this end boot camp sessions can be effective, but it may also be necessary to replace some of the team's members.

An information manager in the discrete manufacturing business (Case VII) states:

> So far client satisfaction is the only element in the assessment of our IT outsourcing partnership's 'soft side'. The results are included in the balanced scorecard for the partnership as a whole. With the help of a consulting firm we are now thinking of introducing several more 'soft' aspects, such as trust. First we must find a way to measure them objectively, then they must be included in the scorecard.

Other soft elements that may be included in assessment scorecards used for IT outsourcing relationships are innovation or governance proposals. Innovation proposals contain suggestions for improving the service delivery; on the basis of a business case the recipient can decide to accept the offer or not. Since service providers obviously have a commercial interest in these proposals, it can be difficult to assess their value. Governance proposals may include agreements on support given by the service provider in professionalizing their client's demand management. The provider will not take over demand management as such, but they will contribute their knowledge and know-how to set it up to maximum effect. A difficulty in this respect is that it is hard for service recipients to estimate either the value of their supplier's contribution or the effects of such professionalization efforts.

8.4.4 Aligning frames of reference

Apart from profit, turnover and market penetration goals, many companies wish to act on their social responsibilities. Environmental care is one point of attention, and it may be explicitly included in the partnership contract. Laying down an environmental protection code helps the partners find their bearings in this field – not just the recipient but also their providers (DesJardins 1998). Such codes may include aspects like ink cartridge re-use, paper use (double-sided or single, recycling, etc.) and stimulating the use of public transport rather than private automobiles. In a similar vein, social policies with respect to employees may be included. Even though service providers are unlikely to exploit their staff or use child labour, setting clear standards will help generate mutual understanding and trust.

An information manager working for a global niche-food company (Case XX) feels it is important for his company to show that it cares for the environment:

We pay attention to this aspect in all our external communication efforts, and we report on our actions to our stock holders. We ask our suppliers to act responsibly too. It is mentioned explicitly in our Requests for Information, and during the contract period we ask our providers how they meet these requirements.

8.5 STEERING ORGANIZATIONS

Since so many things must be aligned for a partnership to work well, all these matters must be discussed and then agreed upon. When the steering organizations to do so are set up, it is important that every issue is allocated to the right organizational level – strategic, tactical and operational. This means deciding who talks to whom and about what (Cullen and Willcocks 2003). Of course, a properly functioning partnership requires that there be a well thought-through coherence between these levels. For example: which procedure must be followed when no agreement can be reached on a certain level? How are issues escalated to the level above? Finally, each level has its own conference frequency. Strategic matters are usually discussed only a few times per year, while many operational issues require daily attention. The steering organizations discussed in full in the next four sections of this chapter are summarized in Table 8.2.

An information manager working for a temporary labour agency (Case XIX) considers frequent conferences with their service providers necessary to keep an eye on their service delivery. 'We try to distinguish between major issues and the less important matters. And so, on the operational level we consult one another almost daily, while our strategic conferences are held only twice yearly.'

8.5.1 Steering organizations on the strategic organizational level

On the strategic level three kinds of conference are to be found: the IT board, the partner board and, when needed, the change advisory board. They meet once or twice a year. An IT board is what the Control Objectives for Information and Related Technology (COBIT) calls an IT strategy committee (van Grembergen *et al.* 2003). Generally, only recipient staff are present. These internal steering organizations are used to maximize the contribution of information technology to the company's business processes. Aligning future business requirements and providing business managers with an overview of technical innovations therefore figure prominently on their agenda. Sometimes IT boards are also used to get feedback from business managers on IT strategy drafts, prior to their endorsement. In all cases, the results of IT board discussions are captured in the company's IT strategy. The board is not the place where IT strategy decisions are made, however; that remains the task of the company's management board.

Table 8.2 Steering organizations on all three organizational levels, including the subjects discussed there and the people attending them

Level*	Conference	Subjects discussed	Attendees – service recipient	Meeting frequency**	Attendees – service provider
S	IT Board	• Aligning future business requirements • Providing business managers with an overview of technical innovations	• Chief information officer† • Information managers • Senior business managers (including C-level)	Once a year	• Independent experts (only invited when necessary)
S	Partner Board	• Joint strategic planning • Resolving issues escalated from the tactical level • Relationship building	• Chief information officer • Information managers	Once or twice a year	• Client executives • Customer operations director • Lead technical officer
S	Change Advisory Board	• Change request approvals	• Information managers • Information analysts • Functional application managers • Business management representatives	Every two months	• Service delivery managers • Customer operations manager • Service managers
T	Service Portfolio Board	• The appropriateness of new technologies	• Information managers • Contract managers • Business management representatives	Twice a year	• Lead technical officer • Customer solutions architects
T	Service Review Meeting	• Service provider performance • Improvement plans status	• Information managers • Contract managers	Monthly	• Customer operations director • Service delivery managers
T	Contract Review Meeting	• Advance invoice approval	• Contract manager • Purchasing managers	Monthly	• Client manager • Customer operations director
O	Service Meeting	• Day-to-day service provisioning issues	• Contract manager • Information analysts • Functional application managers • Business management representatives	Weekly	• Customer operations manager • Service delivery manager
O	Change Control Meeting	• Analysing the implications of implementing change requests • Implementing approved change requests	• Information analysts • Functional application managers	Weekly	• Service managers
O	Project Meeting	• Day-to-day project execution issues	• Contract manager • Information analysts • Functional application managers • Business management representatives	Weekly or daily	• Project managers • Customer operations manager

Notes:
* S : strategic; T : tactical; O : operational.
** The meeting frequency depends on the size of the contract (here: annual contract values of more than 10 million euros).
† The underlined attendees are in charge for their respective companies.

As the IT board's discussions involve the company's business strategy, usually no representatives of the company's service providers are present. Resistance to sharing such strategic information with outsiders generally prevents their attendance, as do the service providers' commercial interests. Only real experts, with an in-depth knowledge of certain topics, are sometimes invited: knowledge-based contribution by service providers. But even then there is a preference for independent consultants.

The primary task of partner boards is strategic planning. This involves senior managers from both the recipient and their provider, in order to implement visionary strategies. Partner boards are also the place where issues escalated from the tactical organizational level are decided. These are usually matters concerning service provisioning and mutual contractual obligations. Contracts, after all, provide guidance but they do not cover everything. Both parties must work on this in good faith, and relationship building is therefore an important aspect of the board's work too.

Finally, the interests of both partners may be furthered by setting up a change advisory board, to which independent consultants are often invited. The rationale behind calling such a meeting is that the changes continually made in dynamic partnerships must be implemented with both sides' interests in mind, which requires the careful attention of a separate conference. Adding independent advisors on this strategic governance level ensures that changes in service provisioning and contractual obligations are made with integrity.

A global client executive whose client is a chemicals producer (Case III) felt that at first his participation in the recipient's Corporate Information Platform (as its partner board was called) was not very constructive.

> Its members used my presence only to express worries about operational service delivery issues. Since then, however, the level of the discussions has improved. Today we still discuss service delivery issues, but future services are on the agenda as well. Now my participation really contributes to expanding and improving our outsourcing relation.

8.5.2 Steering organizations on the tactical organizational level

On the tactical level there are three steering organizations as well: the service portfolio board, the service review meeting and the contract review meeting. They meet every month or, in the case of the service portfolio board, every two months. Such a set-up conforms to the IT Infrastructure Library (ITIL) guidelines (CCTA 1993). Issues that cannot be solved on this level are escalated to the strategic boards.

Service portfolio boards explore the appropriateness of new technologies; this is also called technology watch. The characteristics of the recipient's production processes are therefore of prime importance to service portfolio board discussions, as are the company's configuration management and software control and distribution processes. On the basis of the recipient's IT strategy the service provider supplies the board with feasibility studies and pilot projects for new technologies. The board then takes decisions on the implementation of such new technologies. Ideally, however, strategic guidance is not provided by the recipient only: if the recipient is willing to share not only their IT strategy but their business strategy with their provider too, the exploration of appropriate new technologies will be more effective. The initiatives of service portfolio boards have to be approved by their company's partner board; this escalation to the strategic organizational level is necessary because implementing new technologies involves substantial costs.

In service review meetings the performance of the company's service providers is discussed on the basis of reports for the previous month as well as on earlier periods, so that any trends can be discerned. Service level management processes therefore play a major role here. If a provider underperforms, improvement plans must be made, concerning among other matters incident and problem management processes. These plans must then be implemented by the provider, a process that often requires a certain amount of change management. Consequently, the status reviews of such implementation plans and change management processes are discussed in service review meetings as well. A contract manager working for a global financial corporation (Case XXIX) who is responsible for three of his company's suppliers, explains:

> I receive monthly reports, which I use to talk matters through with their account and contract managers. I discuss the reports as well as any issues left undecided the last time we met. These steering organizations are very important to me because they offer me the opportunity to check whether our service suppliers meet their obligations.

Finally, contract review meetings are called to discuss invoices before they are officially sent – the kind of informal consultation mentioned in Section 8.4.1, which serves to prevent payment delays and other difficulties. On the basis of reports and the contractual agreements of the partnership, the provider prepares a concept invoice. During the meeting its elements are discussed, which ensures cost control and transparency. Any complaints are discussed at this meeting too, which means that all complaints and service-level management processes culminate here. Only undisputed elements of the concept invoice are paid; if necessary the disputed elements can be escalated to the strategic level. Contract review meetings are quite frequently combined with service review meetings, in order to save time and resources. This can comfortably be done once the partnership is well under way, since the invoicing process will then have stabilized after the initial aligning during the start-up period.

189

8.5.3 Steering organizations on the operational level

Finally, on the operational level also there are three kinds of conference: service meetings, change control meetings and project meetings – again in line with the ITIL guidelines (CCTA 1993). These meetings have a weekly or daily frequency. Unsolved issues on the operational level are escalated to the tactical level.

In service meetings day-to-day service provisioning issues are discussed. The partnership's service-level management process is therefore very important to these meetings. Since it is essential to keep track of all issues discussed, incident and problem management processes play a major role too. Escalation to the tactical level, if necessary, is to the company's service review meeting.

Change control meetings analyse the implications of carrying out any change requests made. Since the changes requested may be business-driven, business managers sometimes attend these meetings. To be able to make the analyses, the company's present mode of operations, its configuration management and its software control and distribution process are closely involved. On the basis of their analyses change control meetings approve or reject implementation plans for changes, which means that the company's change management process is involved too. Final and financial approval remains the responsibility of the company's partner board, however, as changes involve substantial costs. An IT manager working in discrete manufacturing (Case VII) agrees that these meetings are important:

> We are in the process of rolling out a new ERP system, which we will greatly depend on for our business management. To implement the changes we have drawn up a set of processes and procedures. We hope to be able to implement any future changes smoothly, and so to ensure the continuity of the IT service delivery.

In project meetings, finally, day-to-day project issues are discussed, all of which must be kept track of as the partnership progresses. If any unsolved issues have to be escalated, it will be to the tactical-level service review meeting.

8.5.4 Ensuring coherence between the several steering organizations

For the partnership's success it is, of course, important that this set of boards and meetings is formed into a coherent whole. Each conference's processes and procedures must be aligned with those of the other steering organizations. The ITIL guidelines provide a good connection between the tactical and operational levels (CCTA 1993), while the COBIT guidelines do so for the strategic and tactical levels (van Grembergen *et al.* 2003).

The size of the partnership naturally influences the steering organizations needed. For small-scale partnerships the strategic and tactical levels can be merged.

The operational level will always remain separate, however, since the tasks on this level differ completely from those on the other levels.

A contract manager with responsibility for the management of the mainframe services outsourced by an oil and gas company (Case XIV) appreciates the separation of operational matters from the rest:

> I appreciate not being bothered with operational details. Those are all handled by the provider, on a purely operational level. Of course I keep informed of all that happens; everything out of the ordinary that happens is included in their monthly reports. But I can confine my attention to the main issues. So we have a regular, weekly meeting, and only very rarely do we have to call a crisis meeting.

CASE STUDY

GOVERNANCE AND STEERING ORGANIZATIONS

Summary

In 2002 a globally operating consumer packaged goods (CPG) company based in Europe decided to outsource the European part of its ERP application maintenance services. The roles and responsibilities of interviewees for this case study are detailed in Table 8.2. The provider finally chosen also operated as systems integrator, subcontracting to a hardware supplier for the actual delivery of the services. There were thus three parties involved in the outsourcing partnership.

The recipient's primary reason for outsourcing the maintenance of their ERP systems was that such work was not their core business. Also, with respect to service delivery continuity, they had more confidence in a service provider able to assume responsibility for the whole process than in their internal IT department, dependent as it was on external technical specialists that had to be hired temporarily for the purpose. Finally, the recipient wished to achieve cost savings.

Consequently, the recipient's systems integration and application maintenance tasks were outsourced to their primary provider. The hardware supplier's services were retained, but they now became a subcontractor rather than a direct provider. To achieve the objectives mentioned above, clear agreements then had to be formulated. This meant drawing up contracts but also, equally important, setting up regular steering organizations to discuss all important matters. In this case study students must determine which roles should be assigned to whom, and how a coherent governance structure and the necessary steering organizations can be set up. Their roles and responsibilities are detailed in Table 8.3.

191

Table 8.3 *Interviewees: case study on governance and steering organizations*

The interviewees[2]

Party	Name and job title	Responsibilities	Remarks
Recipient	Ronald Verstraten, Chief Information Officer	• The company's sourcing strategy • ERP outsourcing relationships	• Partner board member • Closely involved in the contracting process
Primary provider	Janneke Steenhuis, Sector Director	• Acquiring the ERP outsourcing contract • ERP outsourcing relationships	
	Udo Parlier, Technical Manager	• The technical design made by the architect • The transfer of the information systems hardware from the recipient to the primary provider's own data centre	
Hardware provider	Karel van Gasteren, Account Manager	• Contracting the supply of information systems hardware • The transfer of this hardware from the recipient to the data centre of the application maintenance provider (the primary provider) • Relationships with this provider	

Introduction

In the spring of 2002 Ronald Verstraten's negotiations to contract out his company's ERP application maintenance to a service provider were discontinued. As CIO of a globally operating consumer packaged goods (CPG) producer he had hoped that setting up an outsourcing partnership with an external party would improve his company's IT services. But alas, the provider he had been talking to could not deliver what he needed, and he was very disappointed. 'I had invested so much time in building this relation. It was frustrating to find that I still had no confidence it would work. However, now I had the chance to make a fresh start.'

The crucial difficulty in the provider's proposal turned out to be the geographical availability of the expertise needed. Verstraten's company was based in Europe but operated globally, and its local subsidiaries were where all final business decisions were made – and, therefore, where all service needs would arise. The service provider had claimed to be able to provide expertise everywhere, since they had many IT professionals available, especially in the USA. However, it then turned out that relationships between the provider's local organizations were anything but cordial. Their staff might simply not always be willing to help their colleagues from another country. 'For me this meant insufficient reliability. I could not enter an outsourcing partnership on this basis.'

Now what? All Verstraten could do was call the number two on his list. He contacted their board and after a few sessions their Sector Director, Janneke Steenhuis, joined the meetings. The central issue at these steering organizations was the division of roles and responsibilities between Verstraten's company as service recipient and Steenhuis' organization as provider. A solution also had to be found for Verstraten's hardware provider, with whom his company had already done business for 15 years. The format found was one in which the new, primary service provider would act as systems integrator and maintenance provider, while the hardware supplier would subcontract from them.

They shook hands on it; the main points of their future partnership were clear. But even though the board was pushing Verstraten to outsource their ERP application maintenance, demanding a contract quickly now, much remained to be taken care of. This put him under quite a lot of pressure. Steenhuis, for her part, was not sure of the deal either. Did this client really want to outsource? After all, they had just broken off their negotiations with another potential partner, after months of deliberations. Perhaps the CIO was afraid he would lose power if these services were delivered by an external provider rather than their internal IT department. She decided not to share these worries with her superiors, however. And so, when she called her commercial director on the way home, she told him:

> We had a good meeting, with a strong focus on the content of the partnership. I think they broke off their negotiations with the previous candidate because they might not have enough IT professionals available. We must make them feel confident about us in that respect. I'll start thinking about the composition of the team that will carry out the delivery once we have a contract.

Company and industry profile

The company and its market

The service recipient in this case study was a Europe-based, globally operating CPG company with a worldwide reputation. Said Janneke Steenhuis, their primary provider's sector director: 'It was the kind of company you like to have among your clients. Having such a name on your list opens doors to other clients.' The recipient's total turnover was 10 billion euros, all of which was realized by one single product group. The relative autonomy of each of its more than 25 European operating companies meant they all had profit and loss responsibility for their business.

The company as a whole grew steadily, both organically and through takeovers, and both in new regions and in countries in which it was active already. This growth was expected to continue. However, while in some countries the company's market grew strongly, in most parts of the world market growth potential was limited. And the company faced substantial market dynamics too, as a result of the sensitiveness of its brand name and image to local and global fashions. Therefore, marketing was of central importance to its management.

IT services

The recipient of our case study used IT services on a very large scale – not just for administrative purposes but also to support its production processes and to manage its logistics. And of course, IT was important in its communication with its customers. The company already contacted its consumers through interactive websites, and it expected the contribution of IT to its marketing efforts to increase significantly in the near future.

Its current IT architecture consisted of a large number of different hardware and software platforms, a result of the relative autonomy of its operating companies, which often made very different choices with respect to the applications they used. However, there was a tendency to centralize such systems, certainly those that were used by several operating companies. Centralization meant that these applications could be standardized too. The move toward outsourcing the company's ERP application maintenance was part of this development.

The freedom of the company's operating companies was what worried Janneke Steenhuis most:

> It was all very fine to discuss matters with their CIO, but at a certain point I really wanted to talk to the business managers of the countries involved. So far, I had no idea of what their plans were. But their buy-in was essential if this outsourcing relation was going to be a success.

Requirements

The recipient's objectives

At the time discussed here, ERP application maintenance and ERP functional application support were no longer considered part of the recipient's core business, which was their first argument for outsourcing. Other arguments were the wish to achieve cost savings and the need to ensure business continuity. The company thought it could guarantee business continuity by clearly allocating end-to-end responsibility for IT services delivery to an external party capable of handling the whole process.

The costs savings desired could mainly be realized by optimizing the number of external consultants responsible for the ERP applications. Prior to the outsourcing arrangement more than 50 per cent of these were external specialists, hired from a large number of service providers. Once this activity was outsourced, the primary provider replaced all of them by their own employees. Ronald Verstraten: 'Doing business with one primary provider at one stroke rid me, as the company's CIO, of all these different external staff.' The volume involved enabled the primary provider to reduce the total cost of ownership. At first, Janneke Steenhuis was slightly worried about this cost reduction objective: 'Of course I like to contribute to any objectives my clients may have. But if cost reductions are their only motive, outsourcing relations don't work. I am glad to say that was not the case here.'

The scope of the services contracted

The geographical scope of the outsourcing relationship was Europe. Janneke Steenhuis:

> Fortunately we had offices in all countries involved. This convinced our client we would be able to deliver the services needed. During the start-up phase, training and recruiting would allow us to upgrade the professionality level in those countries in which it was insufficient, to the level needed for the delivery of the IT services contracted. Our country managers took care of that. Meanwhile, flying in experts from other countries would enable us from day one to deliver as agreed.

With respect to volume, the combined scope of ERP application maintenance and ERP functional application support was a total of more than 10,000 SAP seats. And while only ERP maintenance was included in the contract,[3] this still meant extending the contract with the recipient's current hardware provider.

To ensure its business continuity the recipient had adopted the 'twin data centre' concept: two data and hardware platforms, located at separate physical locations and each able to take over from the other in the unlikely event of a disaster in one of them. The maintenance provider would therefore also have to implement such a twin system. And so the transfer of the data centre from the client to the provider involved making a detailed project plan, including a roll-out progressing country by country. As this was an operation of critical importance to the recipient's business, this project plan was included in the outsourcing contract. It was executed collaboratively by the primary and hardware providers, with the active cooperation of the recipient.

Roles, responsibilities and governance

The service recipient retained responsibility for the development and implementation of its IT strategy, an activity carried out by its corporate information office. Likewise, the recipient themselves implemented their demand management (a collaborative effort of their corporate information office and their corporate IT services centre).

Responsibility for ERP software support and implementation, however, was shared between their corporate IT services centre and the primary provider. The recipient's operating companies remained responsible for their business management.

The primary provider combined two main responsibilities: ERP application maintenance and systems integration. The first task included processing the ERP software involved and managing the recipient's infrastructure environment and help-desk. As systems integrator, the primary provider had to manage the contribution of the hardware service provider.

This third party kept providing the recipient's hardware, as it had done for more than 15 years. It also shouldered responsibility for disaster recovery and break-and-fix services. Finally, apart from the primary provider and the hardware provider, a third supplier was involved in the recipient's ERP processes: a software service provider who took care of all bug fixing, third line support, and implementation projects and support. This provider also developed new ERP software releases, but that activity fell outside the scope of the outsourcing contract discussed here.

In this outsourcing relationship, the allocation of responsibilities is relatively straightforward. Such a simple model was exactly what Ronald Verstraten, the recipient's CIO, was looking for: 'A single systems integrator, who can assume end-to-end responsibility – that is what I needed. At first, however, it wasn't clear what the partnership's governance structure would look like exactly. This involved some more thinking.'

Contract and governance structures

The final negotiations resulted in a three-year contract based on a seat price. A separate contract was drawn up for the transition project. These contracts defined the IT supply to the operating companies as the responsibility of the service recipient's corporate IT service centre. In the words of their CIO, Ronald Verstraten: 'This gave me maximum control over the IT services and the operating companies.' And his provider's sector director believed that:

> It had the advantage that we could make central agreements and yet let customer satisfaction be determined by the business units and not by their corporate IT department. We would, of course, have to pay thorough attention to this issue when defining the partnership model in more detail.

The recipient's contractual relationships with their operating companies were covered in internal contracts with clear descriptions of service levels and settlement methods. Part of the services described the corporate IT service centre sourced from their providers, through contracts which fully covered those made with the operating companies. The recipient's corporate IT service centre thus had contractual relationships with an ERP application maintenance service provider (their primary provider and systems integrator), an ERP software service provider and a functional application support service provider. The direct contract with an information systems hardware service provider, which had run for more than 15 years, was changed into a subcontract with the primary provider. This increased the flexibility of the outsourcing partnership as a whole, and limited the amount of management attention the recipient's corporate IT service centre had to pay to hardware matters. Karel van Gasteren, the hardware provider's account manager, showed himself quite satisfied with the arrangement: 'We had done many large-scale projects with our client. Quick service delivery and reliability were rewarded now, because we remained one of their partners, whereas they might easily have chosen another hardware provider.'

All these service providers were also involved in additional ERP projects, which fell outside the outsourcing partnership's scope and thus had to be contracted separately. Each of these projects averaged about 30 per cent of the recipient's total IT spending on ERP. Janneke Steenhuis: 'These projects were a nice extra bit of business, which made the partnership even more attractive to us.' Karel van Gasteren felt the same way: 'For us these extra projects were important. They generated substantial extra turnover, and I hope this will continue in the future.'

Except for the services supplied by the functional application support provider, all services were captured in framework agreements (Figure 8.1). To this end, the recipient had structured the ERP services needed into clearly defined domains, identifying resources and capabilities. The agreements included clauses on the collaboration

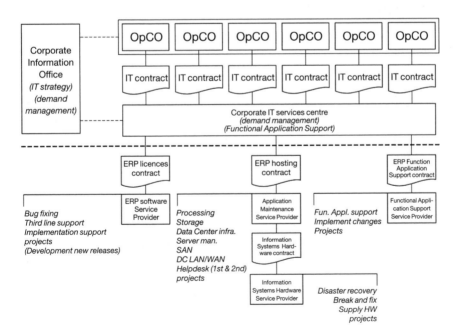

Figure 8.1 *Contractual relationships in the outsourcing partnership*

between the several service providers. Two aspects worth noting were that software and hardware designs were not to be separately charged to the recipient, and that any investments the providers made for their relationships with one another and their client would have to be recouped from the profits on the services delivered.

The service recipient set up a change control board to facilitate the discussions with and between their providers. The meetings of this board thus also became knowledge-sharing occasions. Since third-party enforcement rather than self-enforcement was an important aspect of the governance structure of this partnership, the contracts remained of key importance, however.

The set-up of these governance structures would require much of the partners' attention. Ronald Verstraten: 'I didn't immediately have a clear idea on who would attend these steering organizations. So I began sketching profiles of the expertise needed there.' These profiles included knowledge and know-how as well as the attendees' organizational positions – both for the recipient's and the providers' staff. Janneke Steenhuis: 'We, too, looked closely at the fit between our team members and the recipient's representatives.' A difficulty in this respect was the involvement of so many different parties. Ronald Verstraten: 'Even though we had chosen one provider to be our systems integrator, our corporate IT services centre would still also be talking to the ERP software supplier and the hardware provider, plus our own operating companies.'

The migration project

Karel van Gasteren: 'Discussing the partnership's governance was an important step. But before the partnership could really start, we still had to make the transition from the recipient's data centre to that of their application maintenance provider – a major operation!' Because of the immense risks this migration entailed for the recipient's business continuity, it was timed to coincide with the implementation of new hardware platforms. The hardware platforms used up to the moment of transition could then be used as a fall-back option. Van Gasteren: 'The migration went smoothly, but it was good to have a back-up system you knew would work if needed.'

The transition and its preparations took four months. 'We prepared it with military precision', Karel van Gasteren recalls. 'During the execution, setting up storage facilities would prove to be the most difficult part. CPG producers store immense amounts of data – current and historic – which must all remain immediately retrievable.' And, quite apart from the technical challenges, a project organization had to be set up to prepare and execute the migration. Roles and authority had to be allocated. 'Of course, the systems integrator held final responsibility for this project. But considering the knowledge and know-how needed, they could not have done it without our support as hardware suppliers, or without that of the recipient's corporate IT services centre.'

198

The follow-up: governance and steering organizations

When, after tough but constructive negotiations, the main contracts were signed, the migration project could commence and the ERP service delivery could be set up. Their roll-out would have to progress country by country. Some preliminary talks on governance had been held, but it now remained to set up its structure in detail. What kinds of steering organizations would be needed? How often should they meet? Janneke Steenhuis: 'I know from experience that at the start of an outsourcing partnership you need a high meeting frequency. Many issues come up that you haven't foreseen, and you need to be able to take quick decisions.' Attention also had to be paid to the coherence between the migration project and ERP service delivery. Ronald Verstraten: 'How could we make the temporary project governance structure grow into the permanent governance structure needed afterwards?' This meant it had to be decided who would attend which steering organizations. All parties to the partnership would demand to be represented, so who should represent them and in which meetings? Defining profiles matching the positions in the governance structure would provide a solid basis for the outsourcing relationships entered into.

 LECTURERS' NOTES

CASE STUDY: GOVERNANCE AND STEERING ORGANIZATIONS

Students should work out the governance structure for this IT outsourcing partnership, including the steering organizations needed (Tables 8.4 and 8.5). The parties involved are the recipient, their primary provider and the hardware provider, who subcontracts from the primary provider. Somewhat further removed are the recipient's ERP software provider and their ERP functional application support service provider. The steering organizations needed to make this partnership work should be defined as well as the people attending them. The coherence between the steering organizations must of course be ensured.

A distinction may be made between the project governance organization and that for the ERP maintenance contract, but care must be taken to ensure that they form a coherent whole. To ensure long-term continuity, those involved in the migration project must remain involved in the governance of the ERP maintenance contract. They must people the partnership's partner board, service review board and its service meetings. Attention will also have to be paid to the partner board's discharge of the steering committee.

For the success of the migration project it is essential that all parties participate actively. The system integrator cannot assume sole responsibility for its execution; from operating companies to hardware provider, all must join forces. This aspect,

Table 8.4 Steering organizations to be set up for the governance of the partnership, including the subjects discussed and the people attending them

Level*	Conference	Subjects discussed	Meeting frequency	Attendees – service recipient	Attendees – service provider
S	IT Board	• Aligning future business requirements • Providing business managers with an overview of technical innovations	Twice a year (IT is of strategic importance for the recipient)	• Chief information officer** • The corporate IT office's information managers • The corporate IT centre's IT director • Senior business managers from operating companies	• Note: experts from the service providers (the corporate information office is a mature organization, and fully responsible for IT on behalf of the operating companies)
S	Partner Board	• Joint strategic planning • Resolving issues escalated from the tactical level • Relationship building	Twice a year (ERP service provisioning is of strategic importance for the recipient)	• Chief information officer • The corporate IT office's information managers • The corporate IT centre's IT director • Not: the operating companies' business managers (the corporate information office holds delegated responsibility for IT)	• The primary provider's client executives and possibly their sector director • The primary provider's customer operations director • Possibly: functional application support manager (because of the importance of his services) • Not: representatives of the hardware provider (the primary provider acts as systems integrator) • Not: representatives of the ERP software provider (whose role is limited to delivering licences and support services)
S	Change Advisory Board	• Change requests approvals	Every two months (ERP system dynamics are considerable, so it must be possible to make changes quickly and monitor them well)	• Information managers of the corporate information office • The corporate IT services centre's information analysts and functional application managers • Business managers of the operating companies (they make the requests, which will influence their business management)	• The primary provider's service delivery managers, customer operations manager and service managers • The functional application support provider's service delivery managers, customer operations manager and service managers In this combined meeting, the primary provider (as systems integrator) takes the lead on behalf of all service providers

T	Service Portfolio Board	• The appropriateness of new technologies	Yearly (This partnership concerns ERP only; higher meeting frequencies are unnecessary)	• Information managers • The corporate information office's contract managers • Not: business managers' representatives (the corporate information office holds delegated responsibility for IT)	• The primary provider's lead technical officer (contributes lessons learnt from other partnerships) No Service Portfolio Board meets to discuss ERP licences and ERP functional application support, since their size and dynamics do not require such a conference
T	Service Review Meeting	• Service provider performance • Improvement plan status (Separate Service Review Meetings are held for each outsourcing contract: ERP hosting, ERP functional application support and ERP licences)	• Monthly (ERP hosting and ERP functional application support – being of central importance, these need frequent discussion) • Twice a year (ERP licences – whose changes are limited)	• The corporate information office's contract managers • The corporate information office's information managers This being of central importance, the attention of both is required (for contract aspects and overall responsibility, respectively)	• The primary provider's customer operations director and service delivery managers, who hold final responsibility • The functional application support provider's account manager and service delivery managers, who are responsible for the relationship and the actual delivery of the services, respectively • The ERP software provider's account manager (since this provider's role is limited, their service managers do not attend)
T	Contract Review Meeting	• Advance invoice approval (Separate Contract Review Meetings are held for ERP hosting and ERP functional application support; ERP licensing does not require one)	Monthly (All invoices are calculated and sent monthly, a consequence of the services being delivered continuously)	• The corporate information office's purchasing managers • The corporate information office's contract manager (who must approve the invoices' contents)	• The primary provider's client manager and customer operations director (to explain and to safeguard their commercial interests) • The functional application support provider's account manager and service delivery managers (to explain)

Continued

Table 8.4 Continued

Level*	Conference	Subjects discussed	Meeting frequency	Attendees – service recipient	Attendees – service provider
O	Service Meeting	• Day-to-day service provisioning issues	Weekly	• The corporate information office's <u>contract manager</u> and information analysts • The corporate IT centre's functional application managers • Not: the operating companies' business managers (the corporate information office holds delegated responsibility for IT)	• The primary provider's <u>customer operations manager</u> and service delivery manager • The functional application support provider's service delivery managers • Not: representatives of the ERP software provider (their services being limited) In this combined meeting, the primary provider (as systems integrator) takes the lead on behalf of all service providers
O	Change Control Meeting	• Analysing the implications of implementing change requests • Implementing approved change requests	Weekly	• Information analysts • The corporate IT services centre's functional application managers • Not: the corporate information office (this meeting is too operational in focus)	• The primary provider's <u>service managers</u> • The functional application support provider's service delivery managers In this combined meeting, the primary provider (as systems integrator) takes the lead on behalf of all service providers
O	Project Meeting	• Day-to-day project execution issues Since this meeting concerns new projects, outside the contracts' scopes, the migration project is not discussed here	Weekly or daily (depending on the size and the impact of the projects)	• The corporate information office's <u>contract manager</u> and information analysts • The corporate IT services centre's functional application managers • Not: the operating companies' business managers (the corporate information office holds delegated responsibility for IT)	• The primary provider's <u>project managers</u> and customer operations manager

Notes   * S: strategic; T: tactical; O: operational.
     ** The underlined attendees are in charge for their respective companies.

Table 8.5 Steering organizations to be set up for the migration project, including the subjects discussed and the people attending them

Level*	Conference	Subjects discussed	Meeting frequency	Attendees – service recipient	Attendees – service provider
S	Steering Committee	• Migration project supervision	Monthly (Extra meetings are held on the program manager's request when necessary)	• Chief information officer • The corporate information office's information managers • The operating companies' business managers (required because of the importance of the subject)	• The primary provider's client executives and possibly their sector director** • The hardware supplier's migration manager (for consulting purposes)
T	Programme Management Meeting	• General progress • Project risk management	Weekly	• The corporate information office's information managers • The corporate IT services centre's managers (corporate-level representatives attend tactical-level meetings because of the importance of the subject)	• The primary provider's migration manager • The hardware supplier's migration manager
O	Project Meeting	• Progress • Sub-project risk management	Daily	• The corporate IT services centre's managers	• The primary provider's project leader • The hardware supplier's project leader

Notes: *S: strategic; T: tactical; O: operational.

** The underlined attendees are in charge for their respective companies.

which is of essential importance to the recipient's business continuity, must be included in the students' governance structure.

Considering the strategic importance of the migration project, the recipient's business units will be more closely involved in it than in other parts of the outsourcing set-up. Since the migration will cause the ERP applications to be out of order for a short period, this aspect and its timing will require thorough planning in collaboration with the operating companies (Table 8.6).

Table 8.6 *Overview steering organizations and levels vs ITIL processes*

Conferences and levels		ITIL processes									
Level	Conference	Call management	Incident management	Problem management	Change management	Production	Query management	Configuration management	Complaint management	Service control and distribution	Service level management
T	Service review meeting	X	X	X			X			X	X
T	Contract review board								X		X
T	Service portfolio board					X		X			
O	Service meeting	X	X	X	X	X	X		X		X
O	Change control meeting				X			X		X	
O	Project meeting										

NOTES

1 The staff involved are discussed in Chapters 6 and 7.
2 This case study is based on structured interviews with executives of all three parties, which were held in May 2003, less than 12 months after the outsourcing contract was signed. They were previously published in Beulen and Ribbers (2004: 283–310). The material was rewritten for the purposes of this book. All names are fictional.
3 Functional application support was not included in the outsourcing contract discussed here. Part of it was outsourced to another provider, the rest was carried out by the recipient's internal IT department.

REFERENCES

Barney, J. (1991) 'Firm resources and sustained competitive advantage', *Journal of Management*, 17 (1): 99–120.

Barthelemy, J. (2003) 'The hard and soft sides of IT outsourcing management', *European Management Journal*, 21 (5): 539–548.

Beulen, E. (2000) 'Beheersing van IT-outsourcingsrelaties: een beheersingsmodel voor uitbestedende bedrijven en IT-leveranciers', PhD thesis, Tilburg University (in Dutch).

Beulen, E. (2002) *Uitbesteding van IT-dienstverlening*, Den Haag: Ten Hagen en Stam (in Dutch).

Beulen, E. and Ribbers, P. (2004) 'Value creation in application outsourcing relationships: an international case study on ERP outsourcing', in W. Currie (ed.) *Value Creation from e-Business Models*, Oxford: Butterworth-Heinemann.

CCTA (1993) *The Infrastructure Library: An Introduction*, London: CCTA.

Coase, R. (1937) 'The nature of the firm', *Economica*, 4: 386–405.

Cullen, S. and Willcocks, L. (2003) *Intelligent IT Outsourcing: Eight Building Blocks to Success*, Oxford: Butterworth-Heinemann.

DesJardins, J. (1998) 'Corporate environmental responsibility', *Journal of Business Ethics*, 17 (8): 825–838.

Domberger, S., Fernandez, P. and Fiebig, D.G. (2000) 'Modelling the price, performance and contract characteristics of IT outsourcing', *Journal of Information Technology*, 15 (2): 107–118.

Fama, E. and Jensen, M. (1983) 'Separation of ownership and control', *Journal of Law and Economics*, 26: 301–326.

Fukuyama, F. (1995) *Trust*, London: Hamish Hamilton.

Gadrey, J. and Gallouj, F. (1998) 'The provider–customer interface in business and professional services', *The Service Industries Journal*, 18 (2): 1–15.

Kern, T. and Willcocks, L. (2000) 'Exploring information technology outsourcing relationships: theory and practice', *The Journal of Strategic Information Systems*, 9 (4): 321–350.

Kern, T., Willcocks, L. and van Heck, E. (2002) 'Strategy & organization – the winner's curse in IT outsourcing: – strategies for avoiding relational trauma', *California Management Review*, 44 (2): 47–69.

Kishore, R. (2003) 'A relationship perspective on IT outsourcing', *Communications of the Association for Computing Machinery*, 46 (12): 86–92.

Klepper, R. (1995) 'The management of partnering development in I/S outsourcing', *Journal of Technology*, 10 (4): 249–258.

Lacity, M. and Hirschheim, R. (1993) *Information Systems Outsourcing*, Chichester: Wiley & Sons.

Lacity, M. and Hirschheim, R. (1995) *Beyond the Information Systems Outsourcing Bandwagon*, Chichester: Wiley & Sons.

Langfield-Smith, K. and Smith, D. (2003) 'Management control systems and trust in outsourcing relationships', *Management Accounting Research*, 14 (3): 281–297.

Mouritsen, J. (1999) 'The flexible firm: strategies for a subcontractor's management control', *Accounting, Organizations and Society*, 24 (1): 31–55.

Peppard, J. (1999) 'Managing IT as a portfolio of services', *European Management Journal*, 21 (4): 467–483.

Prahalad, C. and Hamel, G. (1991) 'The core competence of the corporation' in C. Montgomery and M. Porter (eds) *Strategy: 'Seeking and Securing Competitive Advantage'*, Boston, MA: Harvard Business School Press.

Purser, S. (2001) 'A simple graphical tool for modelling trust', *Computers & Security*, 20 (6): 479–484.

Segal, I. (1999) 'Complexity and renegotiation: a foundation for incomplete contracts', *Review of Economic Studies*, 66 (226): 57–82.

Tirole, J. (1989) *The Industry of Organizations*, Cambridge, MA: MIT Press.

van Grembergen, W., De Haes, S. and Guldentops, E. (2003) 'Using COBIT and the Balanced Scorecard as instruments for service level management', *The Information Systems Control Journal*, 4: 56–62.

Willcocks, L. and Fitzgerald, G. (1994) *A Business Guide to Outsourcing IT*, London: Business Intelligence.

Williamson, O. (1975) *Markets and Hierarchies*, New York: Free Press.

Chapter 9

Offshore outsourcing

- Offshore outsourcing introduces extra risks for both the service recipient and their provider.
- Different risk profiles apply for software development and infrastructure management.
- Recipients must determine which kind of offshore outsourcing is best for their purposes: captive, native or foreign service-provisioning.

9.1 INTRODUCTION

Offshore outsourcing, the transfer of IT service delivery responsibility to a provider operating from a continent different from the recipient, is experiencing a growth period with double-digit figures. In comparison with ordinary outsourcing, however, it does require some extra governance. And since not all offshore outsourcing relationships are going well, there is a need to understand these governance aspects better. To that end, the authors have attempted to outline in this chapter the knowledge and know-how collected in the large amount of business literature (Lacity and Hirschheim 1993, 1995; Klepper 1995; McFarlan and Nolan 1995; Rajkumar and Dawley 1997; Carmel 1999; Beulen and Ribbers 2003) in which researchers have reported on the difficulties of managing such relationships. We will first, in Section 9.2, take a look at the market developments influencing the rise of offshore outsourcing. Then the risks associated with it will be discussed in Section 9.3. The two most important kinds of IT services involved, software development and infrastructure management, are the subject of Section 9.4, with an emphasis on their characteristics and risk profiles. On this basis the risk-mitigating strategies of Section 9.5 are elaborated. Finally, the recipient's and provider's responsibilities are discussed in Sections 9.6 and 9.7.

9.2 OFFSHORE OUTSOURCING – MARKET DEVELOPMENTS

Offshore outsourcing may be defined as the transfer of the responsibility for delivering IT services to a provider who delivers these services from a continent different from where the recipient operates (after Carmel 1999). The difference with ordinary outsourcing is this geographic distance between provider and recipient. Sometimes an intermediary kind of outsourcing is distinguished: nearshore outsourcing, which is then taken to be outsourcing to a provider operating from a low-wage country on the same continent as that of the recipient. The issues facing companies who engage in nearshore outsourcing are very similar to those of offshore outsourcing, however, and the difference will therefore not be discussed further here.

The long-term business strategies of many West European and North American multinationals of today incorporate offshore outsourcing as an essential component. Shell recently announced its collaboration with IBM Global Services and Wipro (McDougall 2004), for example, while Procter & Gamble (DiCarlo 2003) and General Motors (Copeland 2002) have also offshored substantial parts of their IT services. The most important reasons for doing so are cost savings and globalization (Vijayan 1996; Carmel 1999; Marshall and Cohan 2003; Robinson and Kalakola 2004). Most services that are outsourced are delivered from India (Nasscom and McKinsey 2002). In addition, China also offers reasonably qualified resources, and in almost inexhaustible quantities (Dedrick and Kraemer 2001; Qu and Brockelehurst 2003). East European countries such as Russia, Hungary, Poland and the Czech Republic are suitable candidates for offshore outsourcing as well, as is Ireland (Marriot 2004). Providing outsourced IT services makes a major contribution to these countries' economies (Carmel and Agarwal 2002).

Offshore outsourcing is not an isolated phenomenon. Related developments, such as globalization, the increasing differentiation on the supply side and the socio-political developments caused by offshoring, must therefore be looked into briefly. Nowadays many companies have relationships with suppliers and clients located at much greater distances than before. This process is called globalization, and specialization and scale increases enhance this trend. The step towards collaboration with IT providers operating from low-wage countries has thus become small, especially since the ongoing technological developments render distances less and less of a problem. The growing maturity of the IT services market also contributes to the potential for offshore outsourcing relationships. Of course, multinationals were the first to engage in them, since they were already used to international relationships and their management. But medium-large and small companies are also beginning to consider offshoring. The limiting factor usually is the volume of the services to be delivered. Offshore outsourcing governance involves extra coordination costs, and if the volume is insufficient these cannot be recouped.

At first, only service providers located in low-wage countries offered offshore outsourcing services. These were companies like Cognizant, Tata, CS Wipro, IMR and Xansa. Now, however, the supply side is differentiating. Providers headquartered in Western countries, such as Atos Origin, CSC, EDS and IBM, have also set up subsidiaries in low-wage countries. Potentially, these offer them a competitive advantage because, while they already know their clients' world and therefore their needs, the new subsidiaries enable them to offer their services much more inexpensively than before. Another differentiating development is the increase in the number of companies setting up shared IT service centres in low-wage countries. General Electric, General Motors and the World Bank have done so in India, from where they deliver to all their branches in the world. This increases the volume of services that are offshored significantly.

Offshore outsourcing also raises new organizational and societal issues (Fitzgerald 2003; Hierbert and Slater 2003). Even though economists emphasize the benefits of offshoring (Schwartz and Wright 2004), quite a number of jobs for highly qualified staff disappear because of it. Labour unions and employees' councils therefore have placed this subject high on their agendas. In Europe this issue is made even more topical by the East European countries who have joined the Union recently. They have become very attractive as offshore oursourcing locations because the barriers for doing business with them have largely been removed. The social unrest this development causes expresses itself in, for example, the 'Buy American' movement in the United States or on websites such as www.outsourceoutrage.com, where attention is drawn to American IT professionals who have lost their jobs. Such lobbying has understandably made many companies hesitant about offshore outsourcing: they do not want the negative publicity that lay-offs would bring. As yet, such a strong anti-offshoring lobby is an American phenomenon only, but other countries may soon follow. In this respect one has to recognize, however, the fact that offshore outsourcing not only costs jobs; it also creates positions. Extra staff are needed to coordinate service delivery from the provider to the client, which involves crossing borders and large distances. These are project and contract management tasks, for which more people are now needed than before. It nevertheless remains true that many operational-level jobs are transferred away from the high-wage countries in which the recipients are located.

Politics have also naturally become involved in this debate. The number of politicians demanding protectionist measures – perhaps somewhat under the influence of the fact that positions at a rather high qualification level are concerned – is remarkable. It is also noticeable that few governments have engaged in offshore outsourcing yet. In fact, governments traditionally do not outsource much at all. This can partly be explained from the fact that, for instance, privacy security laws have much greater consequences for governments than they do for businesses. Moving certain tasks to locations outside the European Union, for example, is subject to a number of very limiting conditions. Nevertheless, this situation is changing gradually. Several Dutch ministries have outsourced not only their data centres and networks but their entire infrastructure management and application development. Offshore outsourcing may be the next step for them too.

9.3 OFFSHORE OUTSOURCING – THE RISKS

The risks associated with offshore outsourcing are diverse. There are cultural differences to contend with, the people involved speak different languages and work in different time zones – to name but a few. An extensive list of these risks is presented in Table 9.1.

9.4 RISK PROFILES FOR SOFTWARE DEVELOPMENT AND INFRASTRUCTURE MANAGEMENT

There are many kinds of IT services (Buck-Lew 1992; Klepper 1995; Aubert et al. 2004), but for the purpose of a risk assessment with respect to offshore outsourcing it is software development and infrastructure management that are especially important. Their characteristics will therefore be discussed in the next subsections (summarized in Table 9.2), and on that basis we will attempt to distinguish the risks associated with offshoring them (Figure 9.1). One characteristic can already be mentioned here: to achieve cost benefits from offshoring software development, the contract value must exceed 500,000 euros per annum; for infrastructure management, which is less labour intensive, the threshold is one million euros.

9.4.1 Software development

Software development, also called application development, means that new applications are custom-made in order to enhance functionality; it may also take the form of modifying or enhancing customized or packaged applications. The integration, detailed design and implementation of those applications and the management needed to link them to each other and the recipient's current or planned IT infrastructure are included in this definition; so are services provided to support their implementation and roll-out (Sadlowski 1998). An example of how such an outsourcing relationship works is provided by a service delivery manager working for a US-based software producer (Case XXX; see Appendix, p. 268, for all Case details):

> Apart from application management we provide customer-specific software codes that provide additional functionality to our client's software products. We meet them weekly for detailed discussions on the applications' specifications. Such a frequency is necessary to ensure the functionality of the applications and the continued alignment of our services with their changing needs.

Table 9.1 *Risks associated with offshore outsourcing (based on Beulen et al. 2005)*

Risk category	Description
Culture (Aeh 1990; Meadows 1996; Rajkumar and Dawley 1997; Ramarapu et al. 1997; Carmel 1999)	Cultural differences – derived from both national and corporate cultures – influence offshore outsourcing relationships.
Language barriers (Aeh 1990; Ravichandran and Ahmed 1993; Meadows 1996; Vijayan 1996; Rajkumar and Dawley 1997; Carmel 1999; Raval 1999)	A limited understanding of English (as that of non-native speakers) may hinder the service delivery process.
Time-zone differences (Aeh 1990; Ravichandran and Ahmed 1993; Smith et al. 1996; Rajkumar and Dawley 1997; Carmel 1999; van Fenema 2002)	The interaction between the recipient's representatives and those of their provider may be hindered by time-zone differences.
Managing scope changes (McFarlan and Nolan 1995; Vijayan 1996; van Fenema 2002)	Changes in the scope of the offshore outsourcing contract have consequences for the service delivery process. Attention must therefore be paid to uniform service delivery processes and certification support.
Human capital (Barney 1991; Ramarapu et al. 1997; Feeny and Willcocks 1998)	The provider may not have employees with the right skills and competences, thus limiting the quality of the service delivery process.
Rotating onshore resources (Meadows 1996; Carmel and Argarwal 2002)	Due to staff rotation the team responsible for delivery may lack stability, hindering the service delivery process.
Infrastructure (Carmel and Argarwal 2002; Khan et al. 2003)	If the supporting infrastructure (for telecommunications, data, etc.) lacks stability, the service delivery process may be hindered.
Security and privacy (Smith et al. 1996; Carmel 1999; Khan et al. 2003)	Both parties' physical assets and intellectual property must be protected to ensure the continuity of the service delivery process.

Continued

Table 9.1 *Continued*

Risk category	Description
Knowledge transfer (Carmel 1999; Rajkumar and Mani 2001; van Fenema 2002)	Knowledge transfer processes between provider and recipient essential to the service delivery process are at risk. In addition knowledge transfer is vulnerable to cultural, language and communications risks.
Understanding the recipient's business processes (Livingstone 1992; Rajkumar and Dawley 1997)	If the provider and their staff do not understand their client's business processes, the service delivery process may be hindered.
Geopolitical risks (Aeh 1990; Smith et al. 1996; Smith et al. 1996; Carmel 1999)	War, terrorism and internal armed conflicts may disturb the continuity of the delivery, which might impact on investments of the service provider. Reasonably stable regions are preferred as provider locations.
Service volume (Carmel 1999; Robb 2000; Cullen and Willcocks 2003)	The size of the contract must be substantial for the service provider to recover their coordination costs.
Contract duration (Williamson 1975; Smith et al. 1996; Aubert et al. 2004)	The duration of the contract period determines how much opportunity the provider has to recover his costs, such as investments. Short-term contracts will make proper service provisioning difficult, but long-term contracts involve the risk of lock-in effects for either party or both. A balance must be sought.

As this example shows, software development is characterized by short-term contracts, frequent interaction with end users and dynamic requirements. The main risks associated with offshoring are language barriers, time-zone differences and cultural clashes (Sinha and Terdiman 2002). Geopolitical risks are relevant too (Smith *et al.* 1996) because it is expensive and time-consuming to move software development to another geographical location. The risks associated with immature telecommunication infrastructures are less important, for software development is not a very time-critical activity (Sinha and Terdiman 2002). Online transaction processing, for example, must be carried out real-time, but in software development a downtime of a day is no problem. This also implies that security risks are relatively unimportant (van Fenema 2002).

9.4.2 Infrastructure management

Infrastructure management consists of operational services, application management services and helpdesk management services. It therefore includes preventive and remedial services for the physical reparation or optimization of hardware (including telephones); technical trouble-shooting; and all fee- and warranty-based assistance in setting up and upgrading hardware (computers, DASD, tape products, network products, terminals, printers and copiers). Online or telephonic trouble-shooting, installation assistance and basic usability assistance (concerning operating systems for desktop computers, networks and servers; application software for personal productivity, that is, for word processing, making presentations and using databases; and systems and network management software and tools and utilities, such as performance monitoring and virus detection) are also included (Sadlowski 1998).

Infrastructure management is characterized by long-term contracts, a limited interaction with one's end users, and process-driven and stable requirements. The service delivery manager of a large European-based discrete-manufacturing company (Case VII) explains why their relationships with their clients have long contract periods: 'We run ERP applications for our customers. The costs of setting up and implementing these services are substantial. Therefore we have contracted for 36 months, with an annual renewal option.' The most important risks associated with offshoring infrastructure management, then, are either of a geopolitical nature (Sinha and Terdiman 2002), or associated with security (Fitzgerald 2003) or the immaturity of telecommunication infrastructures (Carmel and Agarwal 2002). Geopolitical risks generally are countered by operating several service provisioning centres; if one of them is unexpectedly unable to deliver, another can take over to ensure the agreed service levels are met. Nevertheless, in such cases the provider suffers significant losses, for the depreciation on their investments (Currie and Willcocks 1998; Robb 2000) is substantial. Telecommunication infrastructure and security have to function at the highest possible level because infrastructure management is a very time-critical affair requiring real-time actions. On the other

Table 9.2 *The characteristics of software development and infrastructure management (based on Beulen et al. 2005)*

Characteristics	Software development	Infrastructure management
Service types (Johnson and Andrew 1994; Sadlowskie 1998; Tardugno *et al.* 2000;	Projects (12-month contracts maximum)	Continuous services (36-month contracts minimum)
Service levels (Beaver 1985; Duncombe 1992; David *et al.* 2002)	Measured by checking the project deliverables and their timing	Measured continuously during the entire contract period
Interaction between providers, end users and their managers (Ocker *et al.* 1998; Carter 1999; Gruhn and Schope 2002; Olsson 2004)	High frequency, in order to ensure the continued alignment of services and requirements	Low frequency – only when the service delivery is disturbed
Requirement dynamics (Abdel-Hamid 1993; Besson and Rowe 2001; Appelgate *et al.* 2003)	High – business requirements change constantly, so the client's IT service requirements do too	Low – stability during the entire contract period
Components of the total service provisioning costs (Paul 1998; Ross *et al.* 1999; Tardugno *et al.* 2000; David *et al.* 2002; Gerlach *et al.* 2002)	Mainly labour-related costs	Labour and investments costs
Benchmarking possibilities (Schwartz 1998; Tardugno *et al.* 2000; Doll *et al.* 2003)	Limited to the rates paid for the IT professionals involved	Potentially per component (price per server, price per managed SAP-seat, etc.)
Non-contract-specific investments required (Kim *et al.* 2000; Irani 2002; Ross and Beath 2002)	Only for certified service delivery processes	For certified service delivery processes and hardware investments
The importance of security (Badenhorst and Eloff 1989; McGraw 2002; Appelgate *et al.* 2003)	Only for the physical environment in which the development work takes place (physical security)	For the service delivery environment (physical security) and communications (information security)

hand, since infrastructure management providers interact relatively little with their clients, the risks associated with cultural clashes, time-zone differences and language barriers are of minor importance.

9.4.3 Risk profiles

It is now clear that the offshore outsourcing risks listed in Section 9.3 differ in their importance for software development and infrastructure management. In Figure 9.1

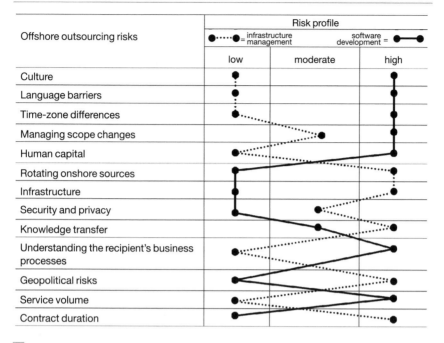

Figure 9.1 *Risk profiles for the offshore outsourcing of software development and infrastructure management (Beulen et al. 2005)*

each risk is scored as high, moderate or low. Companies engaging in offshore outsourcing should pay thorough attention to these risk profiles, as should their providers.

9.5 RISK MITIGATING STRATEGIES

To minimalize the risks associated with offshore outsourcing, several risk-mitigating strategies can be implemented. The six most important of these are:

1 working on the basis of certified processes;
2 using standardized tools;
3 ensuring that one's communication facilities are in good order;
4 selecting reliable local partners;
5 using standardized service-level agreements; and
6 implementing good contract management.

These strategies, which will be discussed in more detail below, must be implemented by the recipient and the provider jointly. Outsourcing companies would therefore do well to verify whether their intended provider does indeed work on the basis of such strategies.

There are several kinds of worldwide certification systems that can be applied to offshore outsourcing processes. The most important of these are the Capability Maturity Model (CMM), which is the standard for application development, and ISO, BS9977 and BS15000 for infrastructure management. These involve extensive audits by independent institutes. They offer outsourcing companies the enhanced safety of controlled security, language, time-zone and culture risks. Even geopolitical risks are diminished by certification, because IT service delivery can more easily be transferred to another location if the provider is certified. At the moment, however, few providers actually work with certified processes, although their number is growing.

Most service providers have adopted the service delivery tools prescribed by the IT Infrastructure Library (ITIL). Thus, it is easier to transfer IT service delivery to professionals in low-wage countries: standardized tools lessen the importance of time, culture and language barriers. And being standardized, these tools also help providers to produce consolidated reports by making it less expensive to do so. For software development the most important tools are those for project management, since they help monitor the project's progress. Which tools are used for the development work itself is less important; it depends strongly on the development platform the provider uses and therefore does not require nearly as much standardization. Within the boundaries of a single project, using standardized tools is, of course, advisable.

Currently there is a worldwide surplus in telecommunication facilities. Service providers can easily lease lines for their service delivery. This means they do not need dedicated lines for every client, since they can simply lease an extra line if the fluctuations in data communication volume demand it. Even if these lines have a limited bandwidth per line, combining them enables providers to serve many clients inexpensively. On the other hand, due to overcapacity, dedicated communication lines are used to reduce security risks of the service provisioning. Overall, then, the infrastructure immaturity risk is limited. And even though providers serving companies in the European Union must be aware that the Union has strict laws on data processing outside its borders, this need not prevent them from engaging in remote infrastructure management if the hardware concerned is physically located in Europe. For software development communication facilities are of less critical importance. But this may change if providers start the remote testing of applications: then reliable communication facilities are of the essence, since this requires real-time actions.

The importance of having reliable local partners is greater for software development than for infrastructure management. In application development projects there are often workload peaks, and the provider must then be able to fall back upon locally available IT professionals. To hire these, providers need local partners they can rely on. In this respect offshore outsourcing is no different from ordinary outsourcing. As we have seen, infrastructure management workloads are a little less dynamic. In this field local partners are needed because some 1 per cent of the tasks must always be carried out by people who are physically present at the client's location. This is no problem for the major hardware suppliers such as Dell, HP or IBM; they have many branches world-wide and can easily send someone from one of those subsidiaries. But even they collaborate with local partners to increase their geographic spread. And for smaller providers this is the only way, since the travelling needed otherwise would be prohibitively expensive in terms of costs and time. All providers therefore need to establish partnerships, that is, long-term relationships with partners with whom they collaborate regularly so that these partners know the provider's processes and procedures. Doing so enhances the quality of the services delivered and it diminishes any culture, language, time-zone and security risks.

In infrastructure management many providers work with catalogues of standardized services with standardized service-level agreements, from which their clients select the ones they need. This enables those providers to deliver their services inexpensively. Also, their professionals can work for several clients at a time, and the standardization decreases the need for communication and so diminishes any culture, language and time-zone risks. The concept of service levels does not really apply to software development: it is project work, the deliverables of which must always be defined uniquely and unambiguously. The Information Services Procurement Library (see www.projekte.fast.de/ISPL/), however, has developed a more or less standardized delivery plan to help the recipient and their provider gain clarity on what should be delivered and when.

Implementing good contract management is of critical importance for both infrastructure management and software development. Doing so requires setting up contract management in both the recipient's country and the low-wage country to which the service delivery has been offshored (a set-up called mirrored contract management), since this enables the provider to react quickly and adequately. Of course, this raises the costs, but these must be considered necessary coordination costs because they diminish the culture, language and time-zone risks involved. The contract manager in the low-wage country should preferably both have affinity with local conditions and circumstances and have work experience in the West. In the case of software development, contract management is often called programme management, but a mirrored set-up remains equally important. The high-wage-country team is frequently called the steering committee and includes the recipient's business managers. The low-wage-country team is then held accountable to them for the project's progress and deliverables.

9.6 THE SERVICE RECIPIENT'S RESPONSIBILITIES

Companies who consider engaging in offshore outsourcing must weigh the pros and cons carefully. This decision always remains their own responsibility, and their deliberations must centre around their business strategy. The IT strategy derived from their business strategy by their chief information officer (CIO) and his information managers defines the contribution IT will make to the company's business processes. It may include guidelines and best practices – such as application standards, hardware brands policies or security policies – especially for those IT services that are used by several of the company's divisions.

From their IT strategy the outsourcing company must in turn derive their sourcing strategy, in which they define which services are to be delivered by their internal IT department and which by external suppliers: the make-or-buy decision. Arguments in favour of outsourcing are gaining access to new technologies, increasing one's flexibility, and enhanced cost predictability. Increased costs, the risk of becoming dependent on providers and the loss of confidentiality, knowledge and know-how argue against it. The make-or-buy decision will turn out differently for each service and each business unit.

Once a buy decision has been taken, the choice remains between ordinary outsourcing and offshore outsourcing. Again, the decision must be taken according to predetermined criteria that include the specific services needed and the nature of the business processes involved. Only if the company's sourcing strategy is considered in the perspective of their business and IT strategies (Figure 9.2) can such decisions be made in a responsible way.

9.6.1 Specific issues: geographical spread and the degree of standardization

If the outsourcing company has decided to offshore certain services, they must consider two extra issues: their geographical spread and its consequences, and the degree

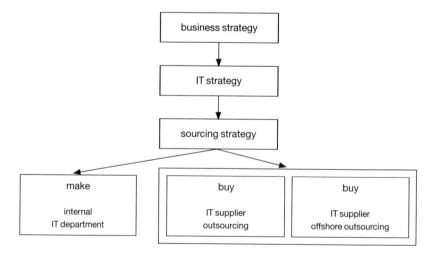

Figure 9.2 *The relationships between companies' business, IT and sourcing strategies and the make-or-buy and onshore–offshore decisions*

to which the services needed have to be standardized. Service recipients who operate out of more than one region or country have to take this aspect into consideration when they engage in offshore outsourcing. Providing services to a recipient with a large geographical spread is complicated. For software development projects much coordination work is needed to cross the multiple culture, time-zone and language barriers; for infrastructure management it is the complexity and insecurity of the communication infrastructure that increases with the recipient's geographical spread. Consequently, providers need global processes and tools to guarantee the governance required in terms of their interaction with their clients (van Fenema 2002). Another complication for geographically widespread companies is presented by the legal consequences of offshore outsourcing. Although international regulations are emerging, countries still have their own laws (Fitzgerald 2003). Both the service recipient and their providers must comply with the laws of every country involved.

Standardization offers the possibility of achieving economies of scale and therefore cost savings. In offshore outsourcing, in which communication plays a major role, standardization is even more desirable: it means that less communication is needed, which decreases the well-known risks of culture, language and time-zone barriers. The degree to which standardization can be implemented depends on both technological choices and governance issues. The recipient's IT strategy provides guidance with respect to the technology to be used – hardware and software platforms, for instance. But the CIO's power is often limited (Cullen and Willcocks 2003) because the company's business managers hold a stronger position, even over its IT budget. Therefore it is sometimes difficult to implement the company's IT strategy, and standardization may be difficult to achieve. Outsourcing organizations should be well aware of this issue because it may jeopardize the success of their offshore relationships.

9.7 THE SERVICE PROVIDER'S RESPONSIBILITIES

The most important issue for service providers to pay attention to is the availability of the resources needed to deliver their services and manage relationships with their clients (Lacity and Hirschheim 1993; Klepper 1995; Beulen 2004). These resources include hardware and software as well as people. In the case of offshore outsourcing, most of the delivery work is done in the low-wage environment of a developing country. This is what makes offshore outsourcing financially attractive. But since today's business dynamics cause frequent changes in the services needed, the provider must have a customer interface near the recipient's location – that is, in the West – in order to react in good time and adequately when such fluctuations occur (Marriot 2004). Having a local customer interface also contributes to keeping the culture, language and time-zone risks under control. Therefore, additional resources are required to coordinate the service delivery and relationship management processes.

Apart from this primary responsibility for their resources, what providers must do depends to a large extent on the kind of offshore outsourcing they provide. Essentially, the choice is between captive outsourcing, native outsourcing and foreign outsourcing. If the recipient's parent company also owns the provider, this is called captive outsourcing, a pattern found with large multinational corporations. A provider that has been set up by its parent specifically for this purpose is often called a shared service centre. Otherwise, the recipient and their provider have a customer–supplier relationship (Carmel and Agarwal 2002). Then the provider may either be a subsidiary of a company headquartered in the same region as their client (native outsourcing) or it may operate from the developing country and have a customer interface subsidiary in the West (foreign outsourcing). Examples of native providers are companies such as Atos Origin (based in France), Logica CMG (UK), and CSC, EDS and IBM (all in the USA). The earliest companies offering offshore outsourcing services, however, were of the third kind: Cognizant, Satyam, Tata Consultancy Services and Xansa are all foreign providers based in India. In the last subsections of this chapter we will take a detailed look into the responsibilities of the provider in each of these situations.

9.7.1 Captive service provisioning

If the provider delivering the IT services is owned by the same parent company as the recipient, this outsourcing pattern is called captive service provisioning, as detailed in Figure 9.3. The recipient's information office is then responsible not only for implementing the company's IT strategy, which has been developed on the basis of its business strategy, but for the overall coordination of the offshore operations involved as well. No local customer interfaces are needed for governance purposes because the provider is familiar with the recipient's company culture, internal politics and business processes. Money can thus be saved on coordination. On the other hand, economies of scale are harder to achieve, so the cost effectiveness of the service delivery itself can be limited.

Setting up captive service provisioning can only be done by companies of a substantial size. And they must have experience with the creation of foreign subsidiaries, as the services are to be delivered from a developing country. Not many companies meet these two conditions. The chief financial officer of Ford Europe, a large automobile corporation, who doubles as its vice-president for strategic planning, provides an example of the size of the operations involved:

> We have concentrated our European accounting services in Chennai, in the Indian province of Madras. This shared service centre employs a staff of 500 who process the reconciliations of 2,000 accounts as well as our payables and receivables. Their services are offered on a 24×7 basis and several European languages are spoken to facilitate the end users.[1]

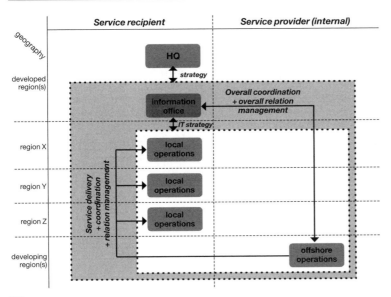

Figure 9.3 *Captive service provisioning*

A financial manager of GE Consumer Finance provided an indication in the same order of magnitude:

> Seventy per cent of our application development work is outsourced, 77 per cent of which is carried out in eight development centres in low-wage countries. And we have also set up a subsidiary in India that employs 16,000 people to deliver business process outsourcing services.[2]

Another condition to be met is that of the substantial minimum service volume. Only if generic IT services can be delivered during a longer period can advantages of scale be achieved. Software development in most cases is an activity for which major workload peaks alternate with relatively quiet periods, and it is therefore not ideal for captive outsourcing. Infrastructure management is more constant in this respect, but it has the disadvantage of being less labour intensive and so less susceptible to advantages of scale. The rule of thumb for an IT department in a low-wage country is that there must be work for a minimum of 50 IT professionals to generate economies of scale and achieve cost savings. But captive service provisioning only becomes really appealing if a staff of more than 250 can be employed. An important aspect here is the relatively high overhead costs of such a department, certainly if expatriates are required as managers.

In many cases, however, it is advisable to appoint an offshore manager who is a native of the low-wage country. Apart from being less expensive than expatriates, they know how to communicate with local governments, authorities and partners, and they are able to recruit better and less expensive local staff. This can be explained from the fact that the social cultures in many developing countries are still strongly family-focused: a local manager always brings his network. And, finally, local managers are often better at managing local staff because they experience no cultural differences.

Some companies engaging in captive service provisioning seek partnerships with existing local IT providers. Such partnerships resemble the pattern of foreign outsourcing (Section 9.7.3). But the collaboration is much closer because these partnership relations are continued also when there are no projects to work on. The outsourcing company thus ensures itself of their partner's loyalty, which means they can rely on their capacity if they need it. And another advantage is that the captive organization's IT professionals can do tasks for other companies if their own does not fill the agendas temporarily. This helps prevent overcapacity problems. An example of this set-up is the joint venture that credit card services provider Mastercard began in June 2004 with Mascon Global Ltd, an offshore IT supplier from Chennai, India, to develop and maintain the software for Mastercard's core business processes: authorization, clearing and settlement.

9.7.2 Native service provisioning

As we have seen in Section 9.6, implementing the recipient's IT strategy, developed on the basis of their business strategy, always remains their own responsibility. But whereas the recipient's information office is in the case of captive outsourcing also responsible for coordinating service delivery, in native outsourcing this is the provider's task, as detailed in Figure 9.4. Providers must therefore dedicate resources to managing their relationship with their client, and these are allocated to their

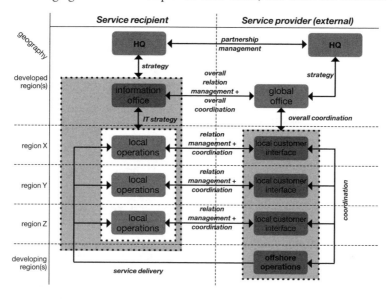

Figure 9.4 Native service provisioning

global office: a customer-specific unit that is responsible for service delivery to that client, for running the local interfaces needed and for the overall coordination of the operations involved. In addition, the global office manages the overall relationships with this client. Guidelines for a global office are derived from the provider's business strategy.

The global office's counterpart in the recipient's organization is the information office; these two represent the tactical level of the outsourcing relationship. On a strategic level the partnership must be anchored collaboratively by both participants' management boards, who also represent the ultimate escalation level should any difficulties arise. On the operational level it is the recipient's offshore operations office who coordinate service delivery to their local business units with the provider's local customer interfaces.

Native service provisioning offers recipients several advantages. For one, the risks of facing culture, language and time-zone barriers are reduced. Or rather, they are absorbed by the provider. For companies with limited international experience and know-how, foreign offshoring is often a bridge too far. They find it much more attractive to continue or extend their outsourcing relationships with native providers who transfer part of their delivery processes to low-wage countries but themselves remain nearby and in charge. In such a set-up, the outsourcing company can gain experience with offshoring without taking too many risks at once, while still achieving direct cost advantages. Many native outsourcing relationships therefore exhibit a mix of onshore and offshore elements. Only the standardized, labour-intensive tasks are then moved to a developing country. Important processes for which it is essential that all those involved understand each other well (such as decision-making on the services needed) can be carried out in an environment without language barriers because the people involved all work in the recipient's country. Indeed, many major IT providers see their offshore outsourcing work grow, especially in their relationships with existing customers. Nevertheless, they offer it to new clients as well in order to maintain their competitive positions vis-à-vis providers operating from low-wage environments.

Another advantage of native outsourcing is that the volume of the contract is much less important than in the case of captive outsourcing. Independent service providers normally have relationships with several customers and therefore reach the scale they need more easily than a subsidiary working only for other branches owned by its parent. This makes this outsourcing pattern much more attractive than captive outsourcing for clients who need very specific services that, while subject to sudden changes in nature and volume, are very important to the continuity of their business processes. In such cases it is generally preferred over foreign outsourcing too, since a native service provider does not have only a local customer interface, but a substantial number of locally available IT professionals who can step in when needed. This means that the culture, language and time-zone risks involved are reduced as well.

Having a native service provider who offshores part of its services also means that the recipient has less need of an extensive, high-level information management office. Controlling, coordinating and managing the recipient's IT suppliers is now to a large extent the provider's responsibility, certainly as far as communications with the offshore locations are concerned. The provider's costs, of course, do increase since they must have managers in both the high-wage and the low-wage countries, but the recipient saves money on FTEs.

Because of these advantages, collaborative partnerships are emerging between offshore suppliers operating out of low-wage countries and traditional IT providers in high-wage countries, especially if the latter lack sufficient offshore capacity themselves. These partnerships profit from the combination of a maximum presence in a Western business environment and a maximum capacity in a developing country. Thus, both communications and cost savings are optimized. Of course, such partnerships also experience specific risks. They must pay extra attention to their mutual communications, even if the Western partner is taking the lead. This involves extra coordination costs. Examples of such partnerships are those of IBM, HP and Sun Microsystems with Tata Consultancy Services. Likewise, IBM and Oracle have relationships with Satyam, and IBM, HP and Microsoft partner with Infosys.

9.7.3 Foreign service provisioning

The major difference between native and foreign outsourcing is the fact that the provider's head office and therefore its global office are located in another part of the world than the recipient. This difference has major consequences for the governance of the outsourcing relationship, as detailed in Figure 9.5. The tasks of the provider's global office are now limited to the coordination of their service delivery because, and more importantly, overall relationship management must now be handled by the provider's customer interface located near the recipient's information office. To this end, senior management presence in the customer interface is required, with a reporting line back to their head office. It is thus much more difficult to anchor the partnership strategically at management board level, as the boards operate on different continents, with all the consequent culture, language and time-zone barriers we have seen before. For this reason several offshore providers have set up regional head offices in Europe and America – not a very cost-effective measure considering the extra overhead, but one that contributes positively to the governance of their outsourcing relationships.

The degree to which culture, language and time-zone barriers play a role in foreign offshoring depends very much on the specific country to which service delivery is transferred. A business manager working for an internationally operating chemicals producer (Case III) tells of their experience:

Our current offshore outsourcing contracts are all with providers in India. Being used to working internationally, we find that collaboration with Indians is no

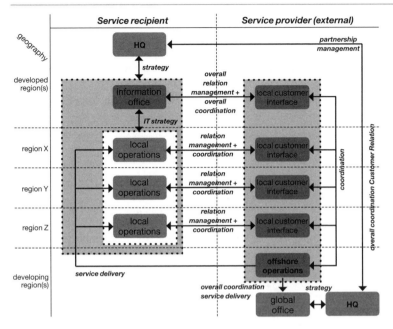

Figure 9.5 *Foreign service provisioning*

problem. However, I recently was in China to set up some new factories and while there I also looked into the possibilities of setting up partnerships with Chinese IT service providers. What I saw didn't inspire much confidence. Language is a major problem and, besides, the Chinese are still much less experienced in the international business world than Indians. So we are considering having the necessary IT services delivered from India. But in a few years, things may have changed. Perhaps the Chinese are then perfectly capable of delivering even our head office's IT services.

In recent years, many other countries in addition to India have become attractive for offshore outsourcing. East European countries such as Poland, Hungary, the Czech Republic, Romania and Russia are growing in importance, with providers like TPSA, Matav, Cesky Telecom, Akela and Luxoft, respectively. The cultural and time-zone differences with these countries are much smaller than those with Asia, which lowers the threshold to do business with providers there. The entry of several of these countries into the European Union has reinforced this trend, as IT professionals can easily travel to West European countries and even be employed there. For the moment, supply from these countries is rather fragmented, as the industry is still developing. But in time large-scale providers will be established, who will be very capable of serving the European market. Their share of foreign service provisioning may therefore be expected to grow quickly during the coming years.

NOTES

1 Presentation during 'Successful business process outsourcing strategies', European Networking Group, 25 and 26 February 2004, Hilton Hotel, Amsterdam.
2 Presentation during 'Successful business process outsourcing strategies', European Networking Group, 25 and 26 February 2004, Hilton Hotel, Amsterdam.

REFERENCES

Abdel-Hamid, T. (1993) 'A multiproject perspective of single-project dynamics', *Journal of Systems and Software*, 22 (3): 151–165.

Aeh, R. (1990) 'Offshore development looking into the future', *Journal of System Management*, 41 (6): 17.

Applegate, L., Austin, R. and McFarlan, W. (2003) *Corporate Information Strategy and Management*, Boston, MA: McGraw Hill.

Aubert, B., Rivard, S. and Patry, M. (2004) 'A transaction cost model of IT outsourcing', *Information & Management*, 41 (7): 921–932.

Badenhorst, K. and Eloff, J. (1989) 'Framework of a methodology for the life cycle of computer security in an organization', *Computers & Security*, 8 (5): 433–442.

Barney, J. (1991) 'Firm resources and sustained competitive advantage', *Journal of Management*, 17 (1): 99–120.

Beaver, J. (1985) 'Approaching service levels', *Computer Decisions*, 17 (November): 74–80.

Besson, P. and Rowe, F. (2001) 'ERP project dynamics and enacted dialogue: perceived understanding, perceived leeway, and the nature of task-related conflicts', *The Database for Advances in Information Systems*, 32 (4): 47–66.

Beulen, E. (2004) 'Governance in IT outsourcing partnerships', in W. van Grembergen (ed.) *Strategies for Information Technologies*, Hershey, PA: Idea Group Publishing.

Beulen, E. and Ribbers, P. (2003) 'A case study of managing IT outsourcing partnerships in Asia', *Communications of the Association of Information Systems*, 11 (21): March.

Beulen, E., van Fenema, P. and Currie, W. (2005) 'From application outsourcing to infrastructure management: extending the offshore outsourcing service portfolio', *European Management Journal*, 23 (2): 133–144.

Buck-Lew, M. (1992) 'To outsource or not?', *International Journal of Information Management*, 12: 3–20.

Carmel, E. (1999) *Global Software Teams, Collaboration Across Borders and Time Zones*, Englewood Cliffs, NJ: Prentice Hall.

Carmel, E. and Agarwal, R. (2002) 'The maturation of offshore sourcing of information technology work', *Management Information Systems Quarterly Executive*, 1: 65–76.

Carter, J. (1999) 'Incorporating standards and guidelines in an approach that balances usability concerns for developers and end users', *Interacting with Computers*, 12 (2): 179–206.

Copeland, L. (2002) 'General Motors drives application development offshore', *Computerworld*, 21 January.

Cullen, S. and Willcocks, L. (2003) *Intelligent IT Outsourcing: Eight Building Blocks to Success*, Oxford: Butterworth-Heinemann.

Currie, W. and Willcocks, L. (1998) 'Analysing four types of IT-outsourcing decisions in the context of scale, client/server, interdependency and risk migration', *Information Systems Journal*, 8 (2): 119–143.

David, J., Schuff, D. and Louis, R. (2002) 'Managing your IT total cost of ownership', *Communications of the Association for Computing Machinery*, 45 (1): 101–106.

Dedrick, J. and Kraemer, K. (2001) 'China IT report', *Electronic Journal on Information Systems in Developing Countries*, 6 (2): 1–10.

DiCarlo, L. (2003) 'The Philippines fights for U.S. business', *Forbus.com*, 22 May.

Doll, W., Deng, X. and Scazzero, J. (2003) 'A process for post-implementation IT benchmarking', *Information & Management*, 41 (2): 199–212.

Feeny, D. and Willcocks, L. (1998) 'Re-designing the IS function around core capabilities', *Long Range Planning*, 31 (3): 354–367.

Fitzgerald, M. (2003) 'At risk offshore', *CIO*, 17 (4): 1.

Gerlach, J., Neumann, B., Moldauer, E., Argo, M. and Frisby, D. (2002) 'Determining the cost of IT services', *Communications of the Association for Computing Machinery*, 45 (9): 61–67.

Gruhn, V. and Schope, L. (2002) 'Software processes for the development of electronic commerce systems', *Information and Software Technology*, 44 (14): 891–901.

Hierbert, M. and Slater, J. (2003) 'In search of a ready scapegoat', *Far Eastern Economic Review*, 166 (45): 14.

Irani, Z. (2002) 'Information systems evaluation: navigating through the problem domain', *Information & Management*, 40 (1): 11–24.

Johnson, B. and Andrew, M. (1994) *Quality Management for IT Securities*, London: HMSO.

Khan, N., Currie, W., Weerakkody, V. and Desai, B. (2003) 'Evaluating offshore IT outsourcing in India: supplier and customer scenarios', Paper presented at 36th Annual Hawaii International Conference on System Science, Hawaii.

Kim, S., Jang, D.H., Lee, D.H. and Cho, S.H. (2000) 'A methodology of constructing a decision path for IT investment', *The Journal of Strategic Information Systems*, 9 (1): 17–38.

Klepper, R. (1995) 'The management of partnering development in I/S outsourcing', *Journal of Technology*, 10 (4): 249–258.

Lacity, M. and Hirschheim, R. (1993) *Information Systems Outsourcing*, Chichester: Wiley & Sons.

Lacity, M. and Hirschheim, R. (1995) *Beyond the Information Systems Outsourcing Bandwagon*, Chichester: Wiley & Sons.

Livingstone, D. (1992) 'Outsourcing: look beyond the price tag', *Datamation*, 15 November.

McDougall, P. (2004) 'Shell inks huge IBM-Wipro offshore-outsourcing deal', *InformationWeek*, 3 May.

McFarlan, F. and Nolan, R. (1995) 'How to manage an IT outsourcing alliance', *Sloan Management Review*, 36 (2): 9–23.

McGraw, G. (2002) 'On bricks and walls: why building secure software is hard', *Computers & Security*, 21 (3): 229–238.

Marriot, I. (2004) 'Offshore sourcing: a framework for success', Presentation at Outsourcing and IT services Summit 2004, Gartner, Royal Lancaster Hotel, London, 26–27 April.

Marshall, J. and Cohan, P. (2003) 'Offshoring drive for savings accelerates', *Financial Executive*, 19 (6): 52.

Meadows, C. (1996) 'Globework: creating technology with international teams', thesis, Harvard University, Boston.

Nasscom and McKinsey (2002) 'The IT industry in India: strategic review 2002', Research report.

Ocker, R., Fjermestad, J. and Hiltz, S. (1998) 'Effects of four modes of group communication on the outcomes of software requirements determination', *Journal of Management Information Systems*, 15 (1): 99–118.

Olsson, E. (2004) 'What active users and designers contribute in the design process', *Interacting with Computers*, 16 (2): 377–401.

Paul, L. (1998) 'What price ownership?', *Datamation*, 44 (1): 88–94.

Qu, Z. and Brockelehurst, M. (2003) 'What will it take for China to become a competitive force in offshore outsourcing? An analysis of transaction costs in the supplier selection', *Journal of Information Technology*, 18: 53–67.

Rajkumar, T. and Dawley, D. (1997) 'Problems and issues in offshore development of software', in L. Willcocks and M. Lacity (eds) *Information Systems Sourcing: Theory and Practice*, Oxford: Oxford University Press.

Rajkumar, T. and Mani, R. (2001) 'Offshore software development: the view from Indian suppliers', *Information Systems Management*, 18 (2): 63–73.

Ramarapu, N., Parzinger, M. and Lado, A. (1997) 'Issues in foreign outsourcing: focus on applications development and support', *Information Systems Management*, 14 (2): 27–31.

Raval, V. (1999) 'Seven secrets of successful offshore software development', *Information Strategy*, 15 (4): 34–39.

Ravichandran, R. and Ahmed, N. (1993) 'Offshore systems development', *Information & Management*, 24 (1): 24–40.

Robb, D. (2000) 'Offshore outsourcing nears critical mass', *InformationWeek*, 12 June: 89–98.

Robinson, M. and Kalakola, R. (2004) *Offshore Outsourcing, Business Models, ROI and Best Practices*, Alpharetta, GA: Mivar Press Inc.

Ross, J. and Beath, C. (2002) 'Beyond the business case: new approaches to IT investment', *MIT Sloan Management Review*, 43 (2): 51–59.

Ross, J., Vitale, M. and Beath, C. (1999) 'The untapped potential of IT charge back', *Management Information Systems Quarterly*, 23 (2): 215–237.

Sadlowski, M. (1998) 'Worldwide services: market definitions', Research report, Dataquest, SVCS-EU-GU-9801.

Schwartz, J. and Wright, R. (2004) 'Offshoring – learn to love it!', *VARbusiness*, 20 (11): 32.

Schwartz, K. (1998) 'Benchmarking for dollars', *Datamation*, 44 (2): 50–57.

Sinha, D. and Terdiman, R. (2002) *Potential Risks in Offshore Sourcing*, Gartner Research, 5th September.

Smith, M., Mitra, S. and Narasinhan, S. (1996) 'Offshore outsourcing of software development and maintenance', *Information & Management*, 31 (3): 165–175.

Tardugno, A., Matthews, R. and Dipasquale, T. (2000) *IT Services: Costs, Metrics, Benchmarking and Marketing*, New York: Prentice Hall.

van Fenema, P. (2002) 'Coordination and control of globally distributed software projects', PhD thesis, Erasmus University Rotterdam, The Netherlands, Erasmus Institute of Management PhD Series Research in Management 19 (http://hdl.handle.net/1765/360) Accessed 29 August 2004.

Vijayan, J. (1996) 'Look before you leap', *Computerworld*, 30 (10): 79–80.

Williamson, O. (1975) *Markets and Hierarchies*, New York: Free Press.

Chapter 10

Contracts

Several contract aspects require careful attention. The most important issues discussed in this chapter are the following:

- A layered contract structure makes it possible to manage IT outsourcing.
- Contract scope, service levels and responsibilities must be defined unambiguously.
- In the case of multiple outsourcing contracts, the responsibilities of the service providers involved must be defined unambiguously in all contracts.
- Contracts have to be flexible and adaptable in order to make global partnerships work.
- Break options, including exit strategies, should be clearly defined.

10.1 INTRODUCTION

Contracts are very important to IT outsourcing partnerships. They enable the participants to manage their relationships (Lacity and Hirschheim 1995; Saunders et al. 1997; Cullen and Willcocks 2003). When contracts are drawn up, it is important that their structure matches the partnership's context: the contract for a relationship with a limited scope and involving only one provider will obviously be very different from that of a worldwide partnership with many parties. Attention must also be paid to the market conformance of the IT services to be delivered. Benchmarking is one of the means by which this may be achieved. Considering the dynamics of many IT outsourcing partnerships, however, it often is not possible to define all aspects right from the start. Service recipients and their providers will therefore have to make agreements on how to change parts of their contracts when needed. By making such changes to the contracts, the fit can be maintained between the recipient's needs and the IT services delivered.

Increasingly, IT outsourcing partnerships involve more than one provider. Then everyone's responsibilities must be clearly delineated, and it is the recipients who must make choices concerning the allocation of those responsibilities. Finally, attention must be paid – right from the beginning – to contract termination. Fewer contracts are renewed, and increasingly contracts are terminated before their running period is complete.[1] This means that the tasks and activities involved must be transferred to other providers. Such transfers must be managed and this is best done by including termination clauses in the contract.

This chapter also includes an extensive case study on contract structuring. This case study explains the way a European-based global conglomerate of companies active in the chemical industry has set up a long-term partnership.

10.2 OBJECTIVES

The most important aim of a contract is laying down the agreements made between the contracting parties. These agreements include descriptions of the services to be delivered and their service levels and prices. Many context aspects are also included, such as tax circumstances, liabilities, contract termination conditions, the contract period and intellectual property rights. Thus, contracts give both recipient and provider control over their partnership, which is important to ensure service delivery continuity.

Contracts should also provide the parties involved with tools to change the agreements made. Such changes, made to contracts during their running period, may be necessary when the business management of one or more of the parties changes, or when unforeseen technological developments occur. By including agreements on how to make changes the contract parties are provided with a common context for handling such circumstances.

Since contracts formalize agreements, they also function to enforce them. Recipients and providers are made explicitly aware of the deal, and know that their partner may go to court in case of default. This possibility alone is generally enough to make the parties keep their promises. Thus, contracts are useful tools for achieving the governance partnerships need.

10.3 CONTRACT STRUCTURE

Normally, IT outsourcing contracts are drawn up on three levels (Beulen *et al.* 2004): strategic, tactical and operational. These are illustrated in Figure 10.1. At the strategic level there are framework agreements and transfer agreements; at the tactical level, service agreements, project agreements and secondment agreements; and at the operational level, service level agreements and secondment contracts. In small-scale partnerships the tactical and operational levels are frequently merged into one; these are also the two levels represented in providers' service portfolios.

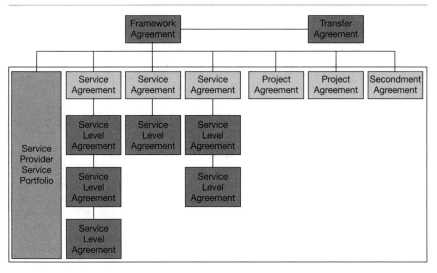

Figure 10.1 *Contract structures for IT outsourcing partnerships*

The framework agreements found at the strategic level define overall issues, such as liabilities, jurisdiction, payment terms, and rate structures and the indexes applied to them. A more complete overview of the major topics involved is presented in Table 10.1. At the same level there are transfer agreements. These formalize the transfer of the former's IT department staff, assets and service contracts from the recipient to the provider. They are therefore closely linked to framework agreements, but with a few important differences: transfer agreements concern a single transaction, whereas framework agreements have contract periods up to more than five years; and transfer agreements have no direct link to the service provisioning that follows the transaction defined in them.

Basically, there are two kinds of transfer agreements: asset deals and share deals. The difference between the two concerns the legal status of the organization transferred. If the IT department is an independent legal entity, the contract will take the form of a share deal; otherwise asset deals are the usual choice. In both cases, shares are transferred from the recipient to the provider and the department's staff are henceforth employed by the provider.

Below the strategic level of framework and transfer agreements is the tactical level. The most important kind of contract here is the service agreement. Services defined in them are found in providers' service portfolios: lists of generic descriptions of services offered to all the provider's clients. These portfolios normally provide a wide assortment of services, described in extensive detail. And they have the advantage that they enable the provider to deliver their services flexibly and thus cost effectively. A disadvantage is that the customization achieved makes it difficult to realize the cost savings that are the result of standardization and economies of scale.

231

Table 10.1 *Major topics included in framework agreements (Beulen 2002: 58–9)*

Topic	Explanation
Objectives	• The parties define what their partnership intends to do and achieve.
IT services	• The IT services to be delivered are described. Details, however, are left to lower-level contracts, dedicated to specific kinds of services. • The level at which these services are to be delivered is laid down as well. Again, details are reserved for lower contract levels, in this case for service level agreements (SLAs). Sometimes it is possible to agree on standard delivery levels for a number of similar services, even if these are delivered for different business processes.
Contract period	• Most contracts have previously agreed running periods. In such temporary contracts renewal procedures should be included. • The alternative is a contract with a period of notice; such permanent contracts are terminated only on the initiative of one of the parties.
Exclusivity	• Is the recipient free to buy services such as those included in the contract from other providers during the contract period? If not, the contract should specify so; if yes, a minimum purchase value may be included.
Prices and changes	• Prices and prices change mechanisms must be specified. Indexes from national institutes or market researchers may be defined as acceptable for this purpose. • Contracts should include tables listing the persons who have the authority to make change agreements. Such tables will have to be updated regularly.
Conferencing and reporting	• Who will meet to discuss what, and how frequently? Again, it should also be clear who has the authority to decide. • The content and formats of service delivery reports should be agreed upon.
Liabilities and damages	• These subjects require careful agreements: maximums per occasion, the liability allocation of direct and consequential damage, etc. • Damages and how to demand them must also be defined.
Contract termination	• Termination conditions must be agreed. It is wise to stay close to current legal terminology such as reasonableness and fairness, and to define these as concretely as possible. • Clauses should be included on the consequences of ownership changes concerning one or more of the parties involved – for example, consequences for the outsourcing contract if business processes are sold to parties with other outsourcing relationships.

Project and secondment agreements also belong to the tactical contract level. Since every project is unique, project agreements must be made for every individual project. They should include all specifications: milestones, conditions, resources allocated by recipient and provider, etc. Secondment agreements are drawn up to enable recipients to use their providers' resources against previously agreed rates – per hour or per occurrence, for instance. They therefore contain well-defined lists of functions and rates. Rates may be differentiated per country, and they will regularly be adapted to ensure market conformance.

Finally, at the operational contract level, there are service level agreements and secondment contracts. Service level agreements or SLAs work out in detail the requirements of service agreements with respect to the outsourced services: the levels at which these services are to be delivered and the variations allowed. Here, too, service portfolios may provide guidance, because the specifications usually include a number of delivery levels in order to provide flexibility. Again, standardizing offers the opportunity of economies of scale, resulting in cost savings. Secondment contracts may essentially be considered the secondment equivalent of SLAs. Working out one's secondment agreements has the advantage of cost efficiency and increased response times when additional resources are needed suddenly.

10.4 MARKET CONFORMANCE

Relationships between service recipients and service providers always contain a certain amount of tension. The recipient wishes to purchase their IT services as cost efficiently as possible, but providers like to make the largest possible margin on the services they deliver. In this game of contrasting interests, both parties would do well to remain reasonable, in order to maintain a collaborative and pleasant partnership (Burden 2003). 'Both clients and vendors tend to behave opportunistically when entering into a contract, and this can lead to mutual disadvantage' (Aubert *et al.* 2003: 183).

Service recipients run their greatest risks when their providers go bankrupt because their margins have been cut back too far. If that happens, service delivery continuity is endangered. Even if it does not quite come to bankruptcy, however, providers who are allowed only minimum margins will be less willing to do all they can for their clients. They will cling to the literal meaning of their contract, rather than acting in its spirit. Coordination will in such circumstances require much more effort, raising the coordination costs and sometimes endangering the partnership.

As one expert remarked:

Some outsourcing companies are too successful in their negotiations with their suppliers. They drive down the margin to the point where their supplier makes almost no money. In the end that ruins their relation, because the supplier then has no room to do anything – even if it is of obvious value to the recipient –

without charging them for every little item. Instead, outsourcing companies should be fair and say: 'I'm happy with the margin you're making, I don't need you to make any less than that. Keep driving down your costs, but keep making an adequate margin too'. Such an approach contributes to a trusting relation between partners. Poverty kills relations.

(Beulen 2004: 231)

However, allowing one's provider their margin should not keep the provider from striving continuously to optimize their services delivery. Improving the effectiveness and efficiency of their services always remains part of the provider's responsibilities, and recipients should not hesitate to specify this in their contracts (Cullen and Willcocks 2003). To do so, several paths can be taken. If fees and rates are defined for the contract period as a whole, much is saved in the way of coordination costs. But recipient and provider must then ahead of time make estimates of the cost developments (including the cost savings potential) for the whole contract period. Market conformance can only be achieved in such a construction if the contract period is around 24 months, preferably shorter. Another set-up involves agreeing on prices for the first 12 months, followed by renegotiations. The consequence may be rising prices, but rates may also go down. Market-conforming prices can be set in this manner, but the coordination costs involved are higher.

In practice, prices are often set for the whole contract period, with the option to benchmark them if one of the parties involves feels this is necessary. Thus, market-conforming prices are established while keeping the coordination costs down. However, benchmarking is not inexpensive either, since it requires the services of a third, independent and neutral party plus a lot of management attention from both parties, who must provide that third party with the information needed. Therefore, contracts often specify that the benchmarking costs are to be borne by the party requesting the investigation, unless the results show that the partnership's price levels deviate more than, say, 10 per cent from market conformance. Such an arrangement stimulates the participants to reach an agreement by themselves, thus keeping down the costs (Aubert et al. 2003).

Sometimes it can be difficult to establish market conformance even through a benchmark investigation (Cullen and Willcocks 2003). For generic services such as desktop management, network management or mainframe processing, enough data are available. But some services are designed especially for the client, which means there are few similar contracts with which to compare prices. Application management is a case in point. Then benchmarking is hard, and it usually comes down to interpreting the results of the investigation – which essentially puts you back where you came from, since this may cause those tough discussions which it was the investigation's objective to prevent. Another circumstance that makes benchmarking difficult is financial engineering by the provider: including extra costs for the salaries of transferred staff, hardware depreciations, transition costs and the like in their rates. Doing so makes price calculations unclear. It is therefore better to include such costs in the transfer contracts, and then charge realistic prices that can be tested against the market at any time.

10.5 COMPLETENESS

The ideal situation is one in which the contract signed at the beginning of one's partnership includes all circumstances, issues and questions that may arise during its running period (Beulen and Ribbers 2003). Then there is no uncertainty left. Attempts to do so, however, almost invariably fail. It simply requires too much effort from both parties – if it is actually possible to foresee every future scenario. A fruitful way of tackling this subject is presented by the 'transaction cost theory' (Klepper 1995), which states that the real question is to what extent both parties are prepared to attempt to be complete. The degree to which completeness is possible for IT outsourcing contracts depends on the following factors: asset specificity, uncertainty and measurement, and transaction frequency (Coase 1937; Aubert et al. 1996; Williamson 1975).

In many outsourcing situations, there is very little chance to incorporate details in the contract. There often is too much time pressure to calculate all costs before signing the contract, especially if the recipient needs the services quickly. Then, procedures for dealing with changes not covered by the contract are included (Gietzmann 1996). These can be set up using the 'liaison model' (Burnett 1998), according to which a previously agreed procedure is used as the basis for formulating amendments to the contract. Another approach is based on the concept of 'ex-post negotiations' (Hart 1995; Segal 1999). But in many circumstances the costs of new negotiations are very high (Parkhe 1993), and they make considerable demands on the maturity of the recipient's contract managers. Fortunately, while at the close of the twentieth century most recipient companies' contract management organizations were quite immature (Heckman 1999), their levels of professionality have now increased significantly because standardized processes have been set up and qualified professionals have been hired. More attention will be paid to contract flexibility and adaptability in the following section of this chapter.

Another important issue to consider when assessing a contract's completeness is the extent to which it matches the requirements of the business. For this purpose a so-called balanced scorecard may be used. Balanced scorecards should not contain many technical details, but be business-oriented. Says the business manager of a utility company (Case XVII; see Appendix, p. 268, for all Case details): 'I'm not interested in an overview of the up-time of the servers in my supplier's data centre, I'm interested in the progress of the billing process. Statistics on the invoicing matter, not the underlying IT services.'

Finally, the degree of completeness desired is influenced by cultural factors as well. North American companies like to cover every possible detail. Consequently, their contracts are big documents and drawing them up requires the assistance of many lawyers. Asian companies focus on trust rather than on the contract, so their contracts are generally much thinner. Europe traditionally takes a middle position. Globalization, however, is levelling these differences.

10.6 FLEXIBILITY AND ADAPTABILITY IN IT OUTSOURCING CONTRACTS

The problem of incomplete contracts is made worse by the market dynamics facing both recipients and providers. These dynamics may have a serious impact on their partnership (Shepherd 1999). Contracts, therefore, must be flexible and adaptable, which puts an even greater stress on the importance of contract management (Lacity and Willcocks 2003). Changes in the partnership's context necessitate 'relational contracting' (Kern and Willcocks 2000). This means that as well as formal contacts, informal conferencing is an important element in controlling one's partnership.

In IT outsourcing partnerships, context changes are caused by business management changes or technological developments. The recipient may, for example, change their business strategy, or acquire or sell business units. The dynamics involved are often hard to catch in formal contracts, which means that much informal contact is needed to adapt and amend the agreements.

A member of a University Board (Case XXXI) remarks:

> Within the University Board I'm responsible for IT services. We recognize the fact that the enabling role of IT will increase in research and education. Also to attract new students IT facilities such as wireless networks on our campus become more and more important. We have outsourced our IT services and we explore innovative opportunities with our service provider. To have this upfront detail in the contract is impossible. Over the years we have made significant changes in the contract and the scope of the contract. This way of working is the only way to successfully maintain an outsourcing relationship.

An example of the changes caused by technological developments is the rise of utility-based computing: providing computer capacity against per-unit prices. This can be done for server management or storage as well as applications. If this phenomenon continues its current development, this will have major consequences for many IT outsourcing contracts. All of their pricing mechanisms and payment procedures will have to be adapted, for instance. Portals are another such development: web interfaces making all applications available to end users. Again, their rise would have a great influence on current IT partnerships. It is therefore important that IT outsourcing contracts include 'technology refresh' clauses. These stipulate that providers are obliged to use the newest technologies available for the delivery of their services. Efficiency and cost effectiveness can thus be realized for the recipient. But since nobody knows the character of future technology developments, such changes will require regular contract adaptations (Turner *et al.* 2002).

Adapting contracts is the shared responsibility of recipient and provider. Providers need time to implement changes, and it is therefore essential that recipient and provider keep each other informed of any adaptations made possible or desirable. To allow for timely contract changes use may be made of the 'rolling forecast mechanism'. The recipient is then obliged to indicate the IT services they need for the coming period, after which the provider makes the resources required available for that period. Typically, such periods are three to six months long. Estimates for longer periods are not very useful, generally. Business and technology dynamics are usually such that longer-term estimates are made quickly obsolete.

10.7 DEFINING RESPONSIBILITIES

Increasingly, IT outsourcing partnerships involve more than one provider: multiple sourcing. Cost savings are an important argument to do so (Lacity and Willcocks 1998). Service recipients must in such partnerships decide which provider is to be responsible for which services. These choices can be made along two dimensions: technology and geography. Sometimes a combination of the two is preferred.

Allocation by technology means that a separate provider is selected for each of the technologies required, such as desktop, network and server management, or application development and management. All business processes and units are then provided with this technology by the same supplier, who has been selected on the basis of their quality in this field. A difficulty with allocation by technology is that all providers to a recipient must make their systems match. This requires interfaces between the technologies, which for this purpose are ordered into International Standards Organization (ISO) layers, so called after the model from which they are derived. There are seven such layers: the application or top layer, the presentation layer, the session layer, the transport layer, the network layer, the data link layer and the physical or bottom layer. Realizing and maintaining the interfaces between these layers requires much effort. But providers collaborating in this way profit because it allows them to standardize, generating economies of scale that enable them to offer their client the best deal.

Another disadvantage of allocation by technology is that only a few providers (such as Accenture, CSC, EDS or IBM) are able to deliver these services globally. For many other providers the solution is to collaborate with colleagues in other countries. This issue is less important for recipients who themselves only operate in a limited number of countries. Then the number of providers able to deliver the services needed is much larger.

Allocation by geography allows the recipient to select strong providers for each of its operational regions. All business processes and units in that region are then serviced

237

by one provider. In this case the task is to ensure a fit between the regions. This requires application-level interfaces, in order for the regions to be able to exchange information. For this purpose Enterprise Resources Planning (ERP) or Customer Relation Management (CRM) packages are often used. With these packages interface implementation and maintenance are usually problem-free and cost efficient.

The contract manager of a service recipient in the chemicals industry as part of the information management (Case III) recalls how they allocate their IT services:

> Our business units have much autonomy, and we have activities in many countries. Integrating our IT services is not, therefore, our main priority. Our sourcing strategy states that all business units themselves decide how their IT services are delivered and, in the case of outsourcing, by which provider. We do offer the opportunity of joining framework agreements made on our corporate level with several providers. And even though it remains the business units' own responsibility to decide, many fortunately realize that coordination pays. Voluntary coordination, after all, works much better than top-down corporate decisions.

10.8 CONTRACT TERMINATION

One thing is certain about all contracts: at some point they come to an end. Even if a contract is renewed, there will be a moment when the service delivery involved is transferred to another provider. Sometimes recipients decide to take service delivery back into their own hands, but that is unusual. Once the competence to do so has been lost or sold, it is difficult to regain. The management attention required is just too great.

Both recipient and provider must be prepared for the eventual termination of the contract. Their preparation begins when the contract of their partnership is drawn up. It should include 'exit clauses' as well as 'hand-over assistance clauses' (Shepherd 1999; Cullen and Willcocks 2003). These must define the responsibilities of both parties, the primary aim being to guarantee service delivery continuity during the transfer. Financial matters must also be arranged, of course. Generally, the provider is paid for their efforts during the transfer. A maximum fee may be agreed, but in practice the transfer is usually organized as a separate project with its own budget, approved ahead of time by the recipient. The provider then sets up a transfer file on the basis of the transition plan included in the contract (Figure 10.2). In this file all knowledge of the IT services delivered is recorded, and during the project it is regularly updated. Using this file the transfer can then be effected at any time. In fact, since contracts do not only end when their running period is complete, it is wise for providers to have such a transfer file ready even if the expected contract termination date is still far away. This requires substantial work, however.

Other aspects deserving attention when contracts are terminated are listed in Boxes 10.1 and 10.2. The first consists of issues that must be decided before the

238

partnership contract is signed, the latter lists matters requiring attention when the contract period is already running.

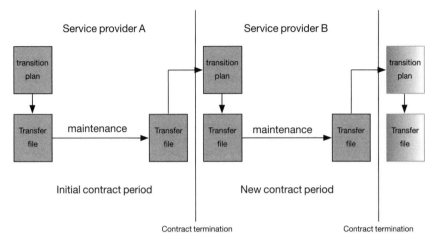

Figure 10.2 *Transferring IT services delivery: transition plans and transfer files* *(Beulen 2003: 154)*

BOX 10.1 CONTRACT TERMINATION ASPECTS TO BE CONSIDERED BEFORE SIGNING THE PARTNERSHIP CONTRACT (Beulen 2003: 152)

1. The recipient must set up its information management function to manage the outsourcing relationship.
2. The recipient groups the service delivery contracts on the basis of the nature of the services to be delivered.
3. The recipient must manage their IT services like a portfolio.
4. The recipient must develop, implement and maintain an IT strategy to direct the use of IT services for its business processes.
5. Prices are normally indexed. Benchmarking by third parties may be used occasionally, to assess market conformance.
6. The contracts should not contain any 'most preferred supplier' clauses.
7. The notice time (three to six months) and a limiting list of contract termination causes must be clearly defined in the contract.
8. Any additional grounds for contract termination must also be listed, including notice times (which should be as short as possible) and financial and other consequences.
9. The transfer period (with a maximum of three months) must be defined in the contract.
10. A transfer file should be drawn up, recording all responsibilities, activities and financial arrangements for the current provider as well as the recipient and any future providers.

BOX 10.2 CONTRACT TERMINATION ASPECTS TO BE CONSIDERED DURING THE RUNNING PERIOD (Beulen 2003:157)

1. After the contract is terminated, the current provider's regularly updated transfer file will become the basis for the new partnership's transition plan.
2. Before the new contract is signed, the new provider's transition plan must be agreed with the recipient's current provider.
3. A business-economical risk inventory must be made, assessing the most critically important business processes and systems.
4. The transition is to be laid down in the new provider's transition plan, which will be an integral part of the new contract.
5. The activities of both the recipient's current and new providers are to be paid on the basis of the transfer file and the new transition plan.
6. The current contract is terminated after agreement has been reached concerning the new outsourcing contract.
7. The recipient will appoint a project leader to coordinate the transition from the current to the new provider.
8. Extra management attention will be paid during the transition period, by the recipient's CIO as well as their business managers.
9. Communication concerning the changes resulting from the transition will require extra management attention.
10. The new provider will use a short transition period (three months) to stabilize service delivery. Only then can the future mode of operation be implemented.

 **CASE STUDY**

CONTRACT STRUCTURING

Summary

In the mid-1990s a European-based global conglomerate of companies active in the chemical industry was looking for an international IT services provider with whom to set up a long-term partnership. The objective was to increase the value added by its IT services. After careful consideration its entire internal corporate IT group, with a staff of nearly 750 IT professionals that had contacts with all of the conglomerate's business groups and units, was sold to a single provider. For the conglomerate itself, its business managers and, of course, the IT professionals involved, this was a major step. The roles and responsibilities of interviewees for this case study are detailed in Table 10.2.

During the negotiations the contract structure was an important subject of discussion. Considering the large number of business groups and units involved and the geographic spread of these subsidiaries, drawing up this structure was no

Table 10.2 *Interviewees for case study*[2]

The interviewees

Party	Name and job title	Responsibilities	Remarks
Recipient	Jean Delcroix, Corporate Information Officer	• Managing the information management department, which is responsible for: • optimizing IT utilization providing business units with guidance on developments in infrastructure and infrastructure tooling, security and vendor management	• Reports directly to his company's board of directors • Personally involved in all contract design and negotiation meetings
	Alain Massenet, Purchasing Officer	• Purchasing IT services	• Works for corporate purchasing department, but closely collaborates with the corporate information management department
Provider	Thierry Dauvergne, Global Client Executive	• Maintaining and improving relationships with the recipient	• Heads a team of global account managers, contract managers, service delivery managers and sales support consultants

easy task. Nevertheless, the contract was signed in 1999, with an initial value of 90 million euros, and it has been renewed several times since. Because of the new market and technology developments that occur all the time, the relationship between the provider and their recipient (including subsidiaries acquired or sold since 1999) is still developing. This case study focuses on the challenges facing internationally operating companies who must keep their IT outsourcing relationships and structures up to date.

Introduction

About a decade ago a large European conglomerate of globally active producers of chemical products decided to outsource its internal corporate IT department. This group, including all its assets such as PCs, networks and mainframes, would now operate under an external provider's supervision. Its services (the management and maintenance of hardware platforms and applications, e-business, application development, SAP services and technical automation) were, of course, very important to the recipient. Purchasing officer Alain Massenet: 'We were used to outsourcing, and collaborated with a great number of external partners. But contracting out our IT services somehow felt strange, since they were so closely related to our business processes.' The change would have a great impact on the work of the company's business managers, and serious consequences for the 750 individuals working for the group. In fact, it would even constitute a major change for the provider.

Selecting the right provider was, therefore, a matter of prime importance. Corporate information officer Jean Delcroix:

> The number of service providers that could handle a job of such magnitude and complexity was very limited. Worldwide there really were only a handful of them. In fact, it cost me a lot of energy to convince our board that it would be possible to find interested parties at all.

But candidates were in fact found, and they all had to be thoroughly vetted. Several safeguards were implemented to find the right one. For example, Jean Delcroix remembers visiting clients of some of their potential partners.

> These visits gave us a better idea of how these service providers performed – a kind of reference material so to speak, providing insight you can never get from a paper proposal. On such visits you get a taste of how a supplier will behave in the context of a partnership.

Thierry Dauvergne, the global client executive of the provider that was chosen, was always confident that his company stood a good chance of being selected.

> Delivering services to a large number of autonomous subsidiaries in more than twenty countries requires flexibility. We were among the few service providers who could offer that flexibility. Nevertheless, laying down all the agreements wasn't easy if we weren't to end up with totally unwieldy contracts.

The negotiations therefore also included discussions about the contract structure needed.

> The strategy chosen was to take over their entire IT department, including all its staff, its assets and its contracts with the recipient's business groups. Thus a basis for our partnership was established. Then, as our collaboration progressed, we would make changes and reinforcements as needed. These changes would of course require additional negotiations.

And so the issues facing the recipient and its provider concerned the way in which such changes were to be made. Jean Delcroix: 'One of the things that kept me occupied was: how could we profit best from any advantages of scale we could achieve, without hindering the fulfilment of our business units' individual IT needs?' At a later time the purchasing officer added that this had to be done, of course, without losing control over the total cost of ownership. All such aspects had to be taken into account.

Company and industry profile

The company

The recipient of this case study was a globally operating conglomerate of companies in the chemical industry. It consisted of three divisions that together realized an annual turnover of more than 10 trillion euros. Its more than 60,000 employees worked in over 80 countries. Every one of the three divisions – chemicals, coatings and pharmaceuticals – was in turn composed of a great number of business units, focused on specific products. Here we will look only at the conglomerate as a whole and its chemicals and coatings divisions.[3]

The recipient's divisions and business units all had their own profit and loss responsibility. This meant they also had their own IT budgets, making them powerful players in the client's negotiations with the provider. Thierry Dauvergne, the provider's global client executive, quickly realized he would have to extend his relationships with the recipient's holding to include a network comprising all their business units.

> And I paid attention to their pharmaceuticals division too. Perhaps we could at some point in the future extend our business with this client by delivering IT services to that division as well. We did so now, incidentally and on a simple hourly-rate basis, but I didn't wish to rule out a more structural form of collaboration.

The market

The company operated in widely differing markets. The chemicals division had recently undergone a major restructuring operation in the sense that selective divestments had been made. Several businesses had been sold, others were up for sale. Dauvergne: 'These changes had our full attention, of course. We had made agreements on how to deal with those business units that are sold.' Jean Delcroix, the recipient's corporate information officer, recalls: 'Our agreements with the provider were of course also intended to support the restructuring operation of our chemicals division.' This operation focused on the coherence of the division's product portfolio as well as on its financial ratios. Another aspect of the complexity involved was that the various chemicals markets also differed very much with respect to their dynamics. All business units had much competition to deal with, though, which put pressure on their prices. And the chemical industry in general was sensitive to conjunctural changes. IT services delivery therefore had to be very efficient.

243

The coatings division offered a completely different picture. Its margins were much higher than those in chemicals. And instead of divestments, acquiring new business units was the rule, causing the division to grow quite spectacularly. Delcroix:

> Such growth also influenced our relations with our IT partner. For us to be able to profit quickly from newly acquired business units, we needed the relevant management information to become available as soon as possible. Therefore, their IT services had to be quickly integrated with those of our other companies. This was one of our provider's main tasks.

In addition, the coatings market experienced a completely different situation from that for chemicals: demand was so great it could hardly be met. For IT services this meant that effectiveness and innovation were of prime importance rather than efficiency.

IT services

The provider under discussion here was the recipient's most important IT services supplier. However, before their contract was signed, the recipient had already outsourced its network services to another provider. Says their purchasing officer, Alain Massenet: 'It is nothing unusual to have deals with multiple suppliers. It prevents you becoming too dependent on any one of them.' Corporate information officer Jean Delcroix agrees. 'Of course, having more than one provider involves some extra coordination work. But my department had enough expertise to tackle that job.'

The services that were delivered consisted of the maintenance and management of hardware platforms and applications (60 per cent), e-business, application development (15 per cent), SAP services (25 per cent) and technical automation. In addition several generic services were delivered (IBM mainframe services, network and generic services, desktop hardware and software services, and LAN management services) plus some dedicated services (mid-range computer services, e-business services, SAP services and miscellaneous services such as helpdesk services, assets charging services and application management for custom-developed applications).

Requirements

The recipient's objectives

The recipient had formulated the ambition to run a business cycle generating above-average economic value. In this respect, they were primarily financially motivated. Explicit attention was paid to the coherence of their product portfolio, in which synergy was the aim. For their IT outsourcing the recipient had consequently formulated three objectives: increasing the IT services' added value; ensuring a better control over the IT services delivered and a better match with the business unit's information requirements; and achieving cost savings. The company's board of directors agreed on all three objectives, which ensured their management support.

With respect to the first objective, corporate information officer Jean Delcroix remarks:

> The ambition to run a business cycle generating above-average added value almost automatically led to the decision to outsource our IT services. This would allow us to focus on our core business, while our IT providers concentrated on increasing the added value of our IT services.

The provider's global client executive, Thierry Dauvergne, adds: 'We were capable of increasing the added value of their IT services because we could utilize our global capabilities.'

Acquiring more control over the conglomerate's IT services and ensuring a better match with the information needs of its business units was especially important in those times of frequent mergers, takeovers and divestments. Only if the contracts drawn up allowed enough flexibility would the provider be able to react to the fluctuating information needs of its client. Dauvergne:

> During the reference visits that our client's executives made to some of our other customers, we paid special attention to this aspect. They visited companies with a similar international spread, where profit and loss responsibility was allocated on a relatively low organizational level and whose business units operated in dynamic markets too.

Finally, cost savings. 'Those are important to virtually all our clients', Dauvergne remarks. 'This contract is almost exceptional in that cost savings are only one of three major objectives.' The agreements between the recipient and their provider contained clear cost savings targets. Purchasing officer Alain Massenet: 'For dedicated services, however, it would be difficult to establish whether the costs had really decreased. When you buy generic services you can benchmark them, for dedicated services that is much harder to do.' The parties therefore agreed that the provider would show the recipient hard figures if the costs of IT service delivery were to rise. That way, the client would have insight in the degree to which their provider realized its cost savings objectives.

The contracting process

After a long and careful decision-making process, the global conglomerate studied here sold its entire corporate IT group to its provider – assets, contracts and staff. It is instructive to take a quick look at the contracting process. Essentially, there were three steps: market research and objectives formulation, request for proposal and selection.

The recipient's global information officer, Jean Delcroix, remembers being charged by his company's board of directors with doing market research into the possibility of outsourcing. 'After my investigations I wrote a recommendation report, the chief conclusion of which was that outsourcing was desirable if the provider could meet a few important requirements. These concerned flexibility and the acceptance of our business units' autonomy.' Having agreed, the board then let the project get underway. The company's corporate purchasing department played a major role in defining the objectives of outsourcing its IT services.

On the basis of these objectives a request for proposal was formulated that was sent to a large number of providers. Purchasing officer Alain Massenet:

> We sent it to our then providers, of course, who at the time effectively subcontracted from our corporate IT department. In addition we invited a few international providers of IT services, companies we felt would be capable of offering a good proposal.

The provider finally chosen was one of the suppliers the recipient already did business with. 'But this earlier business was on a limited scale only', global client executive Thierry Dauvergne recalls. 'The turnover involved was no more than five million euros, concentrated mostly in Europe.'

On the basis of the response to its request for proposals, the recipient selected a single potential provider. Massenet says,

> I would have preferred to do business with several parties, because I feel there's no harm in setting them up for a little competition. But the matter was so complex, we in the end chose to negotiate with only one provider. The advantage of doing so was that we could concentrate on our collaboration and the contract structure required. We laid down our agreements in a couple of statements of principle, which from then on formed the basis of our outsourcing relation.

The services contracted

The scope of the outsourcing contract included the recipient's holding and its chemicals and coatings divisions. Services were to be delivered to business units operating in more than 20 countries. Corporate information officer Jean Delcroix: 'Personally, I think that was the greatest challenge to our provider: having to deliver uniform IT services in so many different countries worldwide. This objective sharply reduced the number of potential partners.'

 246

The structure of the outsourcing relationship contained a number of asset purchase agreements defining the transfer of IT professionals and their tools. The corporate IT department's contracts with the business units were transferred too. These contracts had very different running times. Some involved mainframe services and had 30 months or more of their contract period left; they represented a substantial value. Other contracts, on software development for instance, had no more than a few weeks to go, and thus were valued at some 10,000 euros only. Nevertheless, such a portfolio of contracts was a good basis for an outsourcing relationship.

Other agreements concerned the possibility of extending these contracts. Alain Massenet:

> We certainly realized how important it was for our provider to be able to count on some future business. Nevertheless, we chose not to guarantee any turnover. Our business units are autonomous, and we cannot force them to accept such guarantees. It is their managers who decide, not us.

The provider's global client executive had no problem accepting this.

> Look, of course we like being given turnover guarantees. That way you can be certain you can keep your newly transferred employees at work. But there is a downside to such guarantees. The lack of competition makes you lose attention. You risk becoming sloppy and losing your client altogether. Instead, I felt that the transfer of our client's entire internal IT department offered me enough security. Now we would have to deliver good quality services against realistic prices – the only way towards a good partnership. No, I really don't think turnover guarantees would have improved the situation.

The recipient's information management department played an important role in securing coherence in the services delivered. Jean Delcroix, corporate information manager and the department's head, remarks: 'I was responsible for this outsourcing agreement. I managed it on behalf of our business units, who themselves remained the contracting parties. Our corporate purchasing department and my group together supported them in their negotiations with their various suppliers.' For the provider there was a clear advantage to having only one contact person. 'It gave me a direct link to my client's information management department,' Dauvergne says, 'and through it to their board of directors. My account managers maintained our relations with their individual business units.'

During the first year of the running period, several improvements were made to the contract. Some of these were initiated by the provider, others by the recipient, and together they significantly improved the effectiveness and efficiency of the services delivered. After 12 months, however, the partners took the time to re-attune properly.

Jean Delcroix wanted to look back on the past period and see what changes might be made when setting the course for another year. 'The dynamics of our business environment require that we keep evaluating. Besides, we had laid down regular evaluations in our contracts. So I asked around for a list of suggestions, asking all business units what might be improved.' As it turned out, the business units were reasonably satisfied, but they did have some suggestions as to how the provider's performance could profitably be improved further. Meanwhile, Delcroix had also asked his provider for suggestions:

> Their team, reinforced with extra specialists in the technical field, also made a list. And then, in a two-day session, we put all suggestions together. The result was a shortlist we discussed in further detail with a smaller group of people, to come up with a number of concrete actions.

Such sessions are of great value. It is therefore of essential importance that they are prepared well. And the people attending them must be willing to do business in an open and honest fashion.

The follow-up: how to improve the outsourcing relationship further

Before addressing this question we would do well to take another look at the negotiations phase of the outsourcing relationship. Recipient and provider got together at an early stage to discuss the contract structure needed and to formulate a number of basic agreements. Says corporate information officer Jean Delcroix: 'For me, these agreements still hold.' The student should therefore first establish what these agreements were, formulate important contract clauses and work out their basic assumptions.

Then the main question can be tackled: which of the improvement suggestions should the parties discuss? Also: do you have any suggestions to make the session go well? Alain Massenet:

> Don't get me wrong, but however pleasant such a session is and however well we have collaborated so far, we have interests that are different from those of our partners – interest that may even conflict with theirs. There is the price of the services delivered, of course, but – perhaps even more importantly – service levels and response times too, to name but a few. Sessions such as these are ideal for sharpening everyone up on such matters.

The student should work out which issues the recipients and the provider, respectively, should want to put on the agenda.

APPENDIX: CONTRACT CONTENTS

In the following, the contents of two kinds of contract will be listed: those for service delivery agreements and those for transfer agreements.

SERVICE DELIVERY AGREEMENTS

Preamble

The preamble to a contract defines the contract parties and their legal representatives. The names of the parties are given as registered by the Chamber of Commerce, although abbreviations of their names are frequently used in the rest of the contract. The preamble also defines the objectives of the outsourcing company and their IT supplier. With these definitions the framework for the agreement is set.

1 Contract scope

The first article of the contract contains descriptions of the services to be delivered by the IT provider during the contract period. It is important that these services are described unambiguously, and that those services the recipient will source from their own organization or from other IT suppliers are listed explicitly. Full descriptions may be moved to appendices. The responsibility for any projects already running also must be defined here. If this responsibility is transferred to the IT supplier, they will audit them before accepting.

2 Supplier preference

Two basic relationship types between recipients and providers may be distinguished: preferred supplier and sole supplier. Outsourcing contracts often use a mixture of the two. Then the IT supplier that is party to the contract is sole supplier for the services described in Article 1, and preferred supplier for new services. The position of preferred supplier may be further defined by extra conditions such as 'first call', 'last bid' or 'first call, last bid'. The latter of the three is the most favourable to the supplier, because it gives them a chance to make a second offer if their first is outbid by a competitor.

3 Reports and conferences

The manner in which the parties will confer on their partnership is defined here. This includes the organizational levels of their conferences as well as the subjects discussed there, the people attending them and their frequency. In most outsourcing relationships conferences will be held on three organizational levels: strategic (twice per year, on average), tactical (monthly) and operational (weekly). Reports issued by the IT supplier are to provide the basis for these discussions. Therefore, their formats and contents are defined here too.

4 Contract ranking

Generally, outsourcing agreements may include sub-agreements such as service level agreements and project agreements. If staff or hardware and software are transferred from the recipient to the provider, transfer agreements must also be drawn up. The ranking of these several contracts must be clear, so as to leave no uncertainty about which contract prevails should they not concur. In many cases transfer agreements prevail over service delivery agreements. Service level agreements and project agreements are of a lower order, and are generally attached to the service agreements.

5 Turnover guarantees

In some outsourcing contracts turnover guarantees are given. Often, such clauses are related to the risk the provider takes by taking over staff from the recipient. The scope of these guarantees usually diminishes during the contract period. These clauses may also define the moment when such guaranteed turnovers are to be realized: shifting turnover. Finally, the consequences of default must be defined here. It is reasonable that the recipient will pay part of the unrealized turnover.

6 Prices, benchmarking and payment

It is important to lay down unambiguously which elements are included in the contracts' price agreements. Housing costs are a special category if the IT provider is to use the offices and workspace in the recipient's buildings. In such cases it is best to include housing costs in the prices, and pay the recipient for the use of their accommodation.

This article must also define how the prices agreed are to be adapted during the contract period. Yearly indexing is the most usual method, but benchmarking clauses may be included if indexing is felt not to lead to market conformance. In such cases both the recipient and the provider may decide to have a benchmark performed. Of course it must be defined who is to pay for the benchmark – usually the party who takes the initiative to have it done. Finally, it should be made clear that a benchmark must be carried out by an independent third party. Alternatively, the contract parties may have it done on the basis of a 'third party announcement', which is a more cost efficient option.

The third aspect to be laid down in this article is payment and payment terms. It is reasonable to expect the IT supplier to attach his invoices to his reports, thus providing the recipient with insight into their make-up. The consequences of default may be coupled with legal conditions, such as legally stipulated interest and debt costs. Such terms are important as well in the case of invoices that are disputed. In the latter case, it is reasonable that only the disputed elements are withheld from payment by the recipient.

7 Extra work

Extra work entails extra costs, made by the provider. Normal working hours must therefore be defined, as well as the surcharges for overtime. It is reasonable that the recipient should be asked permission in advance for any extra work expected. This article may also include clauses on consignments.

8 Delivery, property and risks

Apart from IT services, other products also may be supplied, such as hardware or software. In this article the moment of transfer from the provider's ownership to that of the recipient must be defined. It is reasonable to expect the recipient to have completed payment before the property transfer takes effect. As concerns the risks of loss or damage, they may be considered to be the recipient's from the moment of actual physical transfer of the products.

9 Keeping and destroying elements of automated information systems

IT outsourcing relationships often involve the handling of business information for the recipient. The IT provider, of course, then bears responsibility for the information in their care. Procedures must also be defined for the eventual destruction of such information, as should the financial responsibility for this destruction. Preferably, such agreements are also laid down in the contract, or at least put in writing and acknowledged by both parties.

10 Confidential information

In addition to the legal secrecy stipulations with respect to confidential information, the contract parties may include agreements on specifics such as the recipient's IT strategy.

11 Intellectual property

It is of essential importance to define each of the contract parties' intellectual property rights. In principle, these reside with the IT provider, unless the intellectual property has been developed exclusively for the recipient and at their costs. It is, of course, reasonable to prevent intellectual property rights from threatening service delivery continuity if the outsourcing contract is terminated. The IT provider will in case of contract termination have to make the intellectual property available to the recipient and their new provider (internal or external), against reasonable costs.

12 Liability and protective clauses

With respect to liability a distinction may be made between direct and indirect damages. It is reasonable to include the liability for direct damages in the contract. Such liability may be maximized upfront in the contract. Often its value depends on the annual contract value. Extra clauses may be added concerning physical injury.

13 Force majeure

Both parties may under certain circumstances claim force majeure, but this right may by contract be extended to their respective suppliers. Long-term force majeure may lead to contract termination. The consequences of contract termination must, of course, be defined clearly (Article 15).

14 Issues around the millennium transition and the euro

Even though the millennium transition and the introduction of the euro are now several years past, any risks involved with these changes remain the provider's. The contract parties must lay down agreements on the liabilities involved.

15 Premature contract termination

Any service delivery contract should include a limiting list of valid grounds for contract termination, as well as of the consequences of such a termination. These consequences may differ widely: turnover compensation, profit compensation, cost refunds, etc. Likewise, the grounds for termination accepted as valid and their time horizons may also differ. Special circumstances, for instance, may cause the recipient or the provider to terminate the contract. Mergers and takeovers are among such circumstances, as are bankruptcy and the like. Contract termination and the consequent default on one's contractual obligations may lead to demands for compensation.

16 Collaborative efforts

Collaboration between recipient and provider is, of course, part and parcel of outsourcing agreements. If the work to be done by one party has to be carried out on the premises of the other, it is best to include explicit clauses defining such collaborative efforts in the contract.

17 Contract duration

The duration of the contract and the method of termination (preferably by registered mail) must be laid down in the contract.

18 Employees

None of the parties should recruit employees from their partner, since this puts service delivery and business continuity at risk. It is reasonable that this clause should continue in effect for a clearly defined period after the contract is terminated.

19 Guarantees

Guarantees especially concern the software developed for the client. Guarantee periods may be defined in this article, and a period of three months is usually fair. This article is the place, too, to define the acceptance process and the financial consequences.

20 Disputes

Should the recipient and their IT services provider have a difference of opinion concerning their partnership, the dispute should be handled on the appropriate management level. These levels have been defined in Article 3. Such discussions will not always lead to agreement, and the parties should therefore use this article to lay down agreements on binding, independent arbitrage. Arbitrage is a cost efficient and generally quick way to the solution. Should the parties decide to refer their case to the law, they should find clauses here defining which country's laws apply and which court they should take their case to.

TRANSFER AGREEMENTS

Preamble

The preamble to a contract defines the contract parties and their legal representatives. The names of the parties are given as registered by the Chamber of Commerce, although abbreviations of their names are frequently used in the rest of the contract. The preamble also defines the objectives of the outsourcing company and their IT supplier. If the transfer involves employees, it is best to refer explicitly to the approval of the company's employees council. In some European countries an employee transfer agreement must be explicitly linked to the service delivery agreement. With these definitions the framework for the agreement is set.

1 Assets and liabilities

This article should contain a list of the assets and liabilities that are transferred (that is, sold) by the recipient to the provider. This list must have been verified by the provider's due diligence investigation. All assets and liabilities must be physically labelled. Detailed lists may be moved to appendices.

2 Price and payment

The price of the transfer may be a sum of money, paid by the provider to the recipient. In that case it reflects the value of the assets and liabilities, and may include a goodwill remuneration for the services to be delivered. The price may also be a sum of money paid by the recipient. It then reflects the obligations consequent on the transfer of, for instance, employees to the provider. In all cases it is preferable to pay the sums involved at the moment of transfer. If they are included in the prices of the services to be delivered, it will be difficult to attain market conformance for one's prices, which will frequently cause disputes between the partners later. The longer the contract period, the more difficult these disputes tend to be, despite the unambiguous cause of the price differences.

3 Impressions and guarantees

The recipient must safeguard their provider from claims by third parties: general protective clauses. The issues concerned may include taxes and social security costs, as well as specifics concerning the employees transferred (bonuses, pensions, holidays, homework, etc.). Guarantees not to infringe on one another's intellectual and industrial property rights may also be included.

4 Infringements on impressions and guarantees

This article lists the consequences of infringing on the guarantees made to one's partner. It is reasonable that the recipient compensate for any infringements causing their provider damage.

5 Employees and working conditions

The contract should contain a list of activities, with detailed descriptions of the IT services that are to be delivered. Such a list will include estimates of the time needed per service per year. Formulated by the recipient and checked and approved by the provider in the course of their due diligence investigation, the list is preferably laid down in one of the contract's appendices. On the basis of this list another, limiting list is made of the staff who will be responsible for the delivery of these services; it is also included in the transfer agreement. The basis for the transfer of these employees is then laid down in a transfer protocol, which is also included in the transfer agreement. This protocol records generic agreements concerning the transfer as well as specific agreements made with the employees involved (on working hours, holidays and bonuses, for instance). It also defines the allocation of these employees to the organizational and salary levels of the provider's organization. Legal requirements stipulate that the transferred staff's new employment conditions be at least equal to those of their former employer. This equality can be guaranteed by an employment condition comparison made in advance. When such a comparison is made, retirement conditions require extra attention, since these are not included in the legal equality requirements, even though they are a very important component of older employee's working conditions in particular.

6 Contracts

Transfer agreements should contain a list of relevant contracts between the recipient and third parties, such as hardware maintenance and software licence contracts. If the list is extensive, it may be moved to the agreement's appendices; preferably, it is also included in the service delivery agreement. If the contracts concerned are not transferred to the provider, their management remains the responsibility of the recipient. The identification of such third-party contracts is always necessary, however, because the provider must make use of them to deliver their services.

7 No annulment

If any of the transfer agreement's articles or clauses are annulled, all other articles and clauses must remain valid. This constitutes the link between the service delivery agreement and the transfer agreement.

8 Appendices

All lists – of assets and liabilities, employees to be transferred, third-party contracts, etc. – are best moved to appendices. This article should state clearly that such appendices are an integral element of the agreement.

9 Secrecy

A transfer agreement is of another nature than a service delivery agreement. The contents of a service delivery agreement are relevant to the work of a large group of people, since it concerns their tasks and activities over a long period. Transfer agreements, on the other hand, contain privacy-sensitive information and need be known only by the contract partners' senior managers. It is therefore advisable to keep transfer agreements secret.

10 Transfers to third parties

It is advisable to include an article to the effect that neither of the contract parties is allowed, without the other's express permission, to transfer rights or obligations arising from the transfer agreement to third parties.

11 Previous agreements

This article defines the relationship of previous agreements, both in writing and otherwise, to the transfer agreement of this contract. It is important that these matters are made clear. Providers usually prefer contracts that replace all previous agreements with their transfer and service delivery agreements. Such contracts may, however, be challenged on the grounds of fairness.

12 Contract ranking

Generally, outsourcing agreements may include sub-agreements, such as service level agreements and project agreements. If staff or hardware and software are transferred from the recipient to the provider, transfer agreements must also be drawn up. The ranking of these several contracts must be clear, so as to leave no uncertainty about which contract prevails should they not concur. In many cases transfer agreements prevail over service delivery agreements. Service level agreements and project agreements are of a lower order, and are generally attached to the service agreements.

13 Disputes

Should the recipient and their IT services provider have a difference of opinion concerning their partnership, the dispute should be handled on the appropriate management level. Such discussions will not always lead to agreement, and the parties should therefore use this article to lay down agreements on binding, independent arbitrage. Arbitrage is a cost efficient and generally quick way to the solution. Should the parties decide to refer their case to the law, they should find clauses here defining which country's laws apply and which court they should take their case to.

 **LECTURERS' NOTES**

CASE STUDY: CONTRACT STRUCTURING

Students should work out the contract structure and the collaboration principles as established during the negotiation phase. Then, suggestions for improvement must be formulated – from both the recipient's and the provider's perspective. These suggestions may include ideas on how to make their combined session go well.

The negotiation phase

This outsourcing relationship involved the sale of the recipient's internal corporate IT department to the provider. Since this department ran a large number of service delivery contracts with the company's business units, it was important to safeguard the coherence in their portfolio. Next to the asset transfer agreement and associated with it, a framework agreement was therefore set up, defining the principles on which the collaboration between recipient and provider was to be based – principles which were concerned especially with the market dynamics facing the recipient, including takeovers and divestments. All contracts transferred were to be ranged under this framework agreement, as were new and renewed contracts. Thus the IT supplier had some form of guarantee that there would be work for its new staff. Also, a running period had to be established for the framework agreement. Three to five years was considered reasonable, with the possibility to renew every year or for a number of years.

An aspect that also had to be included in the framework agreement was the so-called *termination for convenience*. Takeovers and divestments may sometimes necessitate the termination of a contract before its running period is complete. In such cases, the provider's interests must be cared for. This is especially important if investments have been made for the contract that have not yet been recouped. In this case, if the recipient sold a business unit, they would be obliged to do their utmost to have the buyer accept the provider, so that service delivery could continue. The buyer would thus become the provider's new client.

As we have seen, the collaboration principles did not include turnover guarantees. It was therefore important for the provider that they were given some kind of priority when there was new business to be done. They were, for instance, given the right of 'first call, last bid'. This meant (a) that they were allowed to make the first offer and (b) that if the recipient also wished to ask for other tenders, and one of those turned out to be better, the provider was to be given the opportunity to adapt its proposal to match or outdo the competition. This gave the provider maximum opportunity to acquire new business while still guaranteeing the proposals' market conformity. This mechanism was also used when the recipient bought new business units: they gave their provider no guarantees but full opportunity to make a services delivery proposal and acquire the new business.

Suggestions for improvement

The recipient had two main suggestions: that their provider set up a services catalogue, and that they improve their account management. The idea of a services catalogue arose because the contracts with the business units were so fragmented. A catalogue listing services and their descriptions, service levels and prices would allow the business units to make an informed choice. At the same time it would introduce some uniformity, especially since the recipient's information management department could play a role in setting up the catalogue. Thus, the department would be able to increase the IT services' efficiency and to introduce new technologies. The account management improvements the recipients asked for meant that the provider would listen better to the business units' wishes. To contribute to the business units' success, the provider might need to gain more knowledge of the company and especially its industry.

The provider's suggestions focused on timely information about expected changes and on being allowed more direct contact with the recipient's business units. The market dynamics of the recipient's industry had a major impact on the services delivered by the provider. The sooner the provider was informed of any major changes, the better it could anticipate the consequences for its service delivery. Perhaps the provider could even help their client with some advice. Timelier information would allow the provider to be a better partner. Likewise, contacts with business unit managers would give the provider better insight into their information needs. Having a central contact point (the information management department) gave the provider a direct line to the recipient's senior management, but it also shielded the business units from the provider's view and so made it more difficult to deliver exactly the right services.

Finally, some suggestions for the evaluation session. There are, of course, the basics: timely invitations, a well thought-through agenda and an easily accessible location. Then there is the facilitator. He must be somebody neutral, but with knowledge of and a clear view on the outsourcing relationships. He must be acceptable to both parties, leading them through the day by providing an open atmosphere in which there is time for discussion and in which all participants can express their opinions. These participants, too, must be chosen with care. They must be people with sufficient authority to take decisions that will be accepted by their companies. And there should preferably be no more than ten, since a larger number diminishes the meeting's effectiveness. If it is inevitable that more people

257

attend, there should not only be plenary sessions but workshops and break-out sessions to discuss details as well.

NOTES

1 This need not be caused by conflicts. Takeovers, mergers, market developments – there are many reasons why it may sometimes be better to discontinue even successful partnerships.
2 This case study is based on research published in Beulen (1993), Beulen *et al.* (1994) and Beulen and Ribbers (2002, 2003). These publications include material taken from structured interviews held at different times with several of the recipient's executives. The material was rewritten for the purposes of this book. All names are fictional.
3 The complexity and strictness of the USA Food and Drug Administration's regulations caused the holding to continue the delivery of IT services to its pharmaceuticals division by their own internal IT department. For the sake of simplicity, this division is therefore left out of the discussion.

REFERENCES

Aubert, B., Rivard, S. and Patry, M. (1996) 'A transaction cost approach to outsourcing behaviour: some empirical evidence', *Information & Management*, 30 (2): 51–64.

Aubert, B., Patry, M. and Rivard, S. (2003) 'A tale of two outsourcing contracts: an agency-theoretical perspective', *Wirtschaftsinformatik*, 45 (2): 181–190.

Beulen, E. (1993) 'Outsourcing; een "make or buy" beslissing en een inkoopproces', Master's thesis, Tilburg University (in Dutch).

Beulen, E. (2002) *Uitbesteding van IT-dienstverlening*, Den Haag: Ten Hagen & Stam (in Dutch).

Beulen, E. (2003) 'Lessons learned voor de beeindiging van uit bestedingscontracten', in J. van Bon (ed.) *IT Beheerjaarboek 2003*, Den Haag: Ten Hagen & Stam (in Dutch).

Beulen, E. (2004) 'Governance in IT outsourcing partnerships', in W. van Grembergen (ed.) *Strategies for Information Technologies*, Hershey, PA: Idea Group Publishing.

Beulen, E. and Ribbers, P. (2002) 'Managing complex IT outsourcing – partnerships', Proceedings HICSS-35 conference (US), IEEE, 0–7695–1435–9/02.

Beulen, E. and Ribbers, P. (2003) 'IT outsourcing contracts: practical implications of the incomplete contract theory', Proceedings HICSS-36 conference (Hawaii), IEEE, 0–7695–1874–5/03.

Beulen, E., Ribbers, P. and Roos, J. (1994) *Outsourcing van IT-dienstverlening: een 'make or buy' beslissing*, Deventer: Kluwer Bedrijfswetenschappen (in Dutch).

Beulen, E., Baas, R., Dain, J., Hudson, J., Reitsma, E., Symonds, M. and van der Zee, H. (2004) 'Outsourcing: the Atos Origin outsourcing life cycle – building successful outsourcing relationships', White Paper (www.atosorigin.com/corporate/viewpoint/vp_270104.htm) Accessed 29 August 2004.

Burden, K. (2003) '"We're in it to win it" – negotiating successful outsourcing transactions', *The Computer Law and Security Report*, 19 (6): 478–479.

Burnett, R. (1998) *Outsourcing IT – The Legal Aspects*, Aldershot, Gower.

Coase, R. (1937) 'The nature of the firm', *Economica,* 4: 386–405.

Cullen, S. and Willcocks, L. (2003) 'Intelligent IT Outsourcing, Eight Building Blocks to Success', Oxford: Butterworth-Heinemann.

Gietzmann, M. (1996) 'Incomplete contracts and the make or buy decision: governance design and attainable flexibility', *Accounting, Organization and Society,* 21 (6): 611–626.

Hart, O. (1995) *Contracts and Financial Structure,* Oxford: Oxford University Press.

Heckman, R. (1999) 'Organizing and managing supplier relationships in information technology procurement', *International Journal of Information Management,* 19 (2): 141–155.

Kern, T. and Willcocks, L. (2000) 'Exploring information technology outsourcing relationships: theory and practice', *The Journal of Strategic Information Systems,* 9 (4): 321–350.

Klepper, R. (1995) 'The management of partnering development in I/S outsourcing', *Journal of Technology,* 10 (4): 249–258.

Lacity, M. and Hirschheim, R. (1995) *Beyond the Information Systems Outsourcing Bandwagon,* Chichester: Wiley & Sons.

Lacity, M. and Willcocks, L. (1998) 'An empirical investigation of information technology sourcing practices: lessons from experience', *Management Information Systems Quarterly,* 22 (3): 363–408.

Lacity, M. and Willcocks, L. (2003) 'IT sourcing reflections: lessons for customers and suppliers', *Wirtschafsinformatik,* 45 (2): 115–125.

Parkhe, A. (1993) 'Strategic alliances structuring: a game theoretic and transaction cost examination of interfirm cooperation', *Academy of Management Journal,* 4: 794–829.

Saunders, C., Gebelt, M. and Hu, Q. (1997) 'Achieving success in information systems outsourcing'. *California Management Review,* 39 (2): 63–79.

Segal, I. (1999) 'Complexity and renegotiation: a foundation for incomplete contracts', *Review of Economic Studies,* 66 (226): 57–82.

Shepherd, A. (1999) 'Outsourcing IT in a changing world', *European Management Journal,* 17 (1): 64–84.

Turner, M., Smith, A. and Smith, H. (2002) 'IT outsourcing: the challenge of changing technology in IT outsourcing agreements', *The Computer Law and Security Report,* 18 (3): 181–186.

Williamson, O. (1975) *Markets and Hierarchies,* New York: The Free Press.

Chapter 11

Looking forward

- The outsourcing phenomenon is being pushed by the drive for new business models. These business models concentrate on core competences and collaborative relationships offering products and services that are considered non-core.
- Outsourcing of the execution of activities that are considered non-core is heavily supported by commoditization.
- Future collaboration between service recipients and service providers will be enhanced by the open source movement.
- A direct consequence of focusing on core competences is the outsourcing of entire business processes considered non-core: business process outsourcing. This will affect IT outsourcing relationships since IT is an internal part of most of these processes.

11.1 INTRODUCTION

As we have seen in this book, the dynamics of business management keep increasing. And it is not only the flood of mergers and takeovers that influences business management and, through it, outsourcing relationships (Brown and Renwick 1996). The convergence of IT and telecommunication, and the increasing availability of bandwidth, continue to reduce the transaction and coordination costs associated with old-economy business operations. This enables companies to restructure their value chains and focus on core competences. Thus, new technologies gradually converge with the newly developed business models (Friedman 2005). Globalization is another factor in this process. Together with the rise of network organizations, globalization determines the manner in which companies are organized and how they collaborate. This development also can be noticed in the field of IT outsourcing, where offshore outsourcing is on the increase. In fact, while companies increasingly turn to combinations of onshore, nearshore and offshore outsourcing, the attitude gradually develops into one of global sourcing (Carmel and Tjia 2005), which makes it possible to procure IT services effectively and efficiently. Interestingly, it is especially countries with closed economies and hierarchical political and economic structures that are changing themselves into important suppliers in this market. India, China and Russia are the prime examples, as well as some Eastern European countries (Friedman 2005). Another consequence of this development is that large providers increasingly collaborate in the delivery of IT services.

These developments are expected to continue. Strategic sourcing will take the place of single make-or-buy decisions. This means that not only will the output side of many companies change (into a web-enabled playing field, as it has been called) (Friedman 2005), but the input side will also change. The focus is on standardization, with the aim to realize connectivity and advantages of scale. There will also be a growing accent on flexibility, with respect to both the volume and the nature of the services involved. This means that outsourcing may be expected to continue to grow, in relative as well as in absolute terms. The most important argument in favour of it, the need to focus on core competences, indeed dovetails with the main characteristic of network organizations, which is inter-business relationships (Papazoglou and Ribbers 2005). Most companies have now concluded that IT services are not part of their core competences. Outsourcing and the consequent relationships with other companies therefore have become an integral part of the way in which business management processes are set up.

There are three developments that we feel will play an important role in the near future, in the sense that they will significantly influence outsourcing relationships and their management. These are commoditization, the rise of open source software and the trend towards business process outsourcing. We will take a closer look at these processes in the following sections.

11.2 COMMODITIZATION

Commoditization takes place in two main areas: applications and IT services. Standardizing applications makes it easier for companies to communicate with each other, which is of special importance to companies collaborating in a network organization. Standardized workflow software is the most important aspect there (Friedman 2005). It leads to concentration on the software market. Take, for instance, the developments in the market for electronic resource planning (ERP) systems. PeopleSoft bought JD Edwards only to be bought itself, by Oracle. Likewise, the BAAN Company's perspectives were rather limited in such circumstances, and they are therefore now part of the SSA Global Corporation. Such fusions and collaborative relationships require that the participants communicate adequately across their supply chains (Clark and Lee 2000; Oesterle et al. 2000).

IT services themselves are also being commoditized. Unit prices are common practice for both desktop seats and ERP seats (Beulen and Ribbers 2004). Commercial off the shelf (COTS) solutions are the preferred option and their customization is kept to a minimum. This also reduces the costs of application management. However, if an upgrade is implemented, all interfaces with other applications must be upgraded as well. Usually, this is done by the COTS provider because it saves the recipient money and reduces the risk of data processing faults. While we are on the subject, a few extra remarks may be made concerning COTS solutions. Studies on developments in this field often lack product and project details, and they are frequently founded on uncritically accepted assumptions (Torchiano and Morisio 2004) Furthermore, 'on demand' and 'utility' service provisioning is on its way (Ross and Westerman 2004; Crawford *et al.* 2005), under development by service providers such as Accenture, CSC, EDS, HP and IBM. At present, these concepts are mainly used for marketing purposes, but in the near future service recipients will really have access to the required services at the required volumes – which may, after all, fluctuate during the contract period. The recipients will then only be charged for the services they actually use, a great advantage for companies who experience significant fluctuations in their need for service delivery capacity. This is the case for companies whose business grows or shrinks. But it also applies to companies who are implementing new applications and who must therefore run large testing and quality assurance operations. Such operations may be sizeable, but they are also short-lived. After the first period the company manages with much less capacity.

11.3 OPEN SOURCE SOFTWARE

'Open source' and 'free' are designations applied to software that is made publicly available by the producer without the user having to pay for it. The producer keeps his rights to the product's intellectual property, but users are allowed not only to use it but also to copy, modify and distribute it (Ljungberg 2000). Users often develop modified versions of such software, either for their own specific purposes or simply in an attempt to improve the original. If they add their version to the public domain in order for it to be accessible free of charge, the result is called free software. If they choose to commercialize it and charge a fee for its use, this is called open source because the original remains accessible without paying. The producer of the original may in such cases sometimes set conditions to the commercialization of their source code. A well-known example of open source software is the Linux operating system.

Several characteristics of open source and free software deserve mention. For one, the American Open Source Initiative considers free software a kind of open source software, even though not everybody agrees with them – the American Free Software Foundation, for example, thinks differently. But however one looks at it, most open source software is developed along the lines of the community-based development model, which means that all users may contribute to the product's improvement (www.sourceforce.org). Other possibilities exist, as the free publishing of some proprietary software (Boulanger 2005) has shown, but these are exceptions. Another interesting aspect of open source software is that it is sometimes used to undermine the market dominance of other products. Netscape, for example, uses its freely available browser Navigator to put pressure on a giant like Microsoft.

There are many arguments for the use of open source software. There is a growing reluctance to accept the dominance of a few commercial software providers such as Microsoft, as is evidenced by several anti-trust trials in the USA and Europe. Besides, open source and free software may obviously save the user a substantial amount of money. For many companies this is an argument to use such products (Fuggetta 2003). It even applies to whole countries: it offers an alternative to the use of illegally copied software, something that is currently widely practised in developing countries, who simply cannot afford to buy the products. It has even been argued that open source software might contribute to such countries' economic development, as it generates jobs in the community-based development sphere (O'Donnell 2004).

Nevertheless, the use of open source software is not without its difficulties. The product itself may be free, but one needs people to implement it, to train and support the users, and to maintain and at times update it. And these must still be paid, so using the product cannot be said to be entirely for free. Quality is another matter. To enable users to distinguish between good and bad products, the Open Source Initiative (a non-profit organization) is taking the lead in a trend towards the certification of open source software. Their main conditions are that the licence must be independent of the technology used and that it does not discriminate. They have defined 10 criteria that open source software must meet. Otherwise, the most important aspects of licensing agreements are which laws apply to them and whether their contract clauses form a coherent whole. Certification has another advantage too. It enables service providers to participate in software that has been certified, which means they can use it to develop applications that are recognized as such. In this way, certification contributes to the market's structure. Naturally, one must remain aware that certificates never guarantee the software's quality. When selecting open source software for their use, individuals and companies must therefore pay close attention to this aspect.

Another topic that causes some discussion is that of how to finance innovation if the resulting product is published free of charge. It is often the cycle of innovations–returns–reinvestments that has produced major breakthroughs. And so commercially oriented software industries perhaps cannot be dismissed (Bayrak and Davis 2003). This discussion is nowhere near its conclusion.

The most important change caused by the rise of open source software, however, concerns the way in which service providers and recipients collaborate. The community-based development of open source software can turn users into

263

co-developers (Dahlander and Mckelvey 2005). To this end, provider and recipient will collaborate closely and both will make resources available to have their staff work together on the further development of the software. This fits the concept of network organizations, in which companies as well as individuals collaborate. Doing so requires new process structures, however, which in turn require much management attention. Special attention must be paid, for instance, if one's competitive position is based in part on the use of software that is freely available to everyone – including one's competitors. All projects involved must be monitored continuously. The parties to such collaborative efforts must also be aware of the possibility that conflicts pertaining to industrial law might arise. Everyone who works on the original source code keeps their right to its intellectual property, but those who aid its development do not. This weakens the positions of both the provider and the recipient, but it is an integral aspect of open source software and its use.

11.4 THE GROWTH OF BUSINESS PROCESS OUTSOURCING

Business process outsourcing (BPO) began slowly in the 1980s and matured in the 1990s. Essentially, it may be considered an extension of IT outsourcing: the provider not only delivers IT services but uses those services to carry out one or more of the recipient's entire business processes. There are differences between supportive and core BPO, as we have seen in Section 2.5, but in all cases the collaboration between provider and recipient changes if some of the client's processes are outsourced. All aspects of their relationship must be well anchored in their business management practices, as both companies' business processes are involved. Another interesting aspect is that BPO communication focuses on output rather than on input, unlike IT outsourcing communication, which often concerns technical details (Willcocks *et al.* 2004). Output-oriented discussions are certainly less complex, but the governance of BPO relationships still needs to be investigated in much further detail before hard and fast conclusions can be drawn.

The way in which BPO is offered significantly influences the way in which it is anchored in the companies involved. Currently, many providers who originally only delivered IT services have moved into BPO as well. It was a logical extension of their work. However, it is expected that this will change soon. The trend being to focus on one's core competences, companies who now offer both IT outsourcing and BPO will most likely specialize in one of the two and then network with other companies to offer the complement to their services. IT outsourcing providers thus become subcontractors offering commodities with a relatively low added value to BPO specialists who themselves operate in a market with high added values. Thus, the market is further segmented. For the moment, however, few BPO providers manage to turn a profit, a consequence of their market's lack of maturity. It is to be expected that the large international IT service providers who also have consulting branches, such as Accenture and IBM, will be the ones offering BPO once the market does reach maturity – in five or perhaps ten years. There will then probably be no companies left offering both BPO and IT outsourcing.

Currently, BPO is found mostly in the financial industry (Tas and Sunder 2004). This is a consequence of the information processing intensity that is a characteristic of financial corporations, but also of the fact that they were among the first to computerize their business processes, which is now causing them legacy problems. Their applications have been changed and updated so many times that they have become difficult to maintain. At the same time, the confidentiality needed and the fierce competition in this industry have made financial institutions reluctant to outsource the management and maintenance of such systems. They have now reached the point where such IT outsourcing is no longer enough. Only BPO can help them now that they are losing control over not only their IT services but their business processes too. BPO offers the opportunity of a clean slate. Other information-intensive industries will probably follow soon; the lack of market maturity means that other industries are likely to follow later.

11.5 CONCLUSIONS

Outsourcing is growing up fast. Within the next ten years or so it will be fully institutionalized. And there is no way back either. Service recipients who believe they will at some point be able to insource their IT services again are mistaken. The continuing trend to commoditization makes the necessary advantages of scale almost impossible to achieve for internal IT departments, which will therefore disappear altogether.

For open source software it is early days. There is great potential and the course that future developments will take is clear, since open source software offers an alternative to COTS solutions and enables users to achieve great cost reductions. But we cannot yet say how fast this will go. The competitive position of many companies is still based on the applications they use to support their business. If these applications become available as open source software they are no longer exclusive, which undermines these companies' advantage. The market's capability to organize and regulate itself will determine the speed with which open source software will grow in importance. The authors feel it might easily take more than ten years before it reaches a dominant position.

The segmentation of the BPO market that is to be expected will change the horizons of all service providers significantly. Those who now offer the complete scope from IT outsourcing to BPO will have to make a choice for either of the two and then further between the several kinds that may be distinguished. Such a strategic choice is necessary because it will be almost impossible to keep abreast of the developments in all market segments. Providers who have already gained experience with BPO will probably be the ones to keep offering it. Providers specializing in IT outsourcing will likely have to specialize further, offering only a limited selection of the technologies available only in some parts of the world.

This book aims to provide both a theoretical foundation for and practical insight into the subject of IT outsourcing. For one thing is clear: IT outsourcing may have been a best practice for years now, but its development still hasn't run its full course. We therefore hope that this book contributes to the growth of the IT outsourcing market to its maturity.

REFERENCES

Bayrak, C. and Davis, C. (2003) 'The relationship between distributed systems and open source development', *Communications of the Association for Computing Machinery*, 46 (12): 99–102.

Beulen, E. and Ribbers, P. (2004) 'Value creation in application outsourcing relationships: an international case study on ERP outsourcing' in W. Curry (ed.) *Value Creation from eBusiness Models*, Oxford: Elsevier, Butterworth-Heinemann.

Boulanger, A. (2005) 'The open-source model – open-source versus proprietary software: is one more reliable and secure than the other?', *IBM Systems Journal*, 44 (2): 239–248.

Brown, C. and Renwick, J. (1996) 'Alignment of the IS organization: the special case of corporate acquisitions', *The Database for Advances in Information Systems*, 27 (September): 25–33.

Carmel, E. and Tjia, P. (2005) *Offshore Outsourcing of Information Technology Work*, Cambridge: Cambridge University Press.

Clark, T. and Lee, H. (2000) 'Performance, inter-dependence, and coordination in business to business electronic commerce and supply chain management', *IT and Management*, 1: 85–105.

Crawford, C.H., Bate, G.P., Cherbakov, L., Holley, K. and Tsocanos, C. (2005) 'Toward an on demand service-oriented architecture', *IBM Systems Journal*, 44 (1): 81–108.

Dahlander, L. and Mckelvey, M. (2005) 'Who is not developing open source software? Non-users, users, and developers', *Economics of Innovation and New Technology*, 14 (7): 617–636.

Friedman, T. (2005) *The World is Flat: A Brief History of the Twenty-first Century*, New York: Farrar, Straus and Giroux.

Fuggetta, A. (2003) 'Open source software – an evaluation', *Journal of Systems and Software*, 66 (1): 77–90.

Ljungberg, J. (2000) 'Open source movements as a model for organising', *European Journal of Information Systems*, 9 (4): 208–216.

O'Donnell, C. (2004) 'A case for Indian insourcing: open source interest in IT job expansion', *First Monday*, 9, 11 (http://firstmonday.org/issues/issue9_11/odonnell/index.html) Accessed 29 August 2004.

Oesterle, H., Fleisch, E. and Alt, R. (2000) *Business Networking, Shaping Collaboration Between Enterprises*, 2nd edn, revised and extended, Berlin: Springer.

Papazoglou, M. and Ribbers, P. (2005) *e-Business: Organizational and Technical Foundations*, Chichester: John Wiley.

Ross, J. and Westerman, G. (2004) 'Preparing for utility computing: the role of IT architecture and relationship management', *IBM Systems Journal*, 43 (1): 5–19.

Tas, J. and Sunder, S. (2004) 'New architectures for financial services – financial services business process outsourcing', *Communications of the Association for Computing Machinery*, 47 (5): 50–52.

Torchiano, M. and Morisio, M. (2004) 'Overlooked facts on COTS-based development', *IEEE Software*, 21 (2): 88–93.

Willcocks, L., Hindle, J., Feeny, D. and Lacity, M. (2004) 'IT and business process outsourcing: the knowledge potential', *Information Systems Management*, 21 (3): 7–15.

Overview of the investigated case studies

Case number	Short description of service recipient	Short description of scope of service	Initial contract signed in	Duration of the contract	Contract value	Book chapters
Case I	International tier 1 supplier in photographical products (B2B and B2C), over 75,000 employees worldwide revenue 2005 over 2.5 billion US\$	Application development and network management	1992	Various contracts, duration between 3 and 5 years	< 5 million euros	2
Case II	International tier 1 airliner (including cargo), over 30,000 employees worldwide, revenue 2004 over 6 billion euros	Network management, server management and application development	1990	Various contracts, duration between 3 and 5 years	>10 million euros	2
Case III	Large multinational in coatings, fibres, chemicals and pharmaceuticals, over 60,000 employees, revenue 2004 over 12 billion euros	Full scope of IT services	1999	Purchase of internal IT division	Yearly revenue 90 million US\$ (initial transfer of staff 750 IT professionals)	2, 6, 8, 9, 10
Case IV	International truck manufacturer, over 6,000 employees, revenue is not disclosed	Infrastructure management (including mainframe and midrange services) and partly application management	1992	5-year contract	30 million US\$	2,6
Case V	International manufacturer of copiers, computers and accessories, 21,000 employees, revenue 2004 over 2.5 billion euros	Mainly application development and network management	1991	Various contracts, duration between 3 and 5 years	>10 million euros	2

Case	Description	Scope	Year	Contract	Value	No.
Case VI	Dutch Flower Auction, nearly 2,000 employees, revenue 2003 over 1.5 billion euros	No outsourcing	n.a.	n.a.	n.a.	2
Case VII	International manufacturer including different types of subsidiaries, over 160,000 employees, revenue 2004 over 30 billion euros	Full scope of IT services	1990 onwards	Purchase of internal IT division	Yearly revenue over 300 million US$ (initial transfer of staff 1,500 IT professionals)	2, 4, 6, 7, 8, 9
Case VIII	Dutch automobile leasing company, nearly 3,000 employees, revenue 2004, over 200 million euros	Full scope of IT services	1997	5-year contract	> 5 million euros	2, 6, 7
Case IX	Global starch company, 2,000 employees, revenue 2003/2004 over 700 million euros	Full scope of IT services	2004	3-year contract	< 10 million euros	3, 7
Case X	International CPG company, about 50,000 employees, revenue 2004 over 10 million euros	ERP services	2003	3-year contract	> 10 million euros	3, 4
Case XI	International telecommunication company, over 30,000 employees, revenue 2004 over 9 billion US$	Full scope of IT services	1997	5-year contract	> 20 million euros	3, 4, 6, 8
Case XII	Virgin Mobile UK	Infrastructure Management	2004	5-year contract	Confidential	3
Case XIII	Dutch Utilities company, about 6,000 employees, revenue 2004 nearly 12 billion euros	Infrastructure Management	1996	5-year contract	> 5 million euros	3, 6, 7, 8
Case XIV	Global group of energy and petrochemicals companies	Full scope of IT services (only partly outsourced to multiple service providers)	1985	Large number of contracts	Confidential	4
Case XV	Small utility company, less than 500 employees	Full scope of IT services	2002	3-year contract	< 5 million euros	6, 7

Continued

Appendix *Continued*

Case number	Short description of service recipient	Short description of scope of service	Initial contract signed in	Duration of the contract	Contract value	Book chapters
Case XVI	Design and manufacture of high-tech batteries for industry, about 4,000 employees, revenue 2004 nearly 400 million euros	Full scope of IT services	1999	5-year contract	Confidential	6
Case XVII	Utility company, over 5,000 employees	Full scope of IT services	2000	3 + 2 contract	> 100 million euros	6, 8, 10
Case XVIII	Insurance company, over 10,000 employees	Infrastructure Management	2004	3 + 2 contract	> 100 million euros	6
Case XIX	Temporary and contract staffing organization, over 12,000 employees (corporate staff) and revenue 2004 nearly 6 billion euros	No outsourcing	n.a.	n.a.	n.a.	6, 8
Case XX	Baby food and clinical nutrition company, over 11,000 employees, revenue 2004 over 1.5 billion euros	Full scope of IT services	2003	3-year contract	< 25 million euros	6, 7, 8
Case XXI	Chemical company, less than 25,000 employees, revenue in 2004 over 7.5 billion euros	Desktop services	2002	3-year contract	< 25 million euros	6, 7, 8
Case XXII	Communication company	Full scope of IT services (only partly outsourced to multiple service providers	1990	Large number of contracts	Confidential	6, 7
Case XXIII	Ministry of Housing (the Netherlands), 4.100 employees	Full scope of IT services	2003	3-year contract	Over 60 million euros	7
Case XXIV	Chemical and pharmaceutical group, over 30,000 employees, revenue 2004 over 7.5 billion euros	Full scope of IT services	1996	3-year contract	Over 30 million euros	7

Case	Description	Year	Contract	Value	Ref
Case XXV	KPN	1999	Full scope of IT services (only partly outsourced to multiple service providers	Large number of contracts	Confidential	7, 8
Case XXVI	Global financial institution, nearly 100,000 employees	1990	Full scope of IT services (only partly outsourced to multiple service providers	Large number of contracts	Confidential	7, 8
Case XXVII	Consumer Package Goods company, nearly 100,000 employees	1985	Full scope of IT services (only partly outsourced to multiple service providers	Large number of contracts	Confidential	7
Case XXVIII	Technology company, over 12,000 employees, revenue 2004 nearly 2 billion euros	1993	Full scope of IT services (only partly outsourced to multiple service providers	Large number of contracts	Confidential	8
Case XXIX	Global financial institution, over 115,000 employees	1990	Full scope of IT services (only partly outsourced to multiple service providers	Large number of contracts	Confidential	8
Case XXX	Global software product company, over 1,000 employees	1998	Application management service and helpdesk management services (third level support)	5-year contract	Confidential	9
Case XXXI	Dutch university	2002	Full scope of IT services	3-year contract	< 10 million euros	10

Index